CAMBRIDGE TEXTS IN THE
HISTORY OF PHILOSOPHY

FRIEDRICH NIETZSCHE
The Birth of Tragedy

CAMBRIDGE TEXTS IN THE HISTORY OF PHILOSOPHY

Series editors

KARL AMERIKS

Professor of Philosophy at the University of Notre Dame

DESMOND M. CLARKE

Professor of Philosophy at University College Cork

The main objective of Cambridge Texts in the History of Philosophy is to expand the range, variety and quality of texts in the history of philosophy which are available in English. The series includes texts by familiar names (such as Descartes and Kant) and also by less well-known authors. Wherever possible, texts are published in complete and unabridged form, and translations are specially commissioned for the series. Each volume contains a critical introduction together with a guide to further reading and any necessary glossaries and textual apparatus. The volumes are designed for student use at undergraduate and postgraduate level and will be of interest not only to students of philosophy, but also to a wider audience of readers in the history of science, the history of theology and the history of ideas.

For a list of titles published in the series, please see end of book.

FRIEDRICH NIETZSCHE

The Birth of Tragedy and Other Writings

EDITED BY

RAYMOND GEUSS
University of Cambridge

AND

RONALD SPEIRS
University of Birmingham

TRANSLATED BY

RONALD SPEIRS

CAMBRIDGE
UNIVERSITY PRESS

CAMBRIDGE UNIVERSITY PRESS
Cambridge, New York, Melbourne, Madrid, Cape Town, Singapore, São Paulo,
Delhi, Mexico City

Cambridge University Press
The Edinburgh Building, Cambridge CB2 8RU, UK

Published in the United States of America by Cambridge University Press, New York

www.cambridge.org
Information on this title:www.cambridge.org/9780521639873

First published 1999
15th printing 2012

Printed and bound at MPG Books Group, UK

A catalogue record for this publication is available from the British Library

Library of Congress cataloguing in publication data

Nietzsche, Friedrich Wilhelm, 1844–1900.
[Selections. English. 1999]
The birth of tragedy and other writings / Friedrich Nietzsche;
edited by Raymond Geuss and Ronald Speirs; translated by Ronald Speirs.
p. cm. – (Cambridge texts in the history of philosophy)
Includes bibliographical references and index.
ISBN 0 521 63016 9 (hardback). – ISBN 0 521 63987 5 (pbk.)
1. Philosophy, Modern. I. Geuss, Raymond. II. Speirs, Ronald.
III. Title. IV. Series.
B3312.E5G48 1999
193–dc21   98–35097 CIP

ISBN 978-0-521-63016-0 hardback
ISBN 978-0-521-63987-3 paperback

Contents

Introduction

Cosima Wagner's thirty-third birthday, her first since she and Wagner had married, fell on 25 December 1870. Wagner's present to her was the newly composed 'Siegfried Idyll'. He secretly arranged for a small group of musicians to assemble in the morning on the stairs outside her bedroom and they began to play as she awoke. One of the guests present at this performance was the newly appointed 26-year-old Professor of Classical Philology at the University of Basle, Friedrich Nietzsche. Nietzsche was an ardent admirer of Wagner's music, and he and Wagner shared an enthusiasm for the philosophical pessimism of Arthur Schopenhauer. The world as we know it, Schopenhauer thought, the world of objects in space and time held together by relations of cause and effect, was nothing but a representation, an illusion generated by the unending play of a metaphysical entity which he called 'the Will'. This Will, the underlying reality of the world, expressed itself in a variety of ways in the human world, most keenly in the form of sexual desire; it had each human individual in its grip and drove each of us on to forms of action that inevitably ended either in disgusting satiation or in frustration. The very nature of the universe precluded the possibility of any continuing human happiness. The best we could hope for, Schopenhauer argued, was momentary respite from the continual flux of willing and frustration through the contemplation of art. Aesthetic experience could have this effect because it is radically disinterested and thus extracts us from the world of willing. Music, in particular, is inherently non-representational, and Schopenhauer draws from this fact the stunning conclusion that music both gives us virtually direct access to ultimate reality, and is also one of the best ways available to us of distancing ourselves from the relentless throb of the Will.

This heady combination of extreme pessimism, sexual fantasy presented as metaphysics and the deification of music was irresistible to Wagner, the unemployed kapellmeister who had spent a decade of his life in exile following his participation in the failed revolution of 1849 and who had experienced some difficulty in controlling the attractions the wives of various of his patrons and associates held for him. He was delighted to find a young academic who shared so many of his own passionate interests and Nietzsche became a frequent visitor at Wagner's house in Tribschen, near Lucerne, and an intimate friend of the family. On that Christmas morning he, too, had a present for Cosima, the manuscript of a study entitled 'Die Entstehung des tragischen Gedankens'. In turn he received a copy of Wagner's recent essay 'Beethoven' and a piano reduction of the first act of *Siegfried*. In the evening there were two further performances of the 'Siegfried Idyll', and Wagner read aloud from the text of *Die Meistersinger*. The next day Nietzsche's manuscript was read aloud and discussed. On 1 January 1871 Nietzsche returned to Basle and began work on his first book, *The Birth of Tragedy out of the Spirit of Music,* using some of the material he had originally elaborated in Cosima's birthday present. He dedicated the book to Wagner.

By 1886, when he was preparing a second edition of the work, Nietzsche claimed to have long since changed his mind about Wagner (and about Schopenhauer). As he would later put it, he had eventually overcome these two youthful enthusiasms, exchanging Schopenhauerian pessimism for a fully affirmative attitude towards life and coming to see Wagner as a *décadent* and the embodiment of everything that was to be rejected in modern culture. So the view has sometimes been expressed that the 'mature' Nietzsche became just as committed an anti-Wagnerian as his younger self had been pro-Wagner. This in turn has been taken to mean that one should read the main text of *The Birth of Tragedy* through the eyes of the 1886 Preface in which the mature anti-Wagnerian corrects the errors of his youth. Although the later Nietzsche did doubtless occasionally write things that could be interpreted as putting the matter in these simple terms – that he outgrew a deluded, early admiration for Wagner and his music and moved to a position of clear-sighted, unconditional rejection – it would be a mistake to take passages in which Nietzsche makes claims like this simply at face value. After all, Nietzsche prided himself on his ability to see things from a variety of different perspectives, even (and especially) when that resulted in holding views that to lesser minds would have seemed inconsistent, and he also prided himself on his ability to adopt a variety of different disguises or masks for his own deeper and more considered views. The later anti-Wagnerian pose is one such mask, a particular form of self-dramatization adopted at a certain time for particular reasons, and it must be treated with the same suspicion Nietzsche uses in analysing the self-interpretations of others.

Matters must from the very start have been slightly complicated at least on a personal level for the youthful Wagnerite in Tribschen, if only because Wagner in his own way was just as much an egocentric megalomaniac as Nietzsche was. At the time Cosima noted in her diary that for all his professed admiration of and devotion to Wagner the man and his music, Nietzsche seemed to be making a concerted effort to 'defend himself' against the overwhelming direct impact of Wagner's personality, and she suspected that he was preparing in some way to take revenge (*sich rächen*) for having been thus assaulted.[1] In addition, Nietzsche was in love with Cosima, and if the ageing Wagner had been able to detach her from her husband (the conductor Hans von Bülow), why could not the mustachioed young Professor of Philology and former artillerist, in turn, play Tristan to Wagner's Marke? Finally, Nietzsche fancied himself a composer, going so far as to make presents of various of his compositions to Cosima and to play some of them in the presence of 'the Master' (as he called Wagner, following Cosima's usage). These compositions caused Wagner much amusement, and while Cosima seems to have been well bred enough to confine her slighting comments about them to her diaries, Wagner let no opportunity pass to remind Nietzsche that he was a dilettant, whose 'music' deserved no serious attention. Correspondingly, throughout his life, even when he is writing in his most explicitly anti-Wagnerian mode, there is ample evidence of Nietzsche's continuing love of Wagner's music which clearly had a very powerful hold over him to the very end. Thomas Mann seems to me to get the matter right when he says that even Nietzsche's criticism of Wagner is 'inverted panegyric ... another form of glorification' ('Panegyrikus mit umgekehrtem Vorzeichen ... eine andere Form der Verherrlichung'), an expression of one of the major experiences of Nietzsche's life, his deep love–hate of Wagner and his music.[2] The love was there virtually from the beginning, as was the hate; both lasted to the very end.

[1] *Cf. Wagner-Handbuch*, ed. U. Müller and P. Wapnewski (Stuttgart, Kröner Verlag, 1986), pp. 114f.
[2] Thomas Mann, *Leiden und Größe Richard Wagners*, in *Gesammelte Werke in dreizehn Bänden* (Frankfurt-on-Main, Fischer, 1960), vol. IX, p. 373.

Still, between 1871 and 1886 Nietzsche had clearly changed some of his views very significantly. In the new introduction to the second edition, Nietzsche does criticize some aspects of his youthful work quite severely, especially its breathless, hyperbolic style. He does not, however, completely repudiate it, but rather does his best to integrate some of its central claims into the course his thinking was later to take, to find in it the germs of ideas that he was later to develop more fully. This means that we are invited to read the text from a double perspective: that of the youthful follower of the Master – who, whatever his private reservations might have been, in the 1870s seriously proposed changing his profession to that of travelling lecturer on Wagnerism and propagandist for 'the idea of Bayreuth' – and that of the highly, if ambiguously, critical Nietzsche of the late 1880s.

The Birth of Tragedy is directed at two slightly different issues: on the one hand it is an attempt to answer a number of questions about culture and society: what is a human culture? Why is it important for us to participate in one? Are all human cultures fundamentally of the same type or do they differ in important ways? Under what circumstances will a human culture flourish, and under what circumstances will it become 'decadent' and decay or even 'die'? The highest form of culture we know, Nietzsche thinks, is that of ancient Greece, and the most perfect expression of that culture is fifth-century Attic tragedy, but the depredations of time make our knowledge of that culture at best fragmentary and indirect. Attic tragedy was a public spectacle in which poetry, music, and dance were essential constituents, but the tradition of ancient music and dance has been completely lost, so we cannot know (Attic) tragedy as the ancients would have known it. The most vital contemporary form of culture is Wagnerian music-drama, which is also something to which we have full and immediate access,[3] so it makes sense to study the general questions about the nature of culture by looking at the origin, the flourishing, and the decline of Attic tragedy in the light of our experience of Wagner's music-drama. In this sense *The Birth of Tragedy* is a specific intervention in a debate that was conducted during the nineteenth century about what form modern society and modern culture should take. Roughly speaking, *The Birth of Tragedy* asks: how can we remedy the ills of 'modern' society? Nietzsche's answer is: by constructing a new 'tragic culture' centred on an idealized version of Wagnerism.

---

[3] Although when *The Birth of Tragedy* was written most of Wagner's music-dramas had never been staged and Nietzsche will have known them through piano reductions of the scores.

The second set of issues with which *The Birth of Tragedy* is concerned derives from the tradition of Western philosophical theology. The second basic question is: 'Is life worth living?' Nietzsche's answer is (roughly): 'No (*but* in a tragic culture one can learn to tolerate the knowledge that it is not).' Obviously the two questions are intimately connected.

The argument in the text falls into roughly three parts. The first part (§§ 1–10) describes the origin of tragedy in ancient Greece as the outcome of a struggle between two forces, principles, or drives. Nietzsche names each of these principles after an ancient Greek deity (Apollo, Dionysos) who can be thought of as imaginatively representing the drive in question in an especially intense and pure way. 'Apollo' embodies the drive toward distinction, discreteness and individuality, toward the drawing and respecting of boundaries and limits; he teaches an ethic of moderation and self-control. The Apolline artist glorifies individuality by presenting attractive images of individual persons, things, and events. In literature the purest and most intense expression of the Apolline is Greek epic poetry (especially Homer). The other contestant in the struggle for the soul of ancient Greece was Dionysos. The Dionysiac is the drive towards the transgression of limits, the dissolution of boundaries, the destruction of individuality, and excess. The purest artistic expression of the Dionysiac was quasi-orgiastic forms of music, especially of choral singing and dancing.

Although these two impulses are in some sense opposed to each other, they generally coexist in any given human soul, institution, work of art, etc. (although one will usually also be dominant). It is precisely the tension between the two of them that is particularly creative. The task is to get them into a productive relation to each other. This happens, for instance, when the Dionysiac singing and dancing of a chorus is joined with the more restrained and ordered speech and action of individual players on a stage, as in Attic tragedy. The synthesis of Apollo and Dionysos in tragedy (in which the musical, Dionysiac element, Nietzsche claims, has a certain dominance) is part of a complex defence against the pessimism and despair which is the natural existential lot of humans.

Tragedy consoles us and seduces us to continue to live, but the synthesis it represents is a fragile one, and the second part of Nietzsche's text (§§ 11–15) describes how the balance is upset by the arrival of a new force, principle, or drive, which Nietzsche associated with Socrates. Socrates does not try to attain metaphysical consolation through the dissolution of boundaries (Dionysos) or glory in the loving cultivation of individual appearance (Apollo); rather, his life is devoted to the creation of abstract generalizations and the attainment of theoretical knowledge, and he firmly believes that the use of reason will lead to human happiness. Socratic rationalism upsets the delicate balance on which tragedy depends, by encouraging people not to strive for wisdom in the face of the necessary unsatisfactoriness of human life, but to attempt to use knowledge to get control of their fate. 'Modern culture' arises in direct continuity out of such Socratism.

The third and final part of the text (§§ 16–25) describes the modern (i.e. late nineteenth century) state of crisis in which we are being forced to realize the limits of our Socratic culture and the high price we have had to pay for it. History, Nietzsche believes, is about to reverse direction and move us backward from the Socratic state to one in which tragedy will once again be possible (§ 19). The main evidence for this is recent (as of 1870) developments in philosophy and music. Schopenhauer and Kant show the limits of rationalism, and music, especially the music of Beethoven, has rediscovered the Dionysiac. Wagner's music-dramas are a first attempt to marry the Dionysiac power of the modern symphony orchestra to Apolline epic speech and action (in the interests of a pessimistic philosophy derived from Schopenhauer). At the end of his life Socrates realized that he had missed out completely on something and tried to 'write music';[4] he failed, but we can and should adopt the ideal of the *musiktreibender Sokrates*, of a figure who can integrate art and knowledge into cultural forms that will make our lives tolerable again.

As mentioned above, *The Birth of Tragedy* was one of the last and most distinguished contributions to a Central European debate about the ills of modern society. This was a debate in which many of the participants, oddly enough, were broadly in agreement on a complex diagnosis of the problem, although, of course, they disagreed on the treatment. The diagnosis was that life in the modern world lacks a kind of unity, coherence, and meaningfulness that life in previous societies possessed. Modern individuals have developed their talents and powers in an overspecialized, one-sided way; their lives and personalities are fragmented, not integrated, and they lack the ability to identify with their society in a natural way and play the role assigned to them in the world wholeheartedly. They cannot see the lives they lead as meaningful and good. Schiller, Hölderlin, Hegel, Marx, Wagner, Nietzsche (and many other lesser-known figures) all accept

---

[4] Plato, *Phaedo* 60e 5ff.

versions of this general diagnosis. Theoretical and practical reactions to this perceived problematic state differ enormously. Some (like the later Schiller) thought that what was needed was a new elitist classicism; others (such as Marx) thought that only radical political action directed at changing the basic economic structure of society could deal effectively with the situation. The strand of response to this perceived problem that is most important for the genesis of Nietzsche's views is Romanticism. As Nietzsche himself points out in the introduction to the second edition, *The Birth of Tragedy* is a work of Romanticism. It is concerned with the description of a highly idealized past which is analysed so as to highlight its contrast with and superiority to the 'modern' world, and it ends with a peroration which calls for the utopian construction of a form of society and culture which will break radically with the present and re-embody some of the positively valued features of this past. Earlier Romantics had been obsessed with one or the other of two such idealized past societies. Some gave their allegiance to an idealized antiquity, presenting some version of the the ancient city-state (especially the Athens of the fifth and fourth centuries BC) as the model for a harmonious and satisfying human life; others, and this came to be thought the more characteristically Romantic option, followed the lead of the poet Novalis in praising the purported all-encompassing unity of the Catholic Middle Ages.[5] There are strong elements of both of these views in Wagner, whose ideas about the work of art are strongly informed by his reading of Attic tragedy (especially the *Oresteia*), but who tends to derive the plot and setting of his music-dramas from the Middle Ages (and who, of course, ends his productive life with the *catholisant Parsifal*). Nietzsche belongs firmly in the first of the two camps.

His version of the story begins by distinguishing his view from what he takes to be the assumptions of prevailing humanist accounts of antiquity. The 'ancient world' was not itself a single unitary phenomenon which deserves unqualified and indiscriminate admiration. Rather there is a robust, creative, and admirable part, 'archaic Greece', the period from Homer to some time in the middle of the fifth century, and then a period of decadence and decline. It is 'archaic Greece' that we should study if we wish to see a model of the best kind of society humans can aspire to.

Archaic Greek society, Nietzsche claims, is different from and superior to the modern world because archaic Greece was an *artistic* culture,

---

[5] *Cf.* Novalis, 'Christianity or Europe' in *The Early Political Writings of the German Romantics*, ed. F. Beiser (Cambridge University Press, 1996), pp. 59ff.

whereas modern culture is centred on cognition ('science') and 'morality'. The culture of archaic Greece, Nietzsche claims, was not just 'artistic' in that it produced a lot of excellent art, but it was in some sense fundamentally based on and oriented to art, not theoretical science or a formally codified morality. Art was pervasively integrated into all aspects of life and was perceived to be of fundamental significance. Art told the archaic Greeks who they were and how it was best for them to act. Children were taught not biology, geography, mathematics, and a catechism of rules for behaviour (based either on Revelation or on rational argumentation), but athletics, music, dancing, and poetry. The final standards of evaluation and approbation in more or less any area of life were aesthetic. As adults the basic way people argued about what to do was by citing not statistics or scientific theories, but chunks of Homer, Simonides, or Pindar. Homer, in particular, it was thought, must be the universal expert and authority on everything *because* he was the best poet, i.e. was aesthetically superior to all other poets. Plato's Socrates has an uphill battle in many of the dialogues trying to wean his contemporaries from this habit. As Wagner had emphasized, Attic 'tragedy', the most characteristic form of this ancient artistic culture, was not originally a mere 'aesthetic phenomenon' confined to one rather marginal sphere of life, but was rather a highly public event at the very centre of the political, religious, and social life of Athens. The production of tragedies was publicly funded and attendance at the theatre was such an important part of what it was to be an Athenian citizen, in fact, that indigent citizens eventually would have their tickets paid for them, just as they would eventually be paid to attend the Assembly or to serve on juries. The period of greatest dramatic creativity in Athens was also the period during which Athens held hegemony over the so-called 'Delian League'. The League was a military alliance originally directed against the Persian empire, which, however, eventually became in effect an Athenian empire. Most of the 'allied' members of the League were forced to pay assessed contributions which were used for the upkeep of the Athenian fleet and for public works (such as building the Parthenon) in Athens. The poet Sophocles, we know, in addition to writing tragedies, also served on the board of generals and was one of the overseers entrusted with collecting the contributions from the allies. On the day on which the main dramatic festival began, then, all the citizens (ideally) and representatives of the 'allies' assembled in the theatre in front of the altar to Dionysos which stood in the centre of the theatre and observed the sacrifices which were offered to the god, including a sacrifice by the generals. Then the 'tribute' from the 'allies' was carried across the stage to be stored in the Athenian temples that served as treasuries. Finally the dramatic competition proper could begin.

To the contemporary reader it seems odd that Nietzsche, who, following Wagner, emphasizes so strongly the role tragedy played in unifying Athenian culture, has nothing to say about any possible connection between artistic achievement and that archetypically Athenian institution, democracy. Apoliticism was not a necessary part of Romanticism. Indeed some of the early Romantics (the two Schlegels) had been keen republicans – Nietzsche criticizes them on just this account in *The Birth of Tragedy* (see below pp. 36–7). The Wagnerian *Gesamtkunstwerk*, modelled on Wagner's ideas about Attic tragedy, was to be an institution of spiritual *and* political regeneration. It was, of course, not uncommon in the humanistic tradition at the end of which Nietzsche stands to admire Athens *despite* its 'democratic' institutions (and in earlier and more pervasively Christian periods, also *despite* its paganism). Nietzsche's utter contempt for 'democracy' seems to be one of the most basic features of his intellectual and psychological make-up. It certainly antedated the development of any of his characteristic philosophic views. He is said to have resigned from a student fraternity because he disapproved of its excessively democratic admissions policies. It is true that virtually no one in the nineteenth century would have thought of 'democracy' in the way that has become customary here in Western Europe at the end of the twentieth century, as self-evidently the only justifiable form of political organization,[6] but even by the standards of his period Nietzsche's political views were not enlightened. Wagner's political reputation has been tarnished by his anti-Semitism, by his later accommodation to the political powers-that-be in Germany – he would do almost anything, even kowtow to Bismarck (not to mention King Ludwig of Bavaria), to get his Festspielhaus built – and by the attractiveness of his aesthetics to the National Socialists. He was also first and foremost a creative artist who, although intellectually extremely active and sometimes insightful, was not always terribly clear or consistent in the general ideas he held. Left Hegelian, anarchist, republican, pacifist, 'communist', nationalist, and various other kinds of political ideas jostled one another in his mind without apparently disturbing him too much. Still, he remained

---

[6] *Cf.* John Dunn, 'Conclusion' to *Democracy: The Unfinished Journey*, ed. John Dunn (Oxford University Press, 1992).

committed until the end of his life to the idea of a total revolution (i.e. a cultural *and* political revolution) which would abolish the state and introduce a form of radical social egalitarianism. The Festspielhaus itself in Bayreuth embodies Wagner's egalitarian ideal architecturally in the complete absence of separate boxes or special loges where members of an elite could segregate themselves from the other members of the audience: as in an ancient theatre, there are just plain rows of identical benches with each member of the audience the equal of each other, just as (ideally) among the citizens of the ancient democracies. This is the direct architectural denial of one of Nietzsche's central ideas, that of *Rangordnung,* of 'rank-ordering'.

Although politics is absent from the text as we now have it (apart from the odd *obiter dictum*), a sustained discussion of politics was an integral part of the original series of overlapping projects that eventually became *The Birth of Tragedy*. Thus the essay that has come to be known as *The Greek State* was originally part of an early draft of *The Birth of Tragedy*,[7] and Nietzsche must have made a conscious decision to exclude it from the published version. In this essay Nietzsche expresses his early political views with great clarity and force. In contrast to Wagner's view (as expressed in his *Das Kunstwerk der Zukunft*) that the artistic culture of ancient Greece could not be revived because it *deserved* to perish – founded as it was on slavery – and that a fully satisfactory work of art '*of the future*' could belong only to a society that had abolished not only chattel-slavery but its modern equivalent, the wage-slavery characteristic of capitalist societies, Nietzsche asserts that slavery is an essential feature of any society that aspires to high cultural attainments. He does seem to think it is rather a shame that this is the case, but he never suggests that the price is not worth paying.

'Modern culture', in the sense of that term Nietzsche insists on using, starts in mid-fifth-century Athens with Socrates. It is essentially theoretical or scientific in that it assumes that *knowledge* (not custom or the most aesthetically pleasing words of the best poets) should be our guide in life. The good man (and, on Socrates' reading of it, this means the man who was leading a good life) was the man who had a certain kind of knowledge. To be sure, the 'knowledge' the real historical Socrates sought (as far as we can tell, which is not very far, since the historical Socrates notoriously wrote nothing) is not exactly scientific knowledge, certainly not in the sense that term had come to have by the end of the nineteenth century; it is a kind

---

[7] Reprinted in Nietzsche, *On the Genealogy of Morality,* ed. by K. Ansell-Pearson (Cambridge University Press, 1994), pp. 176ff.

of 'moral knowledge', but Nietzsche assumes that there is a distinct, important, historically continuous line of development from the Socratic quest to the nineteenth-century ideal of the pursuit of objective, scientific knowledge for its own sake. This part of his view is not worked out in any great detail, but Nietzsche clearly holds that it is appropriate to call 'modern' nineteenth-century culture 'Socratic' in the wider sense of being essentially devoted to the pursuit and application of propositionally articulated 'theoretical knowledge' and incapable of conceiving that anything else could be an appropriate guide for how to live. Such Socratism, Nietzsche argues, is a fundamentally optimistic view, and that brings us to the second of the two sets of issues *The Birth of Tragedy* addresses, the question whether life is worth living (and if so for what reasons).

Plato's Socrates explicitly holds that no ill can befall a good man, a man with the appropriate kind of knowledge, and that this knowledge is accessible to humans (through 'dialectic', the give-and-take of argument in the attempt to discover formal definitions of human 'excellence'), and the nineteenth century is unreflectively convinced that the accumulation of scientific knowledge will lead to increased human happiness. Christianity too can be seen as contributing a separate strand to the genesis of the characteristically modern form of optimism:[8] the world is finally created by an omnipotent and all-benevolent God who will take care that in the larger scheme of things all is for the best. It is one of Nietzsche's major claims in *The Birth of Tragedy* that archaic Greece did not share this optimism about knowledge, the Christian metaphysical optimism about the final nature of the universe, or indeed optimism in any form. The archaic equivalent of the biblical claim that God looked on the world and saw that it was good (or the Socratic claim that no harm can ever befall the good man) is the wisdom of Silenus that never to have been is the best state of all for humans. This 'wisdom' was *not* necessarily expressed in propositional form – it was a kind of non-theoretical, non-discursive knowledge, as Aeschylus puts

---

[8] In the Preface to the second edition of *The Birth of Tragedy* Nietzsche claims that the absence of any extended discussion of Christianity in the first edition is a sign that even then he was a committed anti-Christian. This is pretty clearly another instance of Nietzsche's attempt to project views he later developed back on to his early work. To the extent to which there is any reference at all to Christianity in *The Birth of Tragedy* it takes the form of a discussion of the *Dionysiac* standing of at least one strand of Christianity (§ 23, cf. § 17 very end, § 12). In later writings Nietzsche goes out of his way to emphasize that Christianity is a historically composite phenomenon comprising a number of different strands. So there may be a Dionysiac Christian religiosity (speaking in tongues in the early church), and also a more rationalist version of Christianity (Leibniz). In the following discussion 'Christianity' means the kind of Christianity of the roughly 'rationalist' theological tradition (including Aquinas).

it in *Agamemnon* (line 177) a 'pathei mathos', a knowing in and through experiencing/suffering, a knowing embodied perhaps tacitly in one's attitudes and behaviour even if one never formulated it clearly (although, as we have seen, various archaic thinkers *did* formulate it explicitly). The very fact that the Athenians organized so much of their political, social, and religious life around a ritualized representation of catastrophic destruction (i.e. tragedy) shows that they must in some sense have been metaphysical pessimists. How else, Nietzsche argues, could one explain the keen, addictive pleasure the Athenians and, following them, many others through the ages have taken in watching a basically admirable, heroic individual destroy himself in the pursuit of truth and knowledge, as Oedipus does?

One possibility, of course, is to attribute to the Athenians (and to us) some kind of deep-seated sadism – we just, in fact, take such pleasure in making other people suffer that we even enjoy artistic representations of other people's sufferings. The later Nietzsche does propose versions of this view,[9] but in *The Birth of Tragedy* he gives a rather more complex account. People enjoy watching tragedy because they in some sense understand that in watching this ritual self-destruction they are gaining insight into the fundamental human condition (perhaps into the very nature of reality), i.e. because they recognize that Oedipus' fate is *the human fate*, and in particular in some sense *their own fate*. People in some sense take pleasure in knowing this truth. Since, however, this kind of knowledge of the truth is useless in helping them avoid their inevitable fate (death and dissolution), this is a masochistic form of knowledge. The situation, however, is even more complex, because while dissolution of our identity and individuality is in one sense what we fear most, it is *also* potentially the highest and most intense kind of pleasure (Isolde's 'unbewußt / höchste Lust'). Presumably the pleasure results from the fact that in losing our individuality we are (if Schopenhauer is right) returning to our original state, a state which is metaphysically speaking what we always *really* were. Getting back to that fundamentally natural state, after the brief sojourn in the illusory world of 'individuality', is experienced as pleasurable. We take pleasure in watching Oedipus' demise because deep down we know we would experience our *own* dissolution as deeply pleasurable (and also horrible). The pleasure we experience in various mundane orgiastic experiences when the sense of separate, differentiated self is lost is a vague analogue of the real pleasure (and horror) of genuine self-dissolution. Finally, just as dissolution of

---

[9] *Cf. Beyond Good and Evil* § 229f; *Genealogy of Morality*, II. § 7.

identity is both horrible and pleasurable, so equally knowledge that our identity is an illusion doomed imminently to be dissolved is both attractive – which explains partly the appeal of tragedy – and repulsive. In fact, Nietzsche claims, full, undiluted knowledge of the metaphysical truth about the world would be strictly intolerable to humans; it would produce in us a nausea in the face of existence that would literally kill us. The paradoxical duality in tragedy (pain and pleasure:'unbewußt / höchste Lust') mirrors an underlying metaphysical paradox: what we take to be most real about ourselves, our very individuation as separate beings, is nothing but an illusory appearance generated by a non-individuated metaphysical entity (the Will). This is what makes tragedy the highest form of art, and, as such, 'the true *metaphysical* activity' ('An attempt at self-criticism' § 5; *cf.* also 'Foreword to Richard Wagner').

Oedipus' fate, then, is a paradigm instance of what it is to be human and a good artistic representation of a basic metaphysical feature of the universe. First of all, the social identity which Oedipus believes is his and which he takes to be robust and firmly founded – that he is the all-knowing, omnicompetent saviour of Thebes – shows itself in the course of the drama to have been an illusion which gradually is dissolved. This is an artistic expression of the basic metaphysical truth that our prized individuality, even our very spatio-temporal distinctness itself, is only a momentary illusion. Second, Oedipus is shown to be untiring in his attempts to discover the truth, but discovery of that truth does him (and Thebes) ultimately no good at all. By answering the riddle of the Sphinx, he frees the city from her depredations, but the end result of this is the plague with which the tragedy opens. Application of human intelligence has merely replaced one evil with another. The truth about himself, which Oedipus pursues so keenly throughout most of the play, is utterly intolerable to him when he attains it – that is why he blinds himself. That knowledge itself is, as Nietzsche puts it, an 'enormous offence against nature' (§ 9) which nature itself will avenge is the basic mythic truth which tragedy transmits and Oedipus instantiates. This is what makes tragedy literally incomprehensible to the optimistic Socrates with his faith in 'knowledge'.

Even if, however, this cognitive account of tragedy explains why the Athenians were addicted to it, it does not answer the further question. If the knowledge of reality *is* really so terrible that no one can tolerate it, how can the audience in a tragedy survive a performance? The answer is that tragedy transmits the basic pessimistic truth about the world and human life while at the same time enveloping it with an illusory appearance which makes it (just barely) tolerable.

Tragedy originally arises, Nietzsche claims, from the dancing and music-making of a frenzied chorus in the grip of a Dionysiac 'intoxication' (*Rausch*). Collective music-making is the form of art that brings us as close as it is possible for us to come to the experience of the basic truth that our individual identity is an illusion. Pure, unadulterated Dionysiac music, however, is so close to the basic reality of the world that it is dangerous. No one, Nietzsche suggests (falsely, no doubt, but that is another matter), could really survive a simple *listening* to (the Dionysiac truth embodied in) the music to the third act of *Tristan* without the words and staging.

Fully formed tragedy has come into existence when words and stage-action are added to the collective, orgiastic music-making of the chorus. The words and the stage-action as it were deflect and dilute the impact of that reality, making it tolerable to humans. They do this by constructing a realm of what Nietzsche calls *Schein*, i.e. of appearance or semblance.

Tragedy is a constructed realm of *Schein* in two senses. First, the actor on stage is not really the mythic king of Thebes, Oedipus (although he in some sense 'seems' to be), but some Athenian citizen in a mask. One has failed to experience the tragedy if one sees only one's friend and fellow actor up there on the stage parading around in an odd mask. One has also failed if one thinks that it *really is* Oedipus up there, that the blood dripping down from his eyes is real blood, etc.

In a second sense, the words and action in tragedy generate a *Schein* in that they seem to individuate what is happening and give the audience distance from it. What is actually happening in the performance of a tragedy is that each member of the audience is being confronted with a general, but existentially pertinent, truth about what human life is and must be (namely one form of catastrophe or another), but the appearance is created that what is happening on stage is happening to some particular *other* individual, to Oedipus, or Tristan (not to you, the individual member of the audience).

When Pentheus in Euripides' *Bacchae* is torn limb from limb by his mother and her friends, presumably this is already a version *ad usum delphini* of Dionysiac experiences that were even more savage and pleasurable, but which few of the participants survived. This is not yet the deepest form of Dionysiac experience because it is 'already' corrupted and distorted by the principle of individuation, i.e. the pleasure and pain are represented as distributed to *different* individuals at *different* times: physical pain to Pentheus, physical pleasure at one point in time to his mother, but then at a later time distress. The genuine aboriginal Dionysiac experience would be most intense pleasure and most intense pain at the same time and in the same person (or rather in the same collectivity with no distinction of person). So again the best example would be if Isolde at the end of *Tristan* were to sing her part without words, as a kind of *vocalise*, in a performance without a separate audience, apart from the musicians, and the collectivity composed of Isolde and the members of the orchestra expired at the end in a paroxysm of self-inflicted intolerable pleasure-and-pain.

The production of individuated *Schein* is the work of 'Apollo'and it is this work that allows the spectators to survive. Tragedy requires the co-operation of Dionysos with Apollo, of music *and* words. Pure or absolute Dionysiac music (which would have to be purely instrumental music with no accompanying words) would be too direct an expression of this truth; we survive a Wagnerian music-drama (as the ancient Athenians had survived an Aeschylean tragedy) only because of the illusions Apollo creates. Success in tragedy consists in combining appropriately the most deeply Dionysiac music with the most highly articulated and pleasing Apolline illusions. Great tragedy can be a central part of a culture only if the members of that culture are psychically vital and robust enough to tolerate engagement with the truth which tragedy transmits.

Socrates correctly diagnoses tragedy as a purveyor of *Schein*, but fails utterly to see the point of this *Schein*. Part of the reason for this, Nietzsche thinks, is that Socrates is a deeply abnormal, unhealthy man, a man of stunted and perverted instincts and a diseased intellect that has run wild. His abnormality take the form of a kind of hyperintellectualized simple-mindedness. When he looks at tragedy, he fails to see it as an instance of a kind of self-sufficient *Schein* which confronts us with a deep truth about life, and thinks it is *just* a simple lie/illusion. That is not to say that Socratism is not itself a tissue of illusions. 'On Truth and Lying in a Non-Moral Sense' is precisely an extended analysis of the various 'illusions' Nietzsche thinks inherently constitutive of the Socratic way of life. Socrates, Nietzsche thinks, is committed not just to the self-evidently false beliefs that no harm can befall the good man, and that no one does 'wrong' willingly, but also to the equally false view that concepts can tell us something about the essence of the world, that the world is composed of identical cases that can be correctly subsumed under general concepts, and so on.

The human situation, then, is dire indeed if tragedy is an illusion, and the only alternatives to it – Socratism or Christianity – are equally illusions. In fact, according to Nietzsche, the only choice we have is (one or another kind of) illusion *or* death. That is one way of expressing what it means to say that Nietzsche's view is pessimistic. If this is the case, though, what reason can we have to prefer the illusions of a tragic culture to the illusions of Socratism? Why should we bother actively to seek tragedies out? Why should *we* (late-nineteenth-century Central Europeans) try to build theatres to expose ourselves to these illusions? Why should we try to construct a new 'tragic' culture?

There are several interconnected reasons for preferring tragic to Socratic illusions. First, Socratic illusions and the form of life associated with them are not finally stable. In the end even Socrates himself felt the need for 'music',[10] and this will be the fate of every Socratic culture. The history of philosophy also shows a natural development from Socrates to the insight attained in Kant (according to Nietzsche) and Schopenhauer that the everyday world investigated by the scientific optimist is a mere illusion and that one must look beyond it (to Kantian 'faith' or Schopenhauer's pessimism) for any final human meaning. Second, although both tragedy and Socratism are 'illusions', *Schein* (in *one* sense of that highly equivocal term), Nietzsche believes that some kinds of *Schein* can be closer to the truth than others. This is one of Nietzsche's more interesting ideas and it is a shame that he never develops it in any detail. Tragedy, in any case, Nietzsche clearly thinks, is closer to the truth than Socratic 'illusions' are. Finally, Socratic illusions just are not as inherently satisfying as the illusions of a full tragic culture.

That brings us to the second of the two main topics of *The Birth of Tragedy*. Clearly the book is intended as a contribution to philosophical theodicy. The text states several times that 'only as an aesthetic phenomenon can the world be justified'.[11] The task of giving a theodicy in the Western theological tradition was that of trying to show argumentatively that the world, despite appearances to the contrary, really was in essence good, and not just 'good' in some very abstract sense, but good *for us*. By showing this, philosophers thought they could vindicate the claim that human life was potentially worthwhile for those living it, and thus that it was rational for us to adopt a fundamentally optimistic attitude toward our respective lives and toward the world as a whole. The history of

---

[10] *Cf.* above, footnote 4.   [11] § 5, *cf.* 3, 'An attempt at self-criticism' § 5.

philosophical theodicies in the West is long and convoluted, and I will mention only two of the various approaches that have been taken. One historically important strand of argument depends on the claim that the existence of evil is a logically necessary concomitant of the existence of free human choice, and the existence of such free choice is an overriding good. Since whatever evil exists in the world is there for the sake of the realization of the overwhelming good of human freedom, it makes sense to see the world as a whole as good. Another approach claims that the world as a whole was created by a rational god attempting to maximize the number and variety of created beings in the most parsimonious way. This project, it is claimed, is inherently rational and good, and what we call 'evil' can be shown to be a necessary, but subordinate, or merely local aspect of it.

Most of these traditional arguments presuppose the existence of an omnipotent god who created the world as a whole according to a rational plan and who cares for the good of each individual person, and they argue from that to the view that the existence of evil in the world is *compatible with* having an optimistic attitude toward the world as a whole and human life. So 'theodicy' can be a useful exercise for people who *already* have the appropriate religious belief in the existence of an omnipotent, benevolent creator of the world, but Nietzsche in *The Birth of Tragedy* is adopting a post-Christian view which does not assume such a religious belief.

The claim that the world can be justified only as an aesthetic phenomenon is to be read in two ways, negatively and positively. First of all it asserts that none of the traditional ways of justifying existence by reference to formal rationality, the exigencies of freedom of the will, or principles such as parsimony, efficiency, plenitude of being etc. works. Second, it asserts positively that one way of justifying the world (or 'life' or whatever) *does* work, namely contemplation of the world as an aesthetic phenomenon. This presumably means that each feature of the world is justified because *that* feature is one the world must have if it is to present an aesthetically pleasing spectacle (or perhaps, *the* most aesthetically pleasing spectacle) to an appropriately sophisticated observer. The first thing to notice is that the very term 'justification' (*Rechtfertigung*) might be thought to belong to the Socratic sphere which it is purportedly the whole intention of *The Birth of Tragedy* to undercut, because the most normal way (at least now) to take it is as a request for some kind of general theoretically based discursive structure. One could, of course, use 'justify' in a more general sense to mean simply 'to cause to seem to be worthwhile or good'. One must be careful not to go too far down this road, because getting drunk or taking various drugs can be a very effective way for me to be caused to come to see the world as good or various activities as 'worthwhile', but it is not clear that this is a model for 'justification' in any interesting sense. The question is whether there is something between sheer *Rausch* on the one hand, and Socratic argumentation on the other. Nietzsche claims that art is located precisely there and that may well be right, but it is not clear how we can get clarity about where this 'there' is. To give too discursive an account would be self-defeating. Perhaps that is part of the reason for the dithyrambic style of *The Birth of Tragedy*, and Nietzsche's comment in the Preface to the second edition ('An attempt at self-criticism' § 3) that he ought to have expressed himself by singing rather than by speaking in prose is perhaps more than just a joke (although, given what we know about Nietzsche's abilities as a composer, we should probably be very pleased we have the text we do).

In addition, if *The Birth of Tragedy* is to be a satisfactory aesthetic theodicy we need to know who is making the basic aesthetic judgment on which the theodicy rests. The answer to this question is not as obvious as it might seem, because in the main text Nietzsche uses as his example of an aesthetic theodicy the 'Homeric' view that the world is justified *because* it presents an engaging aesthetic spectacle *to* the Olympian gods (§ 5). When Nietzsche later refers to *The Birth of Tragedy* as containing an 'artiste's metaphysics' ('Attempt at self-criticism' § 2) I think he has in mind a metaphysics which is a secularized descendant of this 'Homeric' view. The non-individuated reality behind all appearances, what Nietzsche calls *das Ur-Eine* ('the primordially One') (*passim*), is itself a kind of artist. In an image taken over from Heraclitus (fragment 52 [Diels–Kranz]; *The Birth of Tragedy* § 24; *GM* II.16) Nietzsche writes that this primordial unity is like a child playing in the sand on the beach, wantonly and haphazardly creating individuated shapes and forms and then destroying them, taking equal pleasure in *both* parts of the process, in both creation (Apollo) and destruction (Dionysos). Our world is nothing but a momentary configuration of shapes in the sand. The child's play does not in any significant sense follow 'rational' principles and has no purpose beyond itself. It is 'innocent' and ' beyond good and evil' (to use Nietzsche's own later expression). The only sense that can be made of the whole activity is whatever aesthetic sense it makes for the child to create or erase one form rather than another. From the fact, though, that the world presents a pleasing aesthetic spectacle to certain gods (especially to the wanton Heraclitean child), and is in *this* sense 'justified', it does not obviously follow that *I* will find *my* life worth living, especially if my role in the spectacle is that of victim, and even more so if there are cogent philosophical arguments, such as one finds in the work of Schopenhauer, to the effect that the *only* kind of role available for a human is that of one or another kind of victimization or frustration. The world and life may come to *seem* 'justified' for us to the extent to which we, through various aesthetic experiences, can come close to identifying ourselves in the primordial child and seeing the beauty of the play. Successful (great) tragedy may allow us that momentary identification and vision, but that identification is nonetheless in one important sense an illusion. In *one* sense the child who in metaphysical play creates and destroys the world is our underlying reality (because it is the underlying reality of everything), but in the usual sense of 'identical' we are not 'identical' with that child, 'we' are one of the insubstantial shapes with which it plays.

The important difference between Nietzsche's 'theodicy' and previous Christian ones is that *he* will come increasingly to distinguish three separate things which views like traditional Christianity connect: theodicy ('the world is justified'), optimism ('our life can be worth living') and affirmation. Affirmation is not exactly the same thing as optimism (at least as traditionally understood), if only because it is usually assumed that an 'optimistic' position is one that claims that we can see our lives as they really are, *without* illusions, and still find them worthwhile. Nietzsche, however, thinks that this is not possible for us. However beautiful the play from the point of view of *das Ur-Eine*, *we* are momentary illusory shapes doomed to the ineluctable frustration of the desires we necessarily have, and we cannot even tolerate the knowledge that this is our situation. Metaphysically, then, pessimism is true; what Nietzsche wishes to investigate is whether affirmation in any sense is possible under these circumstances, and he seems to find that possibility embodied in tragedy.

Paradoxically, if Dionysos and Apollo are successfully brought into alliance in a given tragedy, the result will be a transformation of 'pessimism' – not into optimism, to be sure, but into a kind of affirmation; that is, the *Schein* that arises will not sap the audience's strength, paralyse its will or lead to demoralization, but rather will energize the members of the audience to go on living. To be more exact, it requires great strength to produce and appreciate tragedy because it takes us so close to the basic horror of things, but if one can tolerate this, the result is an increase rather than a decrease in one's ability to live vividly (and create further great art – Nietzsche seems sometimes rather to confuse these two).

That tragedy can have this life-enhancing effect is one of the things that permits Nietzsche later (in the 1880s when he writes the Preface to the second edition) to claim that in *The Birth of Tragedy* he had *already* moved beyond Schopenhauer and away from pessimism in the strict sense. It is not hard to see how Nietzsche could have thought this. To admit the existence of a life-enhancing form of pessimism (if such a form did exist) would seem to mean at least that 'pessimism' must be a much more highly ambiguous phenomenon than had previously been thought.

Nietzsche's views on pessimism and its modalities shifted significantly from the early 1870s to the mid-1880s. In the earlier period he is still attempting to assimilate archaic Greece more or less straightforwardly to Schopenhauer, and is satisfied to point out that *both* Schopenhauer and Aeschylus (purportedly) are 'pessimistic' (compared with the optimism of Christianity and the modern belief in science, progress etc.). Later (for instance, in *Human, All Too Human*) he comes to claim that the whole discussion of optimism or pessimism as basic attitudes towards the world makes sense only if one assumes an outmoded theological view of the world. So presumably we should try to adopt a form of life that was 'beyond optimism and pessimism', one which we did not find it necessary to interpret in terms of either of these two concepts. Still later (in the Preface to the second edition of *The Birth of Tragedy* and other writings) he seems to find his way back again to a more complex understanding of the problems associated with 'pessimism'. He claims to find the unitary notion of 'pessimism' (which he had used in the main text of *The Birth of Tragedy*) over-simple, and he distinguishes between different types of pessimism – a pessimism of weakness (Schopenhauer), and a pessimism of strength (archaic Greece). The archaic Greeks are 'pessimists', but 'pessimists of strength', *not*, as Nietzsche claims in the main body of *The Birth of Tragedy*, pessimists in the sense in which Schopenhauer is a pessimist (and what Nietzsche now calls 'pessimism of weakness'). That is, he seems to think that what is finally significant in a philosophy is whether or not it contributes to an affirmation of this world, and that one can in some sense distinguish issues of pessimism/optimism from issues concerning affirmation or negation of *this* world, our world of everyday life. Since both Schopenhauer and Christianity agree that *this* world is not to be affirmed, they are really instances of the same kind of weakness, and the difference in their metaphysical views (that the Christian thinks the underlying *reality* of the world, God, is to be affirmed while Schopenhauer thinks this underlying reality, the Will, is to be negated) is irrelevant.

How exactly are we to construct a new tragic culture? Obviously part of the project will be to get rid of the various forms of optimism that cloud our vision, primarily Christianity and the nineteenth-century 'scientific world view'. The image of the *musiktreibender Sokrates* that dominates the latter parts of *The Birth of Tragedy* might be taken as suggesting that the new tragic world view will not just turn its back completely on the existing 'theoretical culture', but will pass through it, assimilate it completely, and emerge, as it were, beyond on the other side of it. How exactly Wagner and Ranke can be brought together, though, is not completely clear.[12] Perhaps in the new tragic culture people will *know* theoretically, in the way Schopenhauer claims to 'know', that our situation in the world is ultimately hopeless. We will *know* in a grounded way that our choice is illusion or death and will still choose life-invigorating illusions. In this we will differ from the ancients. Apolline art in the ancient world was not a reasoned and theoretically grounded response to the inherent worthlessness of our lives, but an instinctive reaction of exceptionally vital people. We will be able to choose *Schein* knowing in the fullest sense that it is *Schein*.

The relation of a work of philosophical speculation, like *The Birth of Tragedy*, to empirical scholarship is complex. Greece is important in the work primarily because of the tacit assumption that it is the paradigmatic artistic culture, and thus that it will exhibit in an especially transparent way the articulations one will need to grasp in order to understand just what a successful artistic culture would be like. So the *The Birth of Tragedy* could in principle contain a certain number of factual errors, idiosyncratic interpretations, empirically unsupported hypotheses, and wilful conflation of things that do not perhaps really belong together – as, in fact, it does – without losing its value completely. At a certain point, of course, if the number of errors or of unsupported speculative claims became too great, the whole project would collapse, although even then it would not be completely clear that the problem lay in Nietzsche's theory of the three factors in every culture (the Dionysiac, the Apolline, and the Socratic); it might

---

[12] In one of the fragmentary notes Nietzsche wrote while working on the preliminary sketches of *The Birth of Tragedy* he claims that Shakespeare is the 'musiktreibender Sokrates' (*Sämtliche Werke: Kritische Gesamtausgabe*, ed. G. Colli and M. Montinari (Berlin: de Gruyter, 1967ff. 7(131)), but, apart from half a dozen other fragments, he never develops this line of thought any further.

just be that Greece was not as good an instance of a (tragic) culture as we had thought.

Nietzsche's hopes for *The Birth of Tragedy* seem to have been both very exaggerated and very naive. He expected the work to be received with enthusiasm by all young Germans eager for cultural renewal, especially Wagnerians, but he also expected that the more open-minded members of the academic community of philologists would recognize the work as a pathbreaking new way of studying the ancient world. The second of these hopes was very quickly and thoroughly dashed. An initial review by Ulrich von Wilamowitz-Möllendorff was harshly critical, indeed dismissive of Nietzsche's whole project. Apart from various points of detail, Wilamowitz correctly diagnosed and categorically rejected Nietzsche's attempt to do 'philology' in a way that would make it more like philosophy or art than like a strict 'wissenschaft';[13] the proper mode of access to the ancient world, Wilamowitz asserted, was through the painstaking study of history 'in der askese selbstverläugnender arbeit', not through the mystic insights used in *The Birth of Tragedy*. It is of course perfectly true that, given the choice, Nietzsche would prefer *Weisheit* to *Wissenschaft*, so there was no real response he could make to that basic charge. Nietzsche also hoped for at least understanding, and perhaps some more tangible support, from his former teacher and patron Ritschl. Ritschl, after all, had been the person who had obtained for him his unprecedented university appointment in Basle, and, as editor of an influential journal, had been responsible for the publication of Nietzsche's early philological papers, but Ritschl agreed with Wilamowitz in his judgment of *The Birth of Tragedy*, and privately expressed regret that Nietzsche had wandered off the track from his very promising historical research into a fantastic world of religiously inspired enthusiasms. The review of *The Birth of Tragedy* was Wilamowitz's first publication, but he went on to become by far the most significant German classical philologist of the turn of the century, so his condemnation continued to be extremely influential, and Nietzsche's work was not an object of serious consideration in academic philological circles in Germany for 40 years or so. *The Birth of Tragedy* did not succeed in reforming German philology, in changing the way it was done.

With Wagnerians Nietzsche had better luck. Wagner himself was thrilled – not surprisingly, since many of the most central thoughts in *The*

---

[13] When Wilamowitz wrote his criticism of *The Birth of Tragedy* he was a supporter of one of the movements for reform of German orthography, so, contrary to current practice, he used lower-case for the initial letter of nouns.

Birth of Tragedy are culled from Wagner's own earlier writings or from Wagner's idol Schopenhauer and the book as a whole could easily have carried as its motto: 'Only as a Wagnerian is life worth living (to the extent to which it can be said to be worth living at all).' With the wider public, too, Nietzsche's work slowly established itself, starting in the 1890s, and eventually became so pervasively influential that the history of its reception in twentieth-century culture is too rich and complex to recount here even in outline.

It might seem odd that one of the most influential modern books on Greek tragedy was written by a person who had little real, continuing interest in drama, if the same thing were not also true of the ancient world: Aristotle, to judge by the existing evidence, turned a much keener eye to the reproductive organs of sea-creatures than to the fate of tragedy. If one looks at Nietzsche's life as a whole there are topics to which he returns again and again obsessively. These include the psychology of religion – his friend Lou Andreas-Salomé was right to emphasize this as a central concern – the nature of philosophy (especially as embodied in the person of Socrates), music and musicians (especially Wagner as the archetypical musician), and some general issues about how to understand the 'vitality' of cultures; they do not include drama or tragedy. Ancient tragedy became of special importance to him for a very brief moment under the spell of Wagner. As he wrote in the letter to Wagner to accompany the presentation copy of *The Birth of Tragedy* (2 January 1872), the object of the book was to show that Wagner's art was 'eternally in the right' ('daß *Sie* mit *Ihrer Kunst* in Ewigkeit recht haben müssen'). To put it bluntly, Nietzsche found tragedy especially interesting for as long as he thought it a form of the self-evidently most important and inherently significant cultural phenomenon there was – *music* – and he thought tragedy was essentially music to a large extent because Wagner said so. Wagner, in turn, said so because this was his way of asserting the superiority of his own music-drama *as music* over the purely instrumental music of Beethoven and others. To make the construction work, Nietzsche needed the highly implausible thesis that the highest form of music *must* transform itself into sung words if it is to remain humanly tolerable. Once this claim was dropped there was no reason to give pride of place to drama. Nietzsche's fascination with music (and with the psychology of religion) could take more direct and appropriate forms, and tragedy could leave centre-stage and return to the dusty corners of his consciousness. The subtitle added to the second edition (*Hellenism and*

Pessimism) connects Nietzsche's first published book more perspicuously with his continuing philosophical concerns than the original title does.

The idea specifically derived from *The Birth of Tragedy* which has become perhaps most influential in the twentieth century is the conception of the 'Dionysiac' and its role in human life, i.e. the view that destructive, primitively anarchic forces are a part of us (not to be projected into some diabolical Other), and that the pleasure we take in them is real and not to be denied. These impulses cannot simply be ignored, eliminated, repressed, or fully controlled. As Euripides' *Bacchae* shows, they will have their due one way or another and failure to recognize them is just a way of, eventually, giving them free rein to express themselves with special force, destructiveness, and irrationality. In some sense higher culture rests on coming to terms with them, but that does not mean simply letting them play themselves out in a direct and unmodified way. The primitive Dionysiac orgy is *not* an Attic tragedy, and not a form of 'higher culture' at all in this sense, although tragedy is in some sense a development of the orgy. The construction of a higher culture requires *both* a sympathetic recognition of the existence of the Dionysiac *and* an integration of it into an alliance with what Nietzsche calls 'Apollo' and what he calls 'the *daimonion* of Socrates'. Different cultures are different ways of negotiating and renegotiating the terms of this 'alliance', probably a never-ending process.

Reading the later Nietzsche has caused us to be very justifiably suspicious about uncritical use of the concept of progress, but the attempt in the modern world to assimilate or at least to face up to Nietzsche's early views about the Dionysiac seems to me to be not just another instance of the random motion of history, but an undeniably progressive development, difficult as it is to specify exactly what is meant by that. If philosophy, as Nietzsche himself thought, is essentially a matter of asking important questions that no one else had thought to ask, then to have begun to ask the questions he did in *The Birth of Tragedy* is a mark of Nietzsche's significance as a philosopher.

Raymond Geuss

Chronology

1844   Born in Röcken, a small village in the Prussian province of Saxony, on 15 October.

1846   Birth of his sister Elisabeth.

1848   Birth of his brother Joseph.

1849   His father, a Lutheran minister, dies at age thirty-six of 'softening of the brain'.

1850   Brother dies; family moves to Naumburg to live with father's mother and her sisters.

1858   Begins studies at Pforta, Germany's most famous school for education in the classics.

1864   Graduates from Pforta with a thesis in Latin on the Greek poet Theogonis; enters the University of Bonn as a theology student.

1865   Transfers from Bonn, following the classical philologist Friedrich Ritschl to Leipzig where he registers as a philology student; reads Schopenhauer's *The World as Will and Representation*.

1866   Reads Friedrich Lange's *History of Materialism*.

1868   Meets Richard Wagner.

1869   On Ritschl's recommendation is appointed professor of classical philology at Basle at the age of twenty-four before completing his doctorate (which is then conferred without a dissertation); begins frequent visits to the Wagner residence at Tribschen.

1870   Serves as a medical orderly in the Franco-Prussian war; contracts a serious illness and so serves only two months. Writes 'The Dionysiac World View'.

1872   Publishes his first book, *The Birth of Tragedy*; its dedicatory preface to Richard Wagner claims for art the role of 'the highest task and truly metaphysical activity of this life'; devastating reviews follow.

1873   Publishes 'David Strauss, the Confessor and the Writer', the first of his *Untimely Meditations*; begins taking books on natural science out of the Basle library, whereas he had previously confined himself largely to books on philological matters. Writes 'On Truth and Lying in a Non-Moral Sense'.

1874   Publishes two more *Meditations*, 'The Uses and Disadvantages of History for Life' and 'Schopenhauer as Educator'.

1876   Publishes the fourth *Meditation*, 'Richard Wagner in Bayreuth', which already bears subtle signs of his movement away from Wagner.

1878   Publishes *Human, All Too Human* (dedicated to the memory of Voltaire); it praises science over art as the mark of high culture and thus marks a decisive turn away from Wagner.

1879   Terrible health problems force him to resign his chair at Basle (with a small pension); publishes 'Assorted Opinions and Maxims', the first part of vol. 2 of *Human, All Too Human*; begins living alone in Swiss and Italian boarding-houses.

1880   Publishes 'The Wanderer and His Shadow', which becomes the second part of vol. 2 of *Human, All Too Human*.

1881   Publishes *Daybreak*.

1882   Publishes *Idylls of Messina* (eight poems) in a monthly magazine; publishes *The Gay Science*, friendship with Paul Ree and Lou Andreas-Salomé ends badly, leaving Nietzsche devastated.

1883   Publishes the first two parts of *Thus Spoke Zarathustra*; learns of Wagner's death just after mailing part one to the publisher.

1884   Publishes the third part of *Thus Spoke Zarathustra*.

1885   Publishes the fourth part of *Zarathustra* for private circulation only.

1886   Publishes *Beyond Good and Evil*; writes prefaces for new releases of: *The Birth of Tragedy*, *Human, All Too Human*, vols. 1 and 2, and *Daybreak*.

1887   Publishes expanded edition of *The Gay Science* with a new preface, a fifth part, and an appendix of poems; publishes *Hymn to Life*, a musical work for chorus and orchestra; publishes *On the Genealogy of Morality*.

1888   Publishes *The Case of Wagner*, composes a collection of poems, *Dionysian Dithyrambs*, and four short books: *Twilight of Idols*, *The Antichrist*, *Ecce Homo*, and *Nietzsche contra Wagner*.

1889   Collapses physically and mentally in Turin on 3 January; writes a few lucid notes but never recovers sanity; is briefly institutionalized; spends remainder of his life as an invalid, living with his mother and then his sister, who also gains control of his literary estate.

1900   Dies in Weimar on 25 August.

Further reading

I Volume I of the edition of Nietzsche's works edited by G. Colli and M. Montinari, Friedrich Nietzsche, *Sämtliche Werke: Kritische Gesamtausgabe* (Berlin, de Gruyter, 1967–77), contains unpublished writings from the period 1870–3 including several preliminary versions of portions of *The Birth of Tragedy*. Volume 7 of this edition contains fragments from 1869–74, many of them of direct relevance to the understanding and evaluation of *The Birth of Tragedy*; some of these fragments have been translated in *Philosophy and Truth: Selections from Nietzsche's Notebooks of the Early 1870s*, trans. and ed. by Daniel Breazeale (Atlantic Highlands, NJ, Humanities Press, 1979). Nietzsche gives a further retrospective account of *The Birth of Tragedy* in his late autobiographical work *Ecce homo* (trans. W. Kaufmann, New York, Vintage, 1967).

II Since *The Birth of Tragedy* is an attempt to use theses derived from Schopenhauer and Wagner (in conjunction with an interpretation of archaic Greece) to sketch a new form of tragic culture, it is very useful to study the works of Nietzsche's two great predecessors. Schopenhauer's major work *The World as Will and Representation* (in 2 volumes, trans. E.F.J. Payne, available in paperback: New York, Dover Publications, 1969) is required reading. His 2-volume collection *Parerga and Paralipomena* (trans. E.F.J. Payne, Oxford, Clarendon Press, 1974) also contains much of interest. The influence of Wagner's theoretical writings on the early Nietzsche has often been seriously underestimated. The two works by Wagner that are of most direct relevance to *The Birth of Tragedy* are *Opera and Drama* and 'Beethoven', but 'Art and Revolution' and 'Music of the Future' also contain relevant material; all of these are available in *Richard*

Wagner's Prose Works, ed. and trans. W.A. Ellis (London, 1892–9). There is a good chapter on Wagner and Nietzsche in *Wagner-Handbuch*, ed. U. Müller and P. Wapnewski (Stuttgart, Kröner-Verlag, 1986), translated and edited by John Deathridge as *Wagner Handbook* (Cambridge, Mass. and London, Harvard University Press, 1992); the chapter on Wagner and the ancient world is also pertinent. A third figure whose work forms an important part of the background to *The Birth of Tragedy* is Friedrich Schiller. Nietzsche refers several times to Schiller's essay 'On Naive and Sentimental Poetry' (translated under the title *Naive and Sentimental Poetry* by J.A. Elias, New York, Ungar, 1966), and his treatise '*On the Aesthetic Education of Humanity in a Series of Letters*' (available in a marvellous bi-lingual edition edited by L.A. Willoughby and E. Wilkinson, Oxford University Press, 1967) is of great importance.

III   Secondary literature on Nietzsche is massive and uneven but there are a few works of high quality. The following are some of the treatments of *The Birth of Tragedy* in English that seem to me most helpful. M. Silk and J.P. Stern, *Nietzsche on Tragedy* (Cambridge University Press, 1981) gives an encyclopaedic treatment of all aspects of the text. The best general introductory book on Nietzsche is M. Tanner, *Nietzsche* (Oxford University Press, 1994). G. Deleuze, *Nietzsche and Philosophy* (London, Athlone, 1983) presents an extremely stimulating, if (finally) not fully worked out and not fully convincing general view of Nietzsche and contains a long discussion of *The Birth of Tragedy*. J. Young, *Nietzsche's Philosophy of Art* (Cambridge University Press, 1992) is especially good on the relation of Nietzsche to Schopenhauer and in general on the later development of Nietzsche's views on art. Paul de Man, *Allegories of Reading* (Yale University Press, 1979) is a very influential, standard deconstructionist view; it is comprehensively refuted in the 'Appendix' to Henry Staten, *Nietzsche's Voice* (Cornell University Press, 1990), a book which also contains much else of interest. A. Nehamas, *Nietzsche: Life as Literature* (Harvard University Press, 1985) is a systematic philosophical treatment of central strands in Nietzsche's thought, including some to be found in *The Birth of Tragedy*. N. Martin, *Nietzsche and Schiller* (Oxford University Press, 1996) discusses the relation of early Nietzsche to the aesthetics of German classicism. W. Dannhauser, *Nietzsche's View of Socrates* (Cornell University Press, 1974) is the standard and extremely useful work on its chosen topic. Walter Benjamin has a long and critical discussion of

Nietzsche's theory of tragedy in his *Origin of German Tragic Drama*, trans. J. Osborne (London, New Left Books, 1977).

Note on the text

The texts used for this translation are those printed in the now standard edition of Nietzsche's works edited by Giorgio Colli and Mazzino Montinari (Berlin, de Gruyter, 1967–77). Their annotation was very helpful in the preparation of the footnotes to this edition. The commentary by von Reibnitz, *Ein Kommentar zu Friedrich Nietzsches 'Die Geburt der Tragödie aus dem Geiste der Musik' (Kap. 1–12)* (Stuttgart, Metzler, 1992) was also very useful; anyone with a serious interest in Nietzsche's understanding of the Greeks would be well advised to study this work. The editorial notes were prepared by Raymond Geuss and the translator's notes by Ronald Speirs. German terms that appear in the text in parentheses are explained in the Glossary.

The Birth of Tragedy

An Attempt at Self-Criticism[1]

Whatever underlies this questionable book, it must be a most stimulating and supremely important question and, furthermore, a profoundly personal one – as is attested by the times in which it was written, and *in spite of which* it was written, the turbulent period of the Franco-Prussian War of 1870–1. While the thunder of the Battle of Wörth rolled across Europe, the brooder and lover of riddles who fathered the book was sitting in some corner of the Alps, utterly preoccupied with his ponderings and riddles and consequently very troubled and untroubled at one and the same time, writing down his thoughts about the *Greeks* – the core of this odd and rather inaccessible book to which this late preface (or postscript) is to be dedicated. A few weeks later he was himself beneath the walls of Metz and still obsessed with the question marks he had placed over the alleged 'cheerfulness'[2] of the Greeks; until finally, in that extremely tense month when peace was being discussed at Versailles, he too made peace with himself and, whilst recovering slowly from an illness which he had brought back from the field, reached a settled and definitive view in his own mind of the 'Birth of Tragedy from the Spirit of *Music*' – from music? Music and tragedy? Greeks and the music of tragedy? Greeks and the pessimistic work

[1] The first edition of *The Birth of Tragedy out of the Spirit of Music* was published in 1872. In 1886 Nietzsche published a new edition with a slightly modified title: *The Birth of Tragedy. Or Hellenism and Pessimism . . . New Edition with an Attempt at Self-Criticism.* The main body of the second-edition text is virtually unchanged, but the *Attempt at Self-Criticism* is a retrospective addition, written more than ten years after the main text.

[2] Classicizing accounts in the late eighteenth and early nineteenth centuries in Germany often emphasize the 'cheerfulness' of Greek culture in contrast, for instance, with the weighty seriousness of the Middle Ages. Part of Nietzsche's purpose in *The Birth of Tragedy* is to give a more complex account of the phenomenon of Greek cheerfulness which will make it compatible with what Nietzsche takes to be the pessimistic insights of Schopenhauer (*cf.* esp. below, *The Birth of Tragedy* § 11).

3

of art? The finest, most beautiful, most envied race of men ever known, the people who made life seem most seductive, the Greeks – what, they of all people *needed* tragedy? Or even: art? What purpose was served by Greek art?

The reader will have guessed at which point I had placed the great question mark over the value of existence. Is pessimism *necessarily* a sign of decline, decay, malformation, of tired and debilitated instincts – as was the case amongst the Indians and appears to be the case amongst us 'modern men' and Europeans? Is there a pessimism of *strength*? An intellectual preference for the hard, gruesome, malevolent and problematic aspects of existence which comes from a feeling of well-being, from overflowing health, from an *abundance* of existence? Is there perhaps such a thing as suffering from superabundance itself? Is there a tempting bravery in the sharpest eye which *demands* the terrifying as its foe, as a worthy foe against which it can test its strength and from which it intends to learn the meaning of fear?[3] What does the *tragic* myth mean, particularly amongst the Greeks of the best, strongest and bravest period? And the monstrous phenomenon of the Dionysiac? And tragedy, born from the Dionysiac? Conversely, those things which gave rise to the death of tragedy – Socratism in ethics, the dialectics, smugness and cheerfulness of theoretical man – might not this very Socratism be a sign of decline, of exhaustion, of sickness, of the anarchic dissolution of the instincts? And might not the 'Greek cheerfulness' of later Hellenism be simply the red flush across the evening sky? Might not the Epicurean will to *oppose* pessimism be mere prudence on the part of someone who is sick? And science itself, our science – what indeed is the meaning of all science, viewed as a symptom of life? What is the purpose, and, worse still, what is the *origin* of all science? What? Is scientific method perhaps no more than fear of and flight from pessimism? A subtle defence against – *truth*? Or, to put it in moral terms, is it something like cowardice and insincerity? To put it immorally, is it a form of cunning? O, Socrates, Socrates, was that perhaps *your* secret? O, mysterious ironist, was this perhaps your – irony?

2

What I had got hold of at that time was something fearsome and dangerous, a problem with horns, not necessarily a bull, but at any rate a *new* problem; today I would say that it was the *problem of science (Wissenschaft)* itself,

---

[3] In Wagner's *Siegfried* the hero does not know the meaning of fear, and sets out to try to discover it.

science grasped for the first time as something problematic and question-able. But the book in which my youthful courage and suspicion vented itself – what an *impossible* book was bound to grow out of a task so at odds with youth! Constructed entirely from precocious, wet-behind-the-ears, personal experiences, all of which lay at the very threshold of what could be communicated, located in the territory of *art* – for the problem of science cannot be recognized within the territory of science – perhaps a book for artists with some subsidiary capacity for analysis and retrospection (in other words for an exceptional type of artist, a type you would have to go looking for, but one you would not actually care to find), full of psychological inno-vations and the concealments of an artiste,[4] with an artiste's metaphysics in the background, a youthful work full of youthful courage and youthful melancholy, independent, standing defiantly on its own two feet even where it appears to bow before an authority and its own veneration, in short a first book in every bad sense of the word despite its old man's problem, burdened with all the errors of youth, above all with its 'much too long', its 'storm and stress';[5] on the other hand, as far as the success it enjoyed is concerned (particularly with the great artist to whom it addressed itself, in a kind of dialogue, namely Richard Wagner), a book which has *proved* itself, by which I mean one which at least satisfied 'the best of its time'.[6] This fact alone means that it should be treated with some consideration and reticence; nevertheless, I shall not suppress entirely just how unpleasant it now seems to me, how alien it seems, standing there before me sixteen years later – before eyes which are older and a hundred times more spoiled, but by no means colder, nor grown any more of a stranger to the task which this reckless book first dared to approach: *to look at science through the prism of the artist, but also to look at art through the prism of life.*[7]

3

I repeat: I find it an impossible book today. I declare that it is badly written, clumsy, embarrassing, with a rage for imagery and confused in its imagery,

---

[4] *Artistenmetaphysik* is translated here as 'the metaphysics of the artiste' (rather than artist) because Nietzsche chooses *Artist* in preference to the usual term *Künstler*.
[5] The *Sturm und Drang* is the name given to a youthfully rebellious movement in German literature in the 1770s.
[6] Schiller (Prologue to *Wallenstein's Camp*, lines 48ff).
[7] *Optik* is an unusual term which I have rendered as 'prism', but which might also have been translated as 'lens'.

emotional, here and there sugary to the point of effeminacy, uneven in pace, lacking the will to logical cleanliness, very convinced and therefore too arrogant to prove its assertions, mistrustful even of the *propriety* of proving things, a book for the initiated, 'music' for those who were baptized in the name of music, who, from the very beginning, are linked to one another by shared, rare experiences of art, a sign by which blood-relations *in artibus*[8] could recognize one another – an arrogant and wildly enthusiastic book which, from the outset, shuts itself off from the *profanum vulgus*[9] of the 'educated' even more than from the 'common people', but also one which, as its effect proved and continues to prove, knows well enough how to seek out its fellow-enthusiasts and to entice them on to new, secret paths and places to dance. At any rate – and this was admitted with as much curiosity as aversion – a *strange*[10] voice was speaking here, the disciple of an as yet 'unknown god' who concealed himself beneath the cowl of a scholar, beneath the ponderousness and dialectical disinclination of the Germans, even beneath the bad manners of a Wagnerite; here was a spirit with strange needs, nameless as yet, a memory brimming over with questions, experiences, hidden things to which the name Dionysos had been appended as yet another question mark; here one heard – as people remarked distrustfully – something like the voice of a mystical and almost maenadic soul which stammers in a strange tongue, with great difficulty and capriciously, almost as if undecided whether to communicate or conceal itself. It ought to have *sung*, this 'new soul', and not talked! What a pity it is that I did not dare to say what I had to say at that time as a poet; perhaps I could have done it! Or at least as a philologist; even today everything is still there for a philologist to discover and excavate in this area! Above all the problem *that* a problem exists here – and that, for as long as we have no answer to the question, 'What is Dionysiac?', the Greeks will remain as utterly unknown and unimaginable as they have always been . . .

4

Yes, what is Dionysiac? – This book contains an answer to that question – a man who 'knows' speaks here, an initiate and disciple of his god. Perhaps

---

[8] 'In the arts'.

[9] 'The crowd that must stand outside the temple and is allowed no access to the sacred rites performed inside': phrase used by Horace (*Odes*III. 1) of those who are to be excluded from the realm of poetry.

[10] The German term *fremd* has a range of meanings, extending from 'strange' through 'foreign' to 'alien'.

I would now speak more cautiously and less eloquently about such a difficult psychological question as the origin of tragedy amongst the Greeks. One fundamental question concerns the Greeks' relationship to pain, the degree of their sensitivity – did this relationship remain constant, or did it become inverted? – the question of whether the Greeks' ever more powerful *demand for beauty* (*Schönheit*), for festivals, entertainments, new cults, really grew from a lack, from deprivation, from melancholy, from pain. If one supposes that this was indeed the case – and Pericles (or Thucydides) indicates as much in the great funeral oration[11] – what then must have been the source of the opposing demand, which emerged at an earlier point in time, the *demand for ugliness*, the older Hellenes' good, severe will to pessimism, to the tragic myth, to affirm the image of all that is fearsome, wicked, mysterious, annihilating and fateful at the very foundations of existence – where must the origins of tragedy have lain at that time? Perhaps in *desire and delight* (*Lust*), in strength, in overbrimming health, in an excess of plenitude? In this case what is the meaning (in physiological terms) of that madness – Dionysiac madness – from which both the tragic and the comic arts emerged? What? Is madness perhaps not necessarily a symptom of degeneration, of decline, of a culture that has gone on too long? Are there perhaps – and this is a question for psychiatrists – neuroses of *health*, of national youth and youthfulness? What does the synthesis of goat and god in the satyr point to? What experience of their own nature, what impulse compelled the Greeks to think of the Dionysiac enthusiast and primal man as a satyr? And as far as the origin of the tragic chorus is concerned – did perhaps endemic fits exist during those centuries when the Greek body was in its prime and the Greek soul brimmed over with life? Were there visions and hallucinations which conveyed themselves to entire communities, entire cultic assemblies? What? If the Greeks were pessimists and had the will to tragedy precisely when they were surrounded by the riches of youth, if, to quote Plato, it was precisely madness which brought the *greatest* blessings to Hellas,[12] and if, on the other hand and conversely, it was precisely during their period of dissolution and weakness that the Greeks became ever more optimistic, more superficial, more actorly, but also filled with a greater lust for logic and for making the world logical, which is to say both more 'cheerful' and more 'scientific' – could it then perhaps be the case, despite all 'modern ideas' and the prejudices of democratic taste, that the victory of *optimism*, the predominance

---

[11] Thucydides, *Peloponnesian War* II.35ff.   [12] *Phaedrus* 244a.

of *reasonableness*, practical and theoretical *utilitarianism*, like its contemporary, democracy, that all this is symptomatic of a decline in strength, of approaching old age, of physiological exhaustion? And that pessimism is precisely *not* a symptom of these things? Was Epicurus an optimist – precisely because he was *suffering*? – As you see, this book burdened itself with a whole bundle of difficult questions. So let us add the hardest question of all! What, when seen through the prism of *life*, is the meaning of morality?

5

Already in the preface to Richard Wagner it is asserted that art – and *not* morality – is the true *metaphysical* activity of man; several times in the book itself the provocative sentence recurs that the existence of the world is *justified* (*gerechtfertigt*) only as an aesthetic phenomenon. Indeed the whole book acknowledges only an artist's meaning (and hidden meaning) behind all that happens – a 'god', if you will, but certainly only an utterly unscrupulous and amoral artist-god who frees (*löst*) himself from the dire pressure of fullness and *over-fullness*, from *suffering* the oppositions packed within him, and who wishes to become conscious of his autarchic power and constant delight and desire, whether he is building or destroying, whether acting benignly or malevolently. The world as the release and redemption (*Erlösung*) of god, *achieved* at each and every moment, as the eternally changing, eternally new vision of the most suffering being of all, the being most full of oppositions and contradictions, able to redeem and release itself only in *semblance* (*Schein*); one may say that this whole artiste's metaphysics is capricious, otiose, fantastical – but its essential feature is that it already betrays a spirit which will defend itself one day, whatever the danger, against the *moral* interpretation and significance of existence. Here, perhaps for the first time, a pessimism 'beyond good and evil' announces itself, here that 'perverse mentality'[13] is put into words and formulations which Schopenhauer never tired of bombarding (before it had actually emerged) with his most wrathful imprecations and thunderbolts – a philosophy which dares to situate morality itself within the phenomenal world, to degrade it and to place it not merely amongst the phenomena (*Erscheinungen*) (in the sense of the idealist *terminus technicus*), but even amongst the 'deceptions' (*Täuschungen*), as semblance, delusion, error, interpretation, manipulation, art. Perhaps the best indication of the depth

[13] Schopenhauer, *Parerga* 2, 107.

of the *anti-moral* tendency in the book is its consistently cautious and hostile silence about Christianity – Christianity as the most excessive, elaborately figured development of the moral theme that humanity has ever had to listen to. In truth there is no greater antithesis of the purely aesthetic exegesis and justification of the world, as taught in this book, than the Christian doctrine which is, and wants to be, *only* moral, and which, with its absolute criteria (its insistence on god's truthfulness, for example) banishes art, *all* art, to the realm of *lies*, and thus negates, damns and condemns it. Behind this way of thinking and evaluating, which is bound to be hostile to art if it is at all genuine, I had always felt its *hostility to life*, a furious, vengeful enmity towards life itself; for all life rests on semblance, art, deception, prismatic effects, the necessity of perspectivism and error. From the very outset Christianity was essentially and pervasively the feeling of disgust and weariness which life felt for life, a feeling which merely disguised, hid and decked itself out in its belief in 'another' or 'better' life. Hatred of the 'world', a curse on the passions, fear of beauty and sensuality, a Beyond, invented in order better to defame the Here-and-Now, fundamentally a desire for nothingness, for the end, for rest, for the 'Sabbath of Sabbaths'[14] – all this, together with the determination of Christianity to sanction *only* moral values, seemed to me the most dangerous and uncanny of all possible forms of a 'will to decline', at the very least a sign of the most profound sickness, tiredness, distemper, exhaustion, impoverishment of life – for before the court of morality (especially Christian, which is to say unconditional, morality) life *must* constantly and inevitably be proved wrong because life is essentially something amoral; life *must* eventually, crushed by the weight of contempt and the eternal 'no!', be felt to be inherently unworthy, undeserving of our desire. Morality itself – might it not be a 'will to negate life', a secret instinct for annihilation, a principle of decay, belittlement, calumny, the beginning of the end? And consequently the greatest danger of all? Thus my instinct turned *against* morality at the time I wrote this questionable book; as an advocate of life my instinct invented for itself a fundamentally opposed doctrine and counter-evaluation of life, a purely artistic one, an *anti-Christian* one. What was it to be called? As a philologist and man of words I baptized it, not without a certain liberty – for who can know the true name of the Antichrist? – by the name of a Greek god: I called it *Dionysiac*.

---

[14] An eschatological day of complete and perfect rest.

6

I wonder if the reader understands which task I was already daring to undertake with this book? I now regret very much that I did not yet have the courage (or immodesty?) at that time to permit myself a *language of my very own* for such personal views and acts of daring, labouring instead to express strange and new evaluations in Schopenhauerian and Kantian formulations, things which fundamentally ran counter to both the spirit and taste of Kant and Schopenhauer. What, after all, did Schopenhauer think about tragedy? This is what he says in *The World as Will and Representation*, II, p. 495: 'What gives to everything tragic, whatever the form in which it appears, the characteristic tendency to the sublime, is the dawning of the knowledge that the world and life can afford us no true satisfaction, and are therefore *not worth* our attachment to them. In this the tragic spirit consists; accordingly it leads to *resignation*.' How differently Dionysos spoke to me! How alien to me at that time was precisely this whole philosophy of resignation! But there is something much worse about the book which I regret even more than having obscured and ruined Dionysiac intimations with Schopenhauerian formulations, and this is the fact that I had *ruined* the grandiose *Greek problem* in general, as I had come to understand it, by mixing it up with the most modern things. Also the fact that I had attached hopes to things where there was nothing to hope for, where everything pointed all too clearly to an end. And that I should have begun to invent stories about the 'German character', on the basis of the latest German music, as if it were about to discover or re-discover itself – and this at a time when the German spirit, which had recently shown the will to rule Europe and the strength to lead Europe, had *abdicated*, finally and definitively, and, using the pompous pretext of founding an empire, was in a process of transition to mediocrity, democracy, and 'modern ideas'. Since then I have indeed learned to think hopelessly and unsparingly enough about this 'German character', and the same applies to current *German music*, which is Romanticism through and through and the most un-Greek of all possible forms of art; furthermore, as a ruiner of nerves it is in the first rank, a doubly dangerous thing amongst a people who love drink and who honour obscurity as a virtue, particularly for its dual properties as a narcotic which both intoxicates and *befogs* the mind. Setting aside all the premature hopes and the erroneous morals applied to the most contemporary things with which I ruined my first book, however, the great Dionysiac question it poses remains (with regard to music, too) as valid as ever: what would music be like if it were no longer Romantic in its origins, as German music is, but *Dionysiac?*

7

But, Sir, if *your* book is not Romanticism, what on earth is? Can the deep hatred of 'the present', 'reality' and 'modern ideas' be carried further than in your artiste's metaphysics, which would prefer to believe in nothingness or in the devil rather than in 'the present'. Is there not a ground bass[15] of anger and delight in destruction rumbling away beneath all your contrapuntal vocal art and seduction of the ear, a furious determination to oppose the entire 'present', a will that is not too far removed from practical nihilism and which appears to say, 'I would prefer that nothing were true, rather than know that *you* were right, that *your* truth turned out to be right.' Just listen, Mr Pessimist and Deifier of Art, with a more attentive ear to a single passage from your own book, that not un-eloquent dragon-killer passage which can sound enticing and seductive to young ears and hearts; are you telling us that this is not the genuine, true Romantic's confession of 1830 beneath the mask of the pessimism of 1850, behind which one can hear the opening bars of the usual Romantic finale – fracture, collapse, return, and prostration before an old belief, before *the* old god? Is not your pessimist's book itself a piece of anti-Graecism and Romanticism, something which itself 'both intoxicates and befogs the mind', at any rate a narcotic, a piece of music even, of *German* music? Listen to this:

Let us imagine a rising generation with this fearless gaze, with this heroic attraction to what is monstrous, let us imagine the bold stride of these dragon-slayers, the proud recklessness with which they turn their backs on all the enfeebled doctrines of scientific optimism so that they may 'live resolutely',[16] wholly and fully; would not the tragic man of this culture, given that he has trained himself for what is grave and terrifying, be bound to desire a new form of art, the art of metaphysical solace, in fact to desire tragedy as his very own Helen, and to call out along with Faust:

> And shall I not, with all my longing's vigour
> Draw into life that peerless, lovely figure?[17]

[15] A pattern of notes, especially a short melodic phrase, set in the bass and repeated over and over again in the course of a musical composition.
[16] Goethe, *General Confession.*   [17] Goethe, *Faust* II, 7438f.

'Would it not be necessary?' . . . No, three times no, you young Romantics; it should *not* be necessary! But it is very probable that it will *end* like this, that *you* will end like this, namely 'comforted', as it is written, despite all your training of yourselves for what is grave and terrifying, 'metaphysically comforted', ending, in short, as Romantics end, namely as *Christians* . . . No, you should first learn the art of comfort *in this world*, you should learn to *laugh*, my young friends, if you are really determined to remain pessimists. Perhaps then, as men who laugh, you will some day send all attempts at metaphysical solace to Hell – with metaphysics the first to go! Or to put it in the words of that Dionysiac monster who bears the name of *Zarathustra*:

> Lift up your hearts, my brothers, high, higher! And do not forget your legs! Lift up your legs, too, you fine dancers! Even better, stand on your heads!

> This crown of the laughing one, this rosary-crown: I myself set this crown on my head, I myself have sanctified my laughter. I could find no one else today strong enough to do so.

> Zarathustra the dancer, Zarathustra the light one, he who beckons with his wings, he who is ready to fly, beckoning to all the birds, prepared and ready, he who is blissfully frivolous.

> Zarathustra who speaks the truth,[18] who laughs the truth, not impatient, not unconditional, one who loves leaps and deviations: I myself set this crown on my head!

> This crown of the laughing one, this rosary-crown; to you, my brothers, I throw this crown! I have sanctified laughter; you higher men, *learn* to laugh, I beseech you![19]

[18] Nietzsche plays in these verses with the word *wahrsagen*, which means 'to prophesy' (to tell true), by extending it into such new compounds as *wahrlachen*.
[19] *Thus Spoke Zarathustra*, Part IV, 'On the higher man'.

Appoline   vs.   Dionysiac
- didactic   - hedonic
- dreams   - Cochella
- medea/calmness   - a concert
  of a person in trouble - in toxication
- images   - Lupercalia / festivals / parties
- Homer / Iliad

        ‖   ‖
        ∨   ∨
    surface   the path
    limiting   overwhelming
    not "emotional"   leads to destruction
    totally individual   knowledge of suffering / nature
    invention of Greeks invention of Asions

The Birth of Tragedy out of the Spirit of Music
Foreword to Richard Wagner

In order to clear my mind of all the possible concerns, excitements, and misunderstandings which the thoughts assembled in this book will provoke (the peculiar character of our aesthetic public being what it is), and thus be free to write the introduction in that same mood of contemplative delight which has left its traces on every page of this petrifact of good and uplifting hours, I now imagine the moment when you, my revered friend, will receive this work. I see you, perhaps after an evening walk in the winter snow, as you study Prometheus Unbound on the title page, read my name, and immediately feel convinced that, whatever the work may contain, its author has something serious and urgent to say, and also that, while conceiving these thoughts, he was conversing with you constantly, as if you had been present and as if he could only write down things which were appropriate in your presence. As you do so, you will recall that I was collecting myself to frame these thoughts at the same time as you were composing your magnificent celebratory essay on Beethoven,[20] in other words amidst all the terrors and sublimities of the war that had just broken out. Yet if this act of self-collection were to prompt anyone to think of patriotic excitement and aesthetic self-indulgence, or courageous seriousness and serene (*heiter*) play, as opposites, they would be wrong; indeed, if such people really read the work they might realize, to their astonishment, that the matter with which we are concerned is a grave problem for Germany, a problem which we now place, as a vortex and turning-point, into the very midst of German hopes. Perhaps, however, these people will take offence at such serious

---

[20] A translation of this essay, written in 1870, is printed in volume v of *Richard Wagner's Prose Works*, ed. and trans. W. A. Ellis (London 1892–9).

consideration being given to any aesthetic problem at all, particularly if they are incapable of thinking of art as anything more than an amusing sideshow, a readily dispensable jingling of fool's bells in the face of the 'gravity of existence' – as if we did not know what is meant by this contrast with the 'gravity of existence'. Let these serious-minded people take note: my conviction that art is the highest task and the true metaphysical activity of this life is based on an understanding which I share with the man and fighter whose sublime lead I follow and to whom I now wish to dedicate this work.

Basle, end of the year 1871

I

We shall have gained much for the science of aesthetics when we have come to realize, not just through logical insight but also with the certainty of something directly apprehended (*Anschauung*), that the continuous evolution of art is bound up with the duality of the *Apolline* and the *Dionysiac* in much the same way as reproduction depends on there being two sexes which co-exist in a state of perpetual conflict interrupted only occasionally by periods of reconciliation. We have borrowed these names from the Greeks who reveal the profound mysteries of their view of art to those with insight, not in concepts, admittedly, but through the penetratingly vivid figures of their gods. Their two deities of art, Apollo and Dionysos, provide the starting-point for our recognition that there exists in the world of the Greeks an enormous opposition, both in origin and goals, between the Apolline art of the image-maker or sculptor (*Bildner*) and the imageless art of music, which is that of Dionysos. These two very different drives (*Triebe*) exist side by side, mostly in open conflict, stimulating and provoking (*reizen*)[21] one another to give birth to ever-new, more vigorous offspring in whom they perpetuate the conflict inherent in the opposition between them, an opposition only apparently bridged by the common term 'art' – until eventually, by a metaphysical miracle of the Hellenic 'Will', they appear paired and, in this pairing, finally engender a work of art which is Dionysiac and Apolline in equal measure: Attic tragedy.

In order to gain a closer understanding of these two drives, let us think of them in the first place as the separate art-worlds of *dream* and *intoxication*

---

[21] The German term *reizen* is ambiguous; its basic meaning is 'to excite', but the effect can be to delight or to irritate.

(*Rausch*). Between these two physiological phenomena an opposition can be observed which corresponds to that between the Apolline and the Dionysiac. As Lucretius[22] envisages it, it was in dream that the magnificent figures of the gods first appeared before the souls of men; in dream the great image-maker saw the delightfully proportioned bodies of super-human beings; and the Hellenic poet, if asked about the secrets of poetic procreation, would likewise have reminded us of dream and would have given an account much like that given by Hans Sachs in the *Meistersinger*:

> My friend, it is the poet's task
> To mark his dreams, their meaning ask.
> Trust me, the truest phantom man doth know
> Hath meaning only dreams may show:
> The arts of verse and poetry
> Tell nought but dreaming's prophecy.[23]

Every human being is fully an artist when creating the worlds of dream, and the lovely semblance of dream is the precondition of all the arts of image-making, including, as we shall see, an important half of poetry. We take pleasure in dreaming, understanding its figures without media-tion; all forms speak to us; nothing is indifferent or unnecessary. Yet even while this dream-reality is most alive, we nevertheless retain a pervasive sense that it is *semblance*; at least this is my experience, and I could adduce a good deal of evidence and the statements of poets to attest to the frequency, indeed normality, of my experience. Philosophical natures even have a presentiment that hidden beneath the reality in which we live and have our being there also lies a second, quite different reality; in other words, this reality too is a semblance. Indeed Schopenhauer actually states that the mark of a person's capacity for philosophy is the gift for feeling occasionally as if people and all things were mere phantoms or dream-images.[24] A person with artistic sensibility relates to the reality of dream in the same way as a philosopher relates to the reality of existence: he attends to it closely and with pleasure, using these images to interpret life, and practising for life with the help of these events. Not that it is only the pleasant and friendly images which give him this feeling of complete intelligibility; he also sees passing before him things which are grave, gloomy, sad, dark, sudden blocks, teasings of chance, anxious

---

[22] *De rerum natura* 1169ff.   [23] Wagner, *Die Meistersinger*, act III, scene 2.
[24] *Aus Schopenhauers handschriftlichem Nachlaß*, ed. J. Frauenstädt (Leipzig 1874), p. 295.

expectations, in short the entire 'Divine Comedy' of life, including the Inferno, but not like some mere shadow-play – for he, too, lives in these scenes and shares in the suffering – and yet never without that fleeting sense of its character as semblance. Perhaps others will recall, as I do, shouting out, sometimes successfully, words of encouragement in the midst of the perils and terrors of a dream: 'It is a dream! I will dream on!' I have even heard of people who were capable of continuing the causality of one and the same dream through three and more successive nights. All of these facts are clear evidence that our innermost being, the deep ground (*Untergrund*) common to all our lives, experiences the state of dreaming with profound pleasure (*Lust*) and joyous necessity.

The Greeks also expressed the joyous necessity of dream-experience in their Apollo: as the god of all image-making energies, Apollo is also the god of prophecy. According to the etymological root of his name, he is 'the luminous one' (*der Scheinende*), the god of light; as such, he also governs the lovely semblance produced by the inner world of fantasy. The higher truth, the perfection of these dream-states in contrast to the only partially intelligible reality of the daylight world, together with the profound consciousness of the helping and healing powers of nature in sleep and dream, is simultaneously the symbolic analogue of the ability to prophesy and indeed of all the arts through which life is made possible and worth living. But the image of Apollo must also contain that delicate line which the dream-image may not overstep if its effect is not to become pathological, so that, in the worst case, the semblance would deceive us as if it were crude reality; his image (*Bild*) must include that measured limitation (*maßvolle Begrenzung*), that freedom from wilder impulses, that wise calm of the image-making god. In accordance with his origin, his eye must be 'sun-like';[25] even when its gaze is angry and shows displeasure, it exhibits the consecrated quality of lovely semblance. Thus, in an eccentric sense, one could apply to Apollo what Schopenhauer says about human beings trapped in the veil of maya:

Just as the boatman sits in his small boat, trusting his frail craft in a stormy sea that is boundless in every direction, rising and falling with the howling, mountainous waves, so in the midst of a world full of suffering and misery the individual man

---

[25] In early Greek philosophy it was often held that 'like' could be known only by 'like' i.e. that for us to recognize something *as*, say, 'water', there had to be some element of water in our cognitive make-up, presumably because knowing is identifying with what is known (*cf*. Empedocles, Fragment 109). For this particular application to the sun *cf*. Plotinus, '*On the beautiful*' 1.6.9, *cf*. also Goethe '*Zahme Xenien*' III.

calmly sits, supported by and trusting in the *principium individuationis* [. . .]²⁶
(*World as Will and Representation*, I, p. 416)

Indeed one could say that Apollo is the most sublime expression of imperturbable trust in this principle and of the calm sitting-there of the person trapped within it; one might even describe Apollo as the magnificent divine image (*Götterbild*) of the *principium individuationis*, whose gestures and gaze speak to us of all the intense pleasure, wisdom and beauty of 'semblance'.

In the same passage Schopenhauer has described for us the enormous *horror* which seizes people when they suddenly become confused and lose faith in the cognitive forms of the phenomenal world because the principle of sufficient reason, in one or other of its modes, appears to sustain an exception. If we add to this horror the blissful ecstasy which arises from the innermost ground of man, indeed of nature itself, whenever this breakdown of the *principium individuationis* occurs, we catch a glimpse of the essence of the *Dionysiac*, which is best conveyed by the analogy of *intoxication*. These Dionysiac stirrings, which, as they grow in intensity, cause subjectivity to vanish to the point of complete self-forgetting, awaken either under the influence of narcotic drink, of which all human beings and peoples who are close to the origin of things speak in their hymns, or at the approach of spring when the whole of nature is pervaded by lust for life. In the German Middle Ages, too, ever-growing throngs roamed from place to place, impelled by the same Dionysiac power, singing and dancing as they went; in these St John's and St Vitus' dancers we recognize the Bacchic choruses of the Greeks, with their pre-history in Asia Minor, extending to Babylon and the orgiastic Sacaea.²⁷ There are those who,

---

²⁶ Schopenhauer thought that our everyday experience of the world was of separate, distinct empirical objects (i.e. things subject to the 'principle of individuation') and that their distinctness was inherently connected with the applicability of the 'principle of sufficient reason'. Roughly speaking, two things are distinct (individuated) only if we have grounds (sufficient reason) to distinguish them and if we have such grounds they are distinct. However, Schopenhauer also believed that all use of the principle of sufficient reason (and thus all individuation) was a result of the operation of the mind, and hence the everyday world of distinct objects of experience was a mere appearance, in fact an illusion. Schopenhauer was very interested in Indian religion and claimed that his view that the everyday world is an illusion was just a Western version of the Vedantic doctrine that the world we experience is nothing but the 'veil of maya'. Although the everyday world is a mere appearance, there is a reality behind it to which Schopenhauer thinks we sometimes have access. The 'reality' of which our empirical world is an appearance is what Schopenhauer calls 'the Will' and we can have non-empirical access to it in our own willing – we know what we will directly without 'observing' anything – and in certain kinds of aesthetic experience. Since this 'will' is by definition outside the realm within which one can speak of individuation and the distinctness of one 'thing' from another, it has a kind of primordial unity.

²⁷ For Nietzsche's views about these festivals (about which virtually nothing is known) *cf.* also *The Dionysiac World View* § 1.

whether from lack of experience or from dullness of spirit, turn away in scorn or pity from such phenomena, regarding them as 'popular diseases' while believing in their own good health; of course, these poor creatures have not the slightest inkling of how spectral and deathly pale their 'health' seems when the glowing life of Dionysiac enthusiasts storms past them.

Not only is the bond[28] between human beings renewed by the magic of the Dionysiac, but nature, alienated, inimical, or subjugated, celebrates once more her festival of reconciliation with her lost son, humankind. Freely the earth offers up her gifts, and the beasts of prey from mountain and desert approach in peace. The chariot of Dionysos is laden with flowers and wreaths; beneath its yoke stride panther and tiger. If one were to transform Beethoven's jubilant 'Hymn to Joy'[29] into a painting and place no constraints on one's imagination as the millions sink into the dust, shivering in awe, then one could begin to approach the Dionysiac. Now the slave is a freeman, now all the rigid, hostile barriers, which necessity, caprice, or 'impudent fashion'[30] have established between human beings, break asunder. Now, hearing this gospel of universal harmony, each person feels himself to be not simply united, reconciled or merged with his neighbour, but quite literally one with him, as if the veil of maya had been torn apart, so that mere shreds of it flutter before the mysterious primordial unity (*das Ur-Eine*). Singing and dancing, man expresses his sense of belonging to a higher community; he has forgotten how to walk and talk and is on the brink of flying and dancing, up and away into the air above. His gestures speak of his enchantment. Just as the animals now talk and the earth gives milk and honey,[31] there now sounds out from within man something supernatural: he feels himself to be a god, he himself now moves in such ecstasy and sublimity as once he saw the gods move in his dreams. Man is no longer an artist, he has become a work of art: all nature's artistic power reveals itself here, amidst shivers of intoxication, to the highest, most blissful satisfaction of the primordial unity. Here man, the noblest clay, the most precious marble, is kneaded and carved and, to the accompaniment of the chisel-blows of the Dionysiac world-artist, the call of the Eleusinian

---

[28] The term *Bund* can mean a 'bond' and a 'covenant', as in the biblical sense of the Old and the New Covenant.

[29] Beethoven used a version of Schiller's ode *To Joy* for the choral Finale of his Symphony in D minor, opus 125.

[30] Quotation from Schiller's *To Joy*.

[31] Conflation of Euripides *Bacchae* lines 142f and 704–11 with Exodus 3.8.

Mysteries[32] rings out: 'Fall ye to the ground, ye millions? Feelst thou thy Creator, world?'[33]

2

So far we have considered the Apolline and its opposite, the Dionysiac, as artistic powers which erupt from nature itself, *without the mediation of any human artist*, and in which nature's artistic drives attain their first, immediate satisfaction: on the one hand as the image-world of dream, the perfection of which is not linked to an individual's intellectual level or artistic formation (*Bildung*); and on the other hand as intoxicated reality, which has just as little regard for the individual, even seeking to annihilate, redeem, and release him by imparting a mystical sense of oneness. In relation to these unmediated artistic states in nature every artist is an 'imitator', and indeed either an Apolline dream-artist or a Dionysiac artist of intoxication or finally – as, for example, in Greek tragedy – an artist of both dream and intoxication at once. This is how we must think of him as he sinks to the ground in Dionysiac drunkenness and mystical self-abandon, alone and apart from the enthusiastic choruses, at which point, under the Apolline influence of dream, his own condition, which is to say, his oneness with the innermost ground of the world, reveals itself to him *in a symbolic (gleichnishaft) dream-image*.

Having set out these general assumptions and contrasts, let us now consider the *Greeks* in order to understand the degree and level to which those *artistic drives of nature* were developed in them. This will enable us to gain a deeper understanding and appreciation of the relationship between the Greek artist and his models (*Urbilder*), or, to use Aristotle's expression, 'the imitation of nature'.[34] Despite all the dream literature of the Greeks and numerous dream anecdotes, we can speak only speculatively, but with a fair degree of certainty, about the Greeks' *dreams*. Given the incredibly definite and assured ability of their eye to see things in a plastic way, together with their pure and honest delight in colour, one is bound to assume, to the shame of all those born after them, that their dreams, too, had that logical causality of line and outline, colour and grouping, and a sequence of scenes resembling their best bas-reliefs, so that the perfection

---

[32] Mystery-religion celebrated in Eleusis, a small village in southwest Attica. Initiates were given a vision of Demeter and promised a form of life after death.
[33] *To Joy*, lines 33–4.   [34] *Poetics* 1447a16.

of their dreams would certainly justify us, if comparison were possible, in describing the dreaming Greeks as Homers and Homer as a dreaming Greek – and in a more profound sense than if a modern dared were to compare his dreaming with that of Shakespeare.

By contrast, there is no need for speculation when it comes to revealing the vast gulf which separated the *Dionysiac Greeks* from the Dionysiac Barbarians. From all corners of the ancient world (leaving aside the modern one in this instance), from Rome to Babylon, we can demonstrate the existence of Dionysiac festivals of a type which, at best, stands in the same relation to the Greek festivals as the bearded satyr, whose name and attributes were borrowed from the goat, stands to Dionysos himself. Almost everywhere an excess of sexual indiscipline, which flooded in waves over all family life and its venerable statutes, lay at the heart of such festivals. Here the very wildest of nature's beasts were unleashed, up to and including that repulsive mixture of sensuality and cruelty which has always struck me as the true 'witches' brew'. Although news of these festivals reached them by every sea- and land-route, the Greeks appear, for a time, to have been completely protected and insulated from their feverish stirrings by the figure of Apollo, who reared up in all his pride, there being no more dangerous power for him to confront with the Medusa's head than this crude, grotesque manifestation of the Dionysiac. Apollo's attitude of majestic rejection is eternalized in Doric art. Such resistance became more problematic and even impossible when, eventually, similar shoots sprang from the deepest root of the Hellenic character; now the work of the Delphic God was limited to taking the weapons of destruction out of the hands of his mighty opponent in a timely act of reconciliation. This reconciliation is the most important moment in the history of Greek religion; wherever one looks, one can see the revolutionary consequences of this event. It was the reconciliation of two opponents, with a precise delineation of the borders which each now had to respect and with the periodic exchange of honorific gifts; fundamentally the chasm had not been bridged. Yet if we now look at how the power of the Dionysiac manifested itself under pressure from that peace-treaty, we can see that, in contrast to the Babylonian Sacaea, where human beings regressed to the condition of tigers and monkeys, the significance of the Greeks' Dionysiac orgies was that of festivals of universal release and redemption and days of transfiguration. Here for the first time the jubilation of nature achieves expression as art, here for the first time the tearing-apart of the *principium individuationis* becomes an artistic phenomenon. That repulsive witches' brew of sensuality and cruelty was powerless here; the only reminder of it (in the way that medicines recall deadly poisons) is to be found in the strange mixture and duality in the affects of the Dionysiac enthusiasts, that phenomenon whereby pain awakens pleasure while rejoicing wrings cries of agony from the breast. From highest joy there comes a cry of horror or a yearning lament at some irredeemable loss. In those Greek festivals there erupts what one might call a sentimental tendency in nature, as if it had cause to sigh over its dismemberment into individuals. The singing and expressive gestures of such enthusiasts in their two-fold mood was something new and unheard-of in the Homeric-Greek world; Dionysiac *music* in particular elicited terror and horror from them. Although it seems that music was already familiar to the Greeks as an Apolline art, they only knew it, strictly speaking, in the form of a wave-like rhythm with an image-making power which they developed to represent Apolline states. The music of Apollo was Doric architectonics in sound, but only in the kind of hinted-at tones characteristic of the *cithara*. It keeps at a distance, as something un-Apolline, the very element which defines the character of Dionysiac music (and thus of music generally): the power of its sound to shake us to our very foundations, the unified stream of melody and the quite incomparable world of harmony. In the Dionysiac dithyramb[35] man is stimulated to the highest intensification of his symbolic powers; something that he has never felt before urgently demands to be expressed: the destruction of the veil of maya, one-ness as the genius of humankind, indeed of nature itself. The essence of nature is bent on expressing itself; a new world of symbols is required, firstly the symbolism of the entire body, not just of the mouth, the face, the word, but the full gesture of dance with its rhythmical movement of every limb. Then there is a sudden, tempestuous growth in music's other symbolic powers, in rhythm, dynamics, and harmony. To comprehend this complete unchaining of all symbolic powers, a man must already have reached that height of self-abandonment which seeks symbolic expression in those powers: thus the dithyrambic servant of Dionysos can only be understood by his own kind! With what astonishment the Apolline Greeks must have regarded him! With an astonishment enlarged by the added horror of realizing that all this was not so foreign to them after all, indeed that their Apolline consciousness only hid this Dionysiac world from them like a veil.

35 A choral song originally part of the cult of Dionysos.

3

In order to understand this, we need to dismantle the artful edifice of *Apolline culture* stone by stone, as it were, until we catch sight of the foundations on which it rests. The first things we observe here are the magnificent figures of the *Olympian* gods who stand on the gables of this building and whose deeds, represented in reliefs which can be seen gleaming from afar, adorn its friezes. If Apollo is also amongst their number, as just one god alongside others and without laying claim to the leading position, we should not allow this fact to confuse us. The very same drive which assumed sensuous form in Apollo gave birth to that entire Olympian world, and in this sense we are entitled to regard Apollo as its father. What, then, was the enormous need that gave rise to such a luminous company of Olympic beings?

Anyone who approaches these Olympians with another religion in his heart and proceeds to look for signs of moral loftiness in them, or indeed holiness, or incorporeal spirituality, or a loving gaze filled with compassion, will soon be forced to turn his back on them in dismay and disappointment. Nothing here reminds us of asceticism (*Askese*), of spirituality and duty; everything here speaks only of over-brimming, indeed triumphant existence, where everything that exists has been deified, regardless of whether it is good or evil. Thus the spectator may stand in some perplexity before this fantastic superabundance of life, asking himself what magic potion these people can have drunk which makes them see Helen, 'hovering in sweet sensuality',[36] smiling at them wherever they look, the ideal image of their own existence. Yet we must call out to this spectator who has already turned away: 'Do not go away, but listen first to what popular Greek wisdom has to say about this inexplicably serene existence you see spread out before you here.' An ancient legend recounts how King Midas hunted long in the forest for the wise *Silenus*,[37] companion of Dionysos, but failed to catch him. When

---

[36] Goethe, *Faust* I, 2603ff.

[37] It is unclear whether 'Silenus' is originally a proper name or a descriptive term for a kind of forest daemon; Nietzsche takes it as a proper name here. In any case Silenus is (or the silens are) represented on early vase paintings as beings in which properties of the human being and the horse are combined. The distinction between silens and 'satyrs' (also composite creatures with human and equine properties) is also originally unclear. Neither silens nor satyrs have originally any connection with Dionysos, nor do they have any goat-like properties. In the post-classical (Hellenistic) period Silenus tends to establish itself as the proper name for the older leader of a group of satyrs in the service of Dionysus, and both Silenus and the satyrs tend to be confused with another, originally quite distinct, forest daemon, Pan, who had human and goat-like attributes. Nietzsche's great

Silenus has finally fallen into his hands, the King asks what is the best and most excellent thing for human beings. Stiff and unmoving, the daemon remains silent until, forced by the King to speak, he finally breaks out in shrill laughter and says: 'Wretched, ephemeral race, children of chance and tribulation, why do you force me to tell you the very thing which it would be most profitable for you *not* to hear? The very best thing is utterly beyond your reach not to have been born, not to *be*, to be *nothing*. However, the second best thing for you is: to die soon.'[38]

How does the world of the Olympian gods relate to this piece of popular wisdom? The relationship is that of the ecstatic vision of a tortured martyr to his torments.

The Olympian magic mountain now opens up, as it were, and shows us its roots. The Greeks knew and felt the terrors and horrors of existence; in order to live at all they had to place in front of these things the resplendent, dream-born figures of the Olympians. That enormous distrust of the Titanic forces of nature, that *moira*[39] which throned, unpitying, above all knowledge, that vulture of man's great friend, Prometheus, that terrifying lot drawn by the wise Oedipus, that curse upon the family of Atreus[40] which compels Orestes to kill his mother, in short that whole philosophy of the wood-god, together with its mythic examples, which destroyed the melancholy Etruscans – all this was constantly and repeatedly overcome by the Greeks, or at least veiled and withdrawn from view, by means of the artistic *middle world* of the Olympians. In order to be able to live, the Greeks were obliged, by the most profound compulsion, to create these gods. This process is probably to be imagined as taking place gradually, so that, under the influence of the Apolline instinct (*Trieb*) for beauty, the Olympian divine order of joy developed out of the original, Titanic divine order of terror in a series of slow transitions, in much the same way as roses burst forth from a thicket of thorns. How else could that people have borne existence, given their extreme sensitivity, their stormy desires, their unique gift

---

opponent, Wilamowitz-Möllendorff (*see* 'Introduction' above p. xxviii) in his review of *Birth of Tragedy* makes a great fuss about the fact that Nietzsche takes this post-classical conflation of the horse-like Silenus, the satyrs, and the goat-like Pan and projects it back into the period before the origin of Attic tragedy; *see* Wilamowitz-Möllendorff, 'Zukunftsphilologie!' in *Der Streit um Nietzsches 'Geburt der Tragödie'*, ed. K. Gründer (Hildesheim, Olms-Verlag, 1989), pp. 32f, 46f.

[38] Translation of a passage from *Eudemos*, a dialogue by Aristotle of which only fragments survive.

[39] Fate.

[40] The way in which the curse on the house of Atreus works itself out in successive generations (eventually causing Orestes to kill his mother) is the subject of Aeschylus' trilogy *The Oresteia*.

for *suffering*, if that same existence had not been shown to them in their gods, suffused with a higher glory? The same drive which calls art into being to complete and perfect existence and thus to seduce us into continuing to live, also gave rise to the world of the Olympians in which the Hellenic 'Will' held up a transfiguring mirror to itself. Thus gods justify the life of men by living it themselves – the only satisfactory theodicy! Under the bright sunshine of such gods existence is felt to be worth attaining, and the real *pain* of Homeric man refers to his departure from this existence, particularly to imminent departure, so that one might say of them, reversing the wisdom of Silenus, that 'the very worst thing for them was to die soon, the second worst ever to die at all'. If a lament is ever heard, it sings of short-lived Achilles, of the generations of men changing and succeeding one another like leaves on the trees,[41] of the demise of the heroic age.[42] It is not unworthy of the greatest hero to long to go on living, even as a day-labourer.[43] So stormily does the 'Will', on the level of the Apolline, demand this existence, so utterly at one with it does Homeric man feel himself to be, that even his lament turns into a song in praise of being.

At this point it must be said that this harmony, which modern men look on with such longing, this unity of man with nature, to which Schiller applied the now generally accepted art-word 'naive',[44] is by no means such a simple, so-to-speak inevitable condition which emerges of its own accord and which we would be *bound* to encounter at the threshold of every culture, as a human paradise; people could only believe this at a time when they were bent on thinking of Rousseau's Emile as an artist, and entertained the illusion that in Homer they had found just such an artist as Emile, reared at the heart of nature. Wherever we encounter the 'naive' in art, we have to recognize that it is the supreme effect of Apolline culture; as such, it first had to overthrow the realm of the Titans and slay monsters, and, by employing powerful delusions and intensely pleasurable illusions, gain victory over a terrifyingly profound view of the world and the most acute sensitivity to suffering. But how rarely is that complete enthralment in the beauty of semblance which we call the naive actually achieved! And how

---

[41] *Iliad* XXI. 464f.   [42] Hesiod, *Works and Days*, 109ff and 174ff.

[43] When Odysseus meets the shade of Achilles in the underworld (*Odyssey* XI. 487ff.) the latter claims that he would rather be a landless day-labourer on earth than king of all the dead.

[44] In his essay *On Naive and Sentimental Poetry* Schiller distinguishes between works of verbal art that present themselves as direct, immediate, spontaneous responses to nature ('naive' literature), and works that express the author's more-or-less conscious reflection on experience ('sentimental' literature).

ineffably sublime, for this very reason, is *Homer*, who, as an individual, stands in the same relation to that Apolline popular culture as the individual dream-artist does to the people's capacity for dreaming and indeed to that of nature in general. Homeric 'naïveté' can be understood only as the complete victory of Apolline illusion; it is an illusion of the kind so frequently employed by nature to achieve its aims. The true goal is obscured by a deluding image; we stretch out our hands towards the image, and nature achieves its goal by means of this deception. In the Greeks the 'Will' wanted to gaze on a vision of itself as transfigured by genius[45] and the world of art; in order that the Will might glorify itself its creatures too had to feel themselves to be worthy of glorification; they had to recognize a reflection of themselves in a higher sphere without feeling that the perfected world of their vision was an imperative or a reproach. This is the sphere of beauty in which they saw their mirror images, the Olympians. With this reflection (*Spiegelung*) of beauty the Hellenic 'Will' fought against the talent for suffering and for the wisdom of suffering which is the correlative of artistic talent; as a monument to its victory, Homer stands before us, the naive artist.

4

The analogy with dream tells us something about this naive artist. If we imagine the dreamer calling out to himself in the midst of the illusory dream world, but without disturbing it, 'It is a dream, I will dream on', and if this compels us to conclude that he is deriving intense inward pleasure from looking at the dream, but if on the other hand the ability to dream with such inner pleasure in looking depends on us having entirely forgotten the day and its terrible importuning, then we may interpret all of these phenomena, under the guidance of Apollo, the diviner of dreams, roughly as follows. There is no doubt that, of the two halves of our lives, the waking and the dreaming half, the former strikes us as being the more privileged, important, dignified, and worthy of being lived, indeed the only half that truly is lived; nevertheless, although it may seem paradoxical, I wish to assert that the very opposite evaluation of dream holds true for that mysterious ground of our being of which we are an appearance (*Erscheinung*). The more I become aware of those all-powerful artistic drives in nature, and of a fervent longing in them for semblance, for their redemption and release in semblance,

---

[45] By *Genius* here Nietzsche means not just some individual gift, but rather a universal inspirational spirit on which individual artists draw.

the more I feel myself driven to the metaphysical assumption that that which truly exists, the eternally suffering and contradictory, primordial unity, simultaneously needs, for its constant release and redemption, the ecstatic vision, intensely pleasurable semblance. We, however, who consist of and are completely trapped in semblance, are compelled to feel this semblance to be that which truly is not, i.e. a continual Becoming in time, space, and causality – in other words, empirical reality. If we ignore for a moment our own 'reality' and if we take our empirical existence, and indeed that of the world in general, to be a representation (*Vorstellung*) generated at each moment by the primordial unity, we must now regard dream as the *semblance of the semblance* and thus as a yet higher satisfaction of the original desire for semblance. It is for this very reason that the inner-most core of nature takes indescribable pleasure in the naive artist and the naive work of art which is also only the 'semblance of semblance'. *Raphael*, himself one of those immortal 'naive' artists, has depicted for us in a symbolic painting the reduction[46] of semblance to semblance, the primal process of the naive artist and also of Apolline culture. In his *Transfiguration* the lower half of the picture, with the possessed boy, the despairing bearers, and the frightened, helpless disciples, shows us a reflection of the eternal, primal pain, the only ground of the world; here 'semblance' is a reflection of the eternal contradiction, the father of all things. From this semblance there now rises, like some ambrosian perfume, a vision-like new world of semblance, of which those who are trapped in the first semblance see nothing – a luminous hovering in purest bliss and in wide-eyed contemplation, free of all pain. Here, in the highest symbolism of art, we see before us that Apolline world of beauty and the ground on which it rests, that terrible wisdom of Silenus, and we grasp, intuitively, the reciprocal necessity of these two things. At the same time, however, we encounter Apollo as the deification of the *principium individuationis* in which alone the eternally attained goal of the primordial unity, its release and redemption through semblance, comes about; with sublime gestures he shows us that the whole world of agony is needed in order to compel the individual to generate the releasing and redemptive vision and then, lost in contemplation of that vision, to sit calmly in his rocking boat in the midst of the sea.

If one thinks of it as in any sense imperative and prescriptive, this deification of individuation knows just one law: the individual, which is

---

[46] Nietzsche uses a curious word here, *Depotenzierung*, by which he presumably means the opposite of *Potenzierung*, which means to raise something to a higher power.

Transfiguration

→ religion is born from the suffering

two separate entities that feel somehow related

(the top can't exist without the bottom)

to say, respect for the limits of the individual, *measure* in the Hellenic sense. As an ethical divinity Apollo demands measure from all who belong to him and, so that they may respect that measure, knowledge of themselves. Thus the aesthetic necessity of beauty is accompanied by the demands: 'Know thyself' and 'Not too much!',[47] whereas getting above oneself and excess were regarded as the true hostile demons of the non-Apolline sphere, and thus as qualities of the pre-Apolline period, the age of the Titans, and of the extra-Apolline world, that of the barbarians. Prometheus had to be torn apart by vultures on account of his Titanic love for mankind; Oedipus had to be plunged into a confusing maelstrom of atrocities because his unmeasured wisdom solved the riddle of the Sphinx; these examples show how the Delphic god interpreted the Greek past.

The Apolline Greek, too, felt the effect aroused by the *Dionysiac* to be 'Titanic' and 'barbaric'; at the same time he could not conceal from himself the fact that he too was related inwardly to those overthrown Titans and heroes. Indeed he was bound to feel more than this: his entire existence, with all its beauty and moderation, rested on a hidden ground of suffering and knowledge which was exposed to his gaze once more by the Dionysiac. And behold! Apollo could not live without Dionysos. The 'Titanic' and 'barbaric' was ultimately just as much of a necessity as the Apolline! Let us now imagine how the ecstatic sounds of the Dionysiac festival, with its ever more seductive, magical melodies, entered this artificially dammed-up world founded on semblance and measure, how in these melodies all the unmeasurable excess in nature found expression in pleasure, suffering and knowledge, in a voice which rose in intensity to a penetrating shout; let us imagine how little the psalm-singing artist of Apollo and the ghostly sound of his harp could mean in comparison with this daemonic popular song! The Muses of the arts of 'semblance' grew pale and wan when faced with an art which, in its intoxication, spoke the truth; the wisdom of Silenus called out 'Woe, woe!' to the serene Olympians. The individual, with all his limits and measure, became submerged here in the self-oblivion of the Dionysiac condition and forgot the statutes of Apollo. *Excess* revealed itself as the truth; contradiction, bliss born of pain, spoke of itself from out of the heart of nature. Thus, wherever the Dionysiac broke through, the Apolline was suspended and annulled. But it is equally certain that, wherever the first

---

[47] These two imperatives were inscribed over the entrance to the Temple of Apollo at Delphi.

onslaught was resisted, the reputation and majesty of the Delphic god was expressed in more rigid and menacing forms than ever before; for the only explanation I can find for the *Doric* state and Doric art is that it was a permanent military encampment of the Apolline: only in a state of unremitting resistance to the Titanic-barbaric nature of the Dionysiac could such a cruel and ruthless polity, such a war-like and austere form of education, such a defiantly aloof art, surrounded by battlements, exist for long.

Up to this point I have simply expanded the observations I made at the beginning of this account: namely that the Dionysiac and the Apolline dominated the Hellenic world by a succession of ever-new births and by a process of reciprocal intensification; that, under the rule of the Apolline instinct for beauty, the Homeric world evolved from the 'iron' age with its Titanic struggles and its bitter popular philosophy; that this 'naive' magnificence was in turn engulfed by the flood of the Dionysiac when it broke over that world; and that the Apolline, confronted with this new power, rose up again in the rigid majesty of Doric art and the Doric view of the world. If, then, the struggle between these two hostile principles means that earlier Hellenic history breaks down into four great artistic stages, we must now ask what ultimate plan underlies all this to-ing and fro-ing – unless, that is, we are to regard the last of these periods, that of Doric art, as the pinnacle and goal of those artistic drives. At this point our gaze falls on the sublime and exalted art of *Attic tragedy* and the dramatic dithyramb as the common goal of both drives whose mysterious marriage, after a long preceding struggle, was crowned with such a child – who is both Antigone and Cassandra in one.[48]

5

We are now drawing closer to the true goal of our study, the aim of which is to understand the Dionysiac–Apolline genius and its work of art, or at least to gain some tentative intimation of that mysterious unity. At this point our first question is: where in the Hellenic world did that new germ first become evident which later evolved into tragedy and the dramatic dithyramb? Here the ancient world itself gives its reply in the form of

[48] Antigone, the child of the incestuous marriage between Oedipus and his mother, died by enforced suicide before reproducing. Cassandra rejected Apollo's advances; he thereupon caused her accurate prophecies (mostly, it seems, of catastrophes (including her own death)) never to be believed. *Cf.* Aeschylus, *Agamemnon*, lines 1200–15.

imagery, by placing *Homer and Archilochus*[49] side by side on brooches and other works of art as being the progenitors and torch-bearers of Greek poetry, a depiction prompted by the sure sense that only these two equally and entirely original natures, from whom a stream of fire pours out across the entire subsequent Greek world, deserve to be considered in this way. Homer, the hoary dreamer lost in his own inner world, the archetypically Apolline, naive artist, now gazes with astonishment at the passionate head of Archilochus, the warlike servant of the Muses, driven wildly through existence; to which recent aesthetics could only add, by way of interpretation, that here the first 'subjective' artist was contrasted with the 'objective' artist. This interpretation is little help to us, as the only subjective artist we know is the bad artist and the prime demand we make of every kind and level of art is the conquest of subjectivity, release and redemption from the 'I', and the falling-silent of all individual willing and desiring; indeed without objectivity, without pure, disinterested contemplation[50] we are unable to believe that any creation, however slight, is genuinely artistic. Thus our aesthetics must first solve the problem of how the 'lyric poet' can possibly be an artist at all, since he is someone who, so the experience of the ages tells us, always says 'I', and who stands before us singing the entire chromatic scale of his passions and desires. Compared with Homer, this Archilochus frankly terrifies us with his cries of hatred and scorn, with the drunken outbursts of his desire; is not then this artist, the first to be called subjective, the true non-artist? But in this case, why should the Delphic oracle, the very seat of 'objective' art, have expressed such veneration for him, as a poet, in very strange utterances?[51]

Schiller has thrown some light for us on the process of poetic composition, as it affected him, in a psychological observation which seemed inexplicable but which did not worry him; he confesses that, in the state of mind preparatory to the act of writing poetry, what he had before and within him was not, say, a series of images, with his thoughts ordered in causal sequence, but rather a *musical mood*.[52] ('In my case the feeling is

---

[49] Seventh-century poet who sings of his military experiences as a mercenary, his enjoyment of wine, and his various likes and dislikes. The traditional story relates that he was in love with a woman named Neoboule, and subjected her father, Lykambes, who refused to allow a marriage, to poetic abuse so effective he killed himself.

[50] Both Kant and Schopenhauer define the aesthetic experience as one of 'disinterested contemplation'.

[51] Probably a reference to the story reported in Plutarch's *De sera numinis vindicatione* 17 that the priestess of Apollo drove Archilochus' murderer out of the temple on the grounds that he had killed 'a sacred man of the Muses'.

[52] In a letter to Goethe of 18 March 1796.

initially without a definite and clear object; this does not take shape until later. It is preceded by a certain musical mood, which is followed in my case by the poetic idea.') If we add to this the most important phenomenon in the whole of ancient lyric poetry, the combination, indeed identity, of the *lyric poet* with the *musician*, something which was regarded as natural everywhere (and in contrast to which our more recent lyric poetry resembles the statue of a god without a head), we are in a position to explain the lyric poet, on the basis of the aesthetic metaphysics presented above, in the following way. In the first instance the lyric poet, a Dionysiac artist, has become entirely at one with the primordial unity, with its pain and contradiction, and he produces a copy of this primordial unity as music, which has been described elsewhere, quite rightly, as a repetition of the world and a second copy of it; now, however, under the influence of Apolline dream, this music in turn becomes visible to him as in a *symbolic dream-image*. The image-less and concept-less reflection of the original pain in music, with its release and redemption in semblance, now generates a second reflection, as a single symbolic likeness (*Gleichnis*) or *exemplum*. The artist has already given up his subjectivity in the Dionysiac process; the image which now shows him his unity with the heart of the world is a dream scene which gives sensuous expression to the primal contradiction and pain, along with its primal lust for and pleasure in semblance. Thus the 'I' of the lyric poet sounds out from the deepest abyss of being; his 'subjectivity', as this concept is used by modern aestheticians, is imaginary. When Archilochus, the first lyric poet of the Greeks, simultaneously proclaims his crazed love and scorn for the daughters of Lycambes, it is not his passion that dances before us in orgiastic frenzy: we see Dionysos and the maenads, we see the intoxicated enthusiast Archilochus sunk in sleep – as Euripides describes it in the *Bacchae*, a sleep on a high alpine meadow, in the mid-day sun[53] – and now Apollo approaches and touches him with a laurel. The Dionysiac-musical enchantment of the sleeper now pours forth sparks of imagery, as it were, lyric poems which, unfolded to their fullest extent, are called tragedies and dramatic dithyrambs.

Both the sculptor and his relative, the epic poet, are lost in the pure contemplation of images. The Dionysiac musician, with no image at all, is nothing but primal pain and the primal echo of it. The lyric genius feels a world of images and symbols growing out of the mystical state of self-abandonment and one-ness, a world which has a quite different colouring,

[53] Lines 677ff.

causality, and tempo from that of the sculptor and epic poet. Whereas the latter is joyfully contented living in these images and in them alone, and never tires of contemplating lovingly even the minutest details of them, and whereas even the image of the wrathful Achilles is for him merely an image whose wrathful expression he enjoys with the dream-pleasure in semblance (so that he is protected by this mirror of semblance against merging and becoming one with his figures), the images of the lyric poet, by contrast, are nothing but *the poet himself*, merely various objectifications of him, as it were, which is why he can say 'I' as the moving centre of that world. Yet this 'I'-ness is not the same as that of the waking, empirically real human being, but rather the only 'I'-ness which truly exists at all, eternal and resting in the ground of things, and through the images which are copies of that 'I' the lyric genius can see down to that very ground of all things. Now let us consider the poet as he catches sight of *himself* amongst these copies, in his condition as non-genius, which is to say his 'subject', that whole tangle of subjective passions and stirrings of the will directed at some specific thing which it takes to be real; although it may now appear as if the lyric genius and the non-genius connected with him were one being, and as if the former were using that little word 'I' to speak of himself, we will not now be led astray by this semblance as those who have defined the lyric poet as the subjective poet have been led astray. In truth Archilochus, the passionately inflamed, loving and hating human being, is nothing but a vision of the genius itself; this genius is no longer Archilochus but the genius of the world which expresses its primal pain symbolically in the likeness of the man Archilochus; conversely, it is quite impossible for the man Archilochus, with his subjective will and desires, ever to be a poet. However, the lyric poet does not necessarily have to see the eternal Being reflected only in the man Archilochus; indeed, tragedy demonstrates just how far the visionary world of the lyric poet can move away from the phenomenon which, admittedly, is the one closest to him.

Schopenhauer, who did not conceal from himself the difficulty which the lyric poet presents to the philosophical discussion of art, believes he has found a way out which I am unable to take with him; yet his own profound metaphysics of music supplied him with a means of disposing of this difficulty decisively, and this is what I believe I have done here, in his spirit and to his honour. In contrast to my own view, he defines the peculiar essence of the song as follows:

It is the subject of the will, in other words, the singer's own willing that fills his consciousness, often as a released and satisfied willing (joy), but even more often as an impeded willing (sorrow), always as emotion, passion, an agitated state of mind. Besides this, however, and simultaneously with it, the singer, through the sight of surrounding nature, becomes conscious of himself as the subject of pure, will-less knowing, whose unshakable, blissful peace now appears in contrast to the stress of willing that is always restricted and needy. The feeling of this contrast, this alternate play, is really what is expressed in the whole of the song, and what in general constitutes the lyrical state. In this state pure knowing comes to us, so to speak, in order to deliver us from willing and its stress. We follow, yet only for a few moments; willing, desire, the recollection of our own personal aims, always tears us anew from peaceful contemplation; but yet again and again the next beautiful environment, in which pure, will-less knowledge presents itself to us, entices us away from willing. Therefore in the song and in the lyrical mood, willing (the personal interest of the aims) and pure perception of the environment that presents itself are wonderfully blended with each other. Relations between the two are sought and imagined; the subjective disposition, the affection of the will, imparts its hue to the perceived environment, and this environment again imparts in the reflex its colour to that disposition. The genuine song is the copy of the whole of this mingled and divided state of mind. (*World as Will and Representation*, I, p. 295)

Who could fail to see that the lyric is characterized here as an imperfectly achieved art, suspended in mid-flight, as it were, and seldom reaching its goal, indeed as only half an art, the *essence* of which supposedly consists in the strange mixing of willing and pure contemplation, i.e. of the non-aesthetic and the aesthetic states? We maintain on the contrary that the entire opposition between the subjective and the objective (which Schopenhauer, too, still uses to divide up the arts, as if it were some criterion of value) is absolutely inappropriate in aesthetics since the subject, the willing individual in pursuit of his own, egotistical goals, can only be considered the opponent of art and not its origin. But where the subject is an artist, it is already released and redeemed from the individual will and has become, as it were, a medium, the channel through which the one truly existing subject celebrates its release and redemption in semblance. For what must be clear to us above all, both to our humiliation *and* our elevation, is that the whole comedy of art is certainly not performed for us, neither for our edification nor our education, just as we are far from truly being the creators of that world of art; conversely, however, we may very well assume we are already images and artistic projections for the true creator of art, and that our highest dignity lies in our significance as works of art – for only as an *aesthetic phenomenon* is existence and the world eternally *justified* – although, of course, our awareness of our significance in this respect hardly differs from the awareness which painted soldiers have of the battle depicted on the same canvas. Thus our whole knowledge of art is at bottom entirely illusory, because, as knowing creatures, we are not one and identical with the essential being which gives itself eternal pleasure as the creator and spectator of that comedy of art. Only insofar as the genius, during the act of artistic procreation, merges fully with that original artist of the world does he know anything of the eternal essence of art; for in this condition he resembles, miraculously, that uncanny image of fairy-tale which can turn its eyes around and look at itself; now he is at one and the same time subject and object, simultaneously poet, actor, and spectator.

6

Scholars have discovered that Archilochus introduced the *folk song* into literature and that it is for this deed that he deserves his unique position alongside Homer in the general esteem of the Greeks. But what is folk song, as compared with the wholly Apolline epic? Nothing other than the *perpetuum vestigium*[54] of a union of the Apolline and the Dionysiac; the fact that it is so widely distributed amongst all peoples and grew ever more intense in an unbroken succession of births bears witness to the strength of that artistic double drive in nature, a drive which leaves traces of itself in popular song in much the same way as the orgiastic movements of a people are eternalized in its music. Indeed it ought to be possible to demonstrate historically that every period which was rich in the production of folk songs was agitated by Dionysiac currents, since these are always to be regarded as the precondition of folk song and as the hidden ground from which it springs.

But above all else we regard folk song as a musical mirror of the world, as original melody which then seeks for itself a parallel dream-appearance, and expresses this in poetry. Thus *melody is the primary and general element* which can therefore undergo several objectifications in several texts. In the naive estimation of the people it is also by far the more important and essential element. Melody gives birth to poetry, and does so over and over again, in ever new ways; this is what the *strophic form of the folk song*

[54] Permanent trace.

is trying to tell us, a phenomenon which always astonished me until I eventually found this explanation. Anyone who examines a collection of folk songs (such as *Des Knaben Wunderhorn*)[55] with this theory in mind will find countless examples of how the melody, as it gives birth again and again, emanates sparks of imagery which in their variety, their sudden changes, their mad, head-over-heels, forward rush, reveal an energy utterly alien to the placid flow of epic semblance. Seen from the point of view of the epic, this uneven and irregular image-world of the lyric is something which must simply be condemned, as indeed the solemn epic rhapsodes at the Apolline festivals in the age of Terpander[56] undoubtedly did condemn it.

Thus in the poetry of folk song we see language straining to its limits *to imitate music*, which is why Archilochus marks the beginning of a new world of poetry fundamentally at odds with that of Homer. With this observation we have defined the only possible relationship between music, word, and sound: the word, the image, the concept seeks expression in a manner analogous to music and thereby is subjected to the power of music. In this sense we may distinguish two main currents in the linguistic history of the Greek people, depending on whether language imitated the world of appearances and imagery or the world of music. One only has to think more deeply about the linguistic difference in colour, syntactic construction, and lexical material between Pindar and Homer to grasp the significance of this opposition; indeed, as one does so, it becomes palpably clear that between Homer and Pindar the *orgiastic flute melodies of Olympus*[57] must have made themselves heard, melodies which were still inspiring drunken enthusiasm at the time of Aristotle and indeed were doing so in the midst of other music which had reached a far higher stage of development; melodies which, when they made their original impact, must have challenged all the expressive poetic devices known to contemporaries to emulate their effect. Here I would draw attention to a familiar phenomenon from our own time, one which only strikes our aesthetics as offensive. Time after time we hear of a symphony by Beethoven forcing individual listeners to speak in images, even if a combination of the various image-worlds generated by a piece of

---

[55] Romantic collection of purported German 'folk songs' put together in 1804–7 by Achim von Arnim and Clemens Brentano.

[56] A 'rhapsode' was a professional reciter of epic poetry (especially Homer); Terpander was an early (7th century BC) Lesbian musician credited with a number of technical innovations.

[57] Legendary inventor of music for the instrument Nietzsche calls the 'flute'; *cf.* Aristotle, *Politicas* 8.5.1340a10ff.

music produces a fantastically variegated, indeed contradictory result; it is typical of contemporary aesthetics to exercise its meagre wit on such combinations and to overlook the phenomenon that is truly in need of explanation. Even when a musician speaks in images about a composition, as when he describes a symphony as 'pastoral',[58] calling one movement a 'scene by a stream' and another a 'merry gathering of country folk', these too are merely symbolic representations born out of the music (as opposed to the objects imitated by the music), representations which are quite incapable of informing us about the *Dionysiac* content of music, and which indeed have no exclusive value as compared with other images. We now need to imagine what happens when this process of music discharging itself (*entladen*) in images takes place amongst a youthfully fresh, linguistically creative mass of people, in order to get some idea of the origins of the strophic folk song and of how the entire linguistic ability of the people is stimulated by the new principle of the imitation of music.

If we are right in considering lyric poetry to be the imitative effulguration of music in images and concepts, we may now ask: 'As what does music *appear* in the mirror of imagery and concepts?' It *appears as Will*, understood in Schopenhauer's sense, which is to say, in opposition to the aesthetic, purely contemplative, will-less mood. But here one should distinguish as sharply as possible between the concepts of essence and appearance, since music, by its essence, cannot possibly *be* Will, because as such it would have to be banished entirely from the realm of art – for Will is that which is inherently un-aesthetic – but it *appears* as Will. In order to express the Will's appearance in images the lyric poet needs all the stirrings of passion, from the whisper of inclination to the fury of madness; impelled by the drive to speak of music in Apolline symbols, he understands the whole of nature, including himself, to be nothing but that which eternally wills, desires, longs. But by virtue of the fact that he interprets music in images, he himself is at rest on the still, calm sea of Apolline contemplation, no matter how much all those things around him which he contemplates through the medium of music are in the grip of thrusting, driving motion. Indeed, when he catches sight of himself through that same medium his own image presents itself to him as being in a state of unsatisfied feeling; his own willing, longing, groaning, and shouting for joy, is a symbolic likeness with which he interprets music. This is the phenomenon of the lyric poet: as an Apolline genius he interprets music through the image of the

---

[58] Beethoven's Symphony in F major opus 68.

Will, while he himself, completely set free from the greed of the Will, is a pure, unclouded sun-eye.

This whole discussion firmly maintains that, whereas lyric poetry depends utterly on the spirit of music, music itself, in its absolute sovereignty, has no *need* at all of images and concepts but merely *tolerates* them as an accompaniment. Lyric poetry can say nothing that was not already contained, in a condition of the most enormous generality and universal validity, within the music which forced the lyric poet to speak in images. For this reason it is impossible for language to exhaust the meaning of music's world-symbolism, because music refers symbolically to the original contradiction and original pain at the heart of the primordial unity, and thus symbolizes a sphere which lies above and beyond all appearance. In relation to that primal being every phenomenon is merely a likeness, which is why *language*, as the organ and symbol of phenomena, can never, under any circumstances, externalize the innermost depths of music; whenever language attempts to imitate music it only touches the outer surface of music, whereas the deepest meaning of music, for all the eloquence of lyric poetry, can never be brought even one step closer to us.

7

We must now summon to our aid all the principles of art discussed so far in order to find our way through what we are bound to describe as the labyrinth of the *origin of Greek tragedy*. I believe I am not talking nonsense when I assert that this problem of origin has not yet even been posed seriously, far less solved, despite the many attempts to sew together and pull apart again the tattered shreds of ancient historical evidence in various combinations. This evidence tells us most decisively *that tragedy arose from the tragic chorus* and was originally chorus and nothing but chorus. From this we derive the obligation to look into the heart of this tragic chorus as into the true, original drama, rather than simply contenting ourselves with the usual artistic clichés, such as the claim that the chorus is the ideal (*idealisch*) spectator, or that it represents the people in contrast to the princely region of the stage. This last interpretation sounds so lofty to the ears of some politicians, as if the immutable moral law of the democratic Athenians were represented in the popular chorus which was always proved right, beyond all the passionate excesses and indulgences of the kings. But no matter how strongly a remark by Aristotle seems to suggest this,[59] this idea had no influence on the original formation of tragedy, since its purely religious origins preclude the entire opposition between prince and people, and indeed any kind of political–social sphere. Even with regard to the classical form of the chorus familiar to us from the works of Aeschylus and Sophocles, we regard it as blasphemous to speak of the premonition of a 'constitutional popular assembly', although others have been less reluctant to commit this blasphemy. In practice the ancient constitutions know of no constitutional popular assembly, and it is to be hoped that they did not even have a 'premonition' of one in their tragedy.

Much more famous than this political explanation of the chorus is one of A.W. Schlegel's[60] thoughts which recommends us to think of the chorus as, in a certain sense, the quintessence and distillation of the crowd of spectators, as the 'ideal spectator'. When set next to the historical evidence that tragedy was originally only a chorus, this suggestion is revealed for what it really is: a crude, unscientific, but brilliant assertion, but one which derives its brilliance from the concentrated manner of its expression alone, from the characteristic Germanic prejudice in favour of anything that is called 'ideal', and from our momentary astonishment. For when we compare the public in the theatre, which we know well, with that chorus, we are simply astonished and we ask ourselves if it would ever be possible to distil from this public something ideal that would be analogous to the tragic chorus. In the privacy of our own thoughts we deny this possibility and we are as much surprised by the boldness of Schlegel's assertion as we are by the utterly different nature of the Greek public. This is because we had always believed that a proper spectator, whoever he might be, always had to remain conscious of the fact that what he saw before him was a work of art and not empirical reality, whereas the tragic chorus of the Greeks is required to see in the figures on stage real, physically present, living beings. The chorus of the Oceanides[61] really believes that it sees before it the Titan Prometheus, and takes itself to be as real as the god on the stage. Are we then supposed to believe that the highest and purest kind of spectator is one who, like the Oceanides, believes Prometheus to be physically present

---

[59] *Problemata* 19.48.922b18ff.

[60] In his *Lectures on Dramatic Art and Literature* (3 vols., 1809–11), *Fifth Lecture*, Schlegel emphasizes the 'republican spirit' of ancient tragedy and its political content.

[61] The daughters of Oceanus form the chorus of Aeschylus' *Prometheus Bound*. The title page of the original edition of *Birth of Tragedy* had a design depicting the moment when Prometheus is about to be freed from his bondage. (This design is reproduced on the front cover of *Nietzsche on Tragedy* by M. Silk and J. P. Stern (Cambridge University Press, 1981).)

and real? And that it would be the mark of the ideal spectator to run on to the stage and free the god from his tortures? We had believed in an aesthetic public and had gauged the individual spectator's competence by the degree of his ability to take the work of art as art, i.e. aesthetically; but now Schlegel's phrase gave us to understand that the perfect, ideal spectator lets himself be affected by the world on stage physically and empirically rather than aesthetically. Oh, curse these Greeks, we sigh; they turn our aesthetics upside down! As we are accustomed to this, however, we simply repeated Schlegel's dictum whenever the chorus was under discussion.

But the historical evidence explicitly speaks against Schlegel here: the chorus as such, without a stage, which is to say the primitive form of tragedy, is not compatible with that chorus of ideal spectators. What kind of artistic genre would be one derived from the concept of the spectator, one where the true form of the genre would have to be regarded as the 'spectator as such'? The spectator without a spectacle is a nonsense. We fear that the explanation for the birth of tragedy can be derived neither from respect for the moral intelligence of the masses, nor from the concept of the spectator without a play, and we regard the problem as too profound for it even to be touched by such shallow ways of thinking about it.

In his famous preface to the *Bride of Messina*[62] Schiller betrayed an infinitely more valuable insight into the significance of the chorus when he considered it to be a living wall which tragedy draws about itself in order to shut itself off in purity from the real world and to preserve its ideal ground and its poetic freedom.

This is Schiller's main weapon in his fight against the common concept of the natural, against the illusion commonly demanded of dramatic poetry. He argued that, although in the theatre the day itself was only artificial, the architecture symbolic, and metrical speech had an ideal character, on the whole error still prevailed; it was not enough merely to tolerate as poetic freedom something which was, after all, the essence of all poetry. The introduction of the chorus was the decisive step by which war was declared openly and honestly on all naturalism in art. It seems to me that this way of looking at things is precisely what our (in its own opinion) superior age dismisses with the slogan 'pseudo-idealism'. I fear that, with our current veneration for the natural and the real, we have arrived at the

---

[62] What Nietzsche claims here as a property of ancient tragedy is described by Schiller as a specific feature of the use of the chorus in *modern* (as opposed to ancient) times.

opposite pole to all idealism, and have landed in the region of the waxworks. They too contain a kind of art, as do certain of today's popular novels; but let nobody torment us with the claim that, thanks to this art, the 'pseudo-idealism' of Schiller and Goethe has been overcome.

It is admittedly an 'ideal' ground on which, as Schiller rightly saw, the Greek chorus of satyrs, the chorus of the original tragedy, is wont to walk, a ground raised high above the real path along which mortals wander. For this chorus the Greeks built the hovering platform of a fictitious *state of nature* on to which they placed fictitious *creatures of nature*. Tragedy grew up on this foundation, and for this very reason, of course, was relieved from the very outset of any need to copy reality with painful exactness. Yet it is not a world which mere caprice and fantasy have conjured up between heaven and earth; rather it is a world which was just as real and credible to the believing Greek as Olympus and its inhabitants. As a member of the Dionysiac chorus, the satyr lives in a religiously acknowledged reality sanctioned by myth and cult. The fact that tragedy begins with the satyr, and that the Dionysiac wisdom of tragedy speaks out of him, is something which now surprises us just as much as the fact that tragedy originated in the chorus. Perhaps it will serve as a starting-point for thinking about this if I now assert that the satyr, the fictitious creature of nature, bears the same relation to the cultured human being as Dionysiac music bears to civilization. Of the latter Richard Wagner has said that it is absorbed, elevated, and extinguished (*aufgehoben*) by music, just as lamplight is superseded by the light of day.[63] I believe that, when faced with the chorus of satyrs, cultured Greeks felt themselves absorbed, elevated, and extinguished in exactly the same way. This is the first effect of Dionysiac tragedy: state and society, indeed all divisions between one human being and another, give way to an overwhelming feeling of unity which leads men back to the heart of nature. The metaphysical solace which, I wish to suggest, we derive from every true tragedy, the solace that in the ground of things, and despite all changing appearances, life is indestructibly mighty and pleasurable, this solace appears with palpable clarity in the chorus of satyrs, a chorus of natural beings whose life goes on ineradicably behind and beyond all civilization, as it were, and who remain eternally the same despite all the changes of generations and in the history of nations.

The Hellene, by nature profound and uniquely capable of the most exquisite and most severe suffering, comforts himself with this chorus, for

---

[63] In his essay 'Beethoven'.

he has gazed with keen eye into the midst of the fearful, destructive havoc of so-called world history, and has seen the cruelty of nature, and is in danger of longing to deny the will as the Buddhist does. Art saves him, and through art life saves him – for itself.

The reason for this is that the ecstasy of the Dionysiac state, in which the usual barriers and limits of existence are destroyed, contains, for as long as it lasts, a *lethargic* element in which all personal experiences from the past are submerged. This gulf of oblivion separates the worlds of everyday life and Dionysiac experience. But as soon as daily reality re-enters consciousness, it is experienced as such with a sense of revulsion; the fruit of those states is an ascetic, will-negating mood. In this sense Dionysiac man is similar to Hamlet: both have gazed into the true essence of things, they have *acquired knowledge* and they find action repulsive, for their actions can do nothing to change the eternal essence of things; they regard it as laughable or shameful that they should be expected to set to rights a world so out of joint. Knowledge kills action; action requires one to be shrouded in a veil of illusion – this is the lesson of Hamlet, not that cheap wisdom about Jack the Dreamer who does not get around to acting because he reflects too much, out of an excess of possibilities, as it were. No, it is not reflection, it is true knowledge, insight into the terrible truth, which outweighs every motive for action, both in the case of Hamlet and in that of Dionysiac man. Now no solace has any effect, there is a longing for a world beyond death, beyond the gods themselves; existence is denied, along with its treacherous reflection in the gods or in some immortal Beyond. Once truth has been seen, the consciousness of it prompts man to see only what is terrible or absurd in existence wherever he looks; now he understands the symbolism of Ophelia's fate, now he grasps the wisdom of the wood-god Silenus: he feels revulsion.

Here, at this moment of supreme danger for the will, *art* approaches as a saving sorceress with the power to heal. Art alone can re-direct those repulsive thoughts about the terrible or absurd nature of existence into representations with which man can live; these representations are the *sublime*, whereby the terrible is tamed by artistic means, and the *comical*, whereby disgust at absurdity is discharged by artistic means. The dithyramb's chorus of satyrs is the saving act of Greek art; the attacks of revulsion described above spent themselves in contemplation of the intermediate world of these Dionysiac companions.

8

Both the satyr and the idyllic shepherd of modern times were born of a longing for what is original and natural; but how firmly and fearlessly the Greek seized hold of his man of the woods, and how bashful and limp was modern man's flirtation with the flattering image of a tender, flute-playing, soft-natured shepherd! What the Greek saw in his satyr was nature, as yet untouched by knowledge, with the bolts of culture still closed, but he did not for this reason equate the satyr with the monkey. On the contrary, what he saw in the satyr was the original image (*Urbild*) of mankind, the expression of man's highest and strongest stirrings, an enthusiastic celebrant, ecstatic at the closeness of his god, a sympathetic companion in whom the sufferings of the god are repeated, a proclaimer of wisdom from the deepest heart of nature, an emblem of the sexual omnipotence of nature which the Greek habitually regards with reverent astonishment. The satyr was something sublime and divine; and he was particularly bound to seem so to the painfully broken gaze of Dionysiac man. The latter would have felt insulted by the prettified, make-believe shepherd; his eye dwelt in sublime satisfaction on the handwriting of nature, undisguised, robust and magnificent; here the illusion of culture was wiped away by the primal image of man; here, in this bearded satyr shouting up to his god in jubilation, man's true nature was revealed. Faced with the satyr, cultured man shrivelled to a mendacious caricature. Schiller is also right about these beginnings of tragic art: the chorus is a living wall against the onslaught of reality because a truer, more real, more complete image of existence is presented by the chorus of satyrs than by cultured man who generally thinks of himself as the only reality. The sphere of poetry does not lie outside the world, like some fantastical impossibility contrived in a poet's head; poetry aims to be the very opposite, the unvarnished expression of truth, and for this very reason it must cast off the deceitful finery of the so-called reality of cultured man. The contrast between this genuine truth of nature and the cultural lie which pretends to be the only reality is like the contrast between the eternal core of things, the thing-in-itself, and the entire world of phenomena; and just as tragedy, with its metaphysical solace, points to the eternal life of that core of being despite the constant destruction of the phenomenal world, the symbolism of the chorus of satyrs is in itself a metaphorical expression of that original relationship between thing-in-itself and phenomenon. The idyllic shepherd of modern man is merely a counterfeit of the sum of educated illusions which modern man takes to be nature; the Dionysian Greek wants truth and nature at full strength – and sees himself transformed by magic into a satyr.

The agitated mass of Dionysos' servants shouts in jubilation as they are seized by moods and insights so powerful that they transform them before their very own eyes, making them think they are seeing themselves restored to the condition of geniuses of nature, as satyrs. The later constitution of the tragic chorus is the artistic imitation of that natural phenomenon; at this point, admittedly, it was necessary to separate the Dionysiac spectators from those who were under the spell of Dionysiac magic. But it must always be remembered that the audience of Attic tragedy identified itself with the chorus on the *orchestra*, so that there was fundamentally no opposition between public and chorus; the whole is just one sublime chorus, either of dancing and singing satyrs, or of those who allow themselves to be represented by these satyrs. Here the deeper meaning of Schlegel's concept is bound to become apparent. The chorus is the 'ideal spectator' inasmuch as it is the only *seer* (*Schauer*), the seer of the visionary world on the stage. A public of spectators as we know it was something unknown to the Greeks; in their theatres it was possible, given the terraced construction of the theatre in concentric arcs, for everyone quite literally to *overlook* (*übersehen*) the entire cultural world around him, and to imagine, as he looked with sated gaze, that he was a member of the chorus. This insight allows us to describe the chorus, at the primitive stage of its development in the original tragedy, as a self-mirroring of Dionysiac man; the clearest illustration of this phenomenon is to be found in the process whereby a truly gifted actor sees with palpable immediacy before his very eyes the image of the role he has to play. The chorus of satyrs is first and foremost a vision of the Dionysiac mass, just as the world of the stage is in turn a vision of this chorus of satyrs; the strength of this vision is great enough to render the spectator's gaze insensitive and unresponsive to the impression of 'reality' and to the cultured people occupying the rows of seats around him. The form of the Greek theatre is reminiscent of a lonely mountain valley; the architecture of the stage seems like a radiant cloud formation seen from on high by the Bacchae as they roam excitedly through the mountains, like the magnificent frame in which the image of Dionysos is revealed to them.

Given our learned view of the elementary artistic processes, there is almost something indecent about the primal artistic phenomenon adduced here in explanation of the tragic chorus. Yet nothing can be more certain than this: what makes a poet a poet is the fact that he sees himself surrounded by figures who live and act before him, and into whose innermost essence he gazes. Because of the peculiar weakness of modern talent we are inclined to imagine the original aesthetic phenomenon in too complicated and abstract a manner. For the genuine poet metaphor is no rhetorical figure, but an image which takes the place of something else, something he can really see before him as a substitute for a concept. To the poet, a character is not a whole composed of selected single features, but an insistently alive person whom he sees before his very eyes, and distinguished from a painter's vision of the same thing only by the fact that the poet sees the figure continuing to live and act over a period of time. What allows Homer to depict things so much more vividly than all other poets? It is the fact that he looks at things so much more than they do. We talk so abstractly about poetry because we are usually all bad poets. Fundamentally the aesthetic phenomenon is simple; one only has to have the ability to watch a living play (*Spiel*) continuously and to live constantly surrounded by crowds of spirits, then one is a poet; if one feels the impulse to transform oneself and to speak out of other bodies and souls, then one is a dramatist.

Dionysiac excitement is able to transmit to an entire mass of people this artistic gift of seeing themselves surrounded by just such a crowd of spirits with which they know themselves to be inwardly at one. This process of the tragic chorus is the original phenomenon of *drama*[64] – this experience of seeing oneself transformed before one's eyes and acting as if one had really entered another body, another character. This process stands at the beginning of the development of drama. Here we have something different from the rhapsode who does not merge with his images but sees them outside himself, with contemplative eye, much as the painter does; here already we have individuality being surrendered by entering into another nature. What is more, this phenomenon occurs as an epidemic: an entire crowd feels itself magically transformed like this. For this reason the dithyramb is essentially different from any other kind of choral song. The virgins who walk solemnly to the temple of Apollo, bearing laurel branches in their hands and singing a processional hymn as they go, remain who they are and retain their civic names; the dithyrambic chorus is a chorus of transformed beings who have completely forgotten their civic past and their social position; they have become timeless servants of their god,

[64] The Greek word *drama* means 'action'.

43

living outside every social sphere. All other choral poetry of the Hellenes is merely a vast intensification of the individual Apolline singer; in the dithyramb, by contrast, a congregation of unconscious actors stands before us who all look on one another as transformed beings.

Enchantment is the precondition of all dramatic art. In this enchanted state the Dionysiac enthusiast sees himself as a satyr, and *as a satyr he in turn sees the god*, i.e. in his transformed state he sees a new vision outside himself which is the Apolline perfection of his state. With this new vision the drama is complete.

This insight leads us to understand Greek tragedy as a Dionysian chorus which discharges itself over and over again in an Apolline world of images. Thus the choral passages which are interwoven with the tragedy are, to a certain extent, the womb of the entire so-called dialogue, i.e. of the whole world on stage, the drama proper. This primal ground of tragedy radiates, in a succession of discharges, that vision of drama which is entirely a dream-appearance, and thus epic in nature; on the other hand, as the objectification of a Dionysiac state, the vision represents not Apolline release and redemption in semblance, but rather the breaking-asunder of the individual and its becoming one with the primal being itself. Thus drama is the Apolline embodiment of Dionysiac insights and effects, and is thereby separated by a vast gulf from the epic.

The *chorus* of Greek tragedy, the symbol of the entire mass of those affected by Dionysiac excitement, is fully explained by our understanding of the matter. Because we are accustomed to the position of the chorus, particularly the operatic chorus, on the modern stage, we were completely unable to understand how the tragic chorus of the Greeks was supposedly older, more original, indeed more important than the 'action' proper – although this is clearly what the historical evidence says; equally, we could not see how the high importance and originality traditionally attributed to the chorus was to be reconciled with the fact that it was said to be composed of lowly, serving creatures, indeed, initially, only of goat-like satyrs; the placing of the orchestra before the stage remained a constant puzzle to us; now, however, we have come to realize that the stage and the action were originally and fundamentally thought of as nothing other than a *vision*, that the only 'reality' is precisely that of the chorus, which creates the vision from within itself and speaks of this vision with all the symbolism of dance, tone, and word. This chorus sees in its vision its lord and master Dionysos, and is therefore eternally the *serving* chorus; it sees how the god suffers and is glorified, and thus does not itself *act*. Despite its entirely subservient position in relation to the god, however, the chorus is nevertheless the highest, which is to say Dionysiac, expression of *nature*, and therefore speaks in its enthusiasm, as does nature herself, oracular and wise words; the chorus which *shares in suffering* is also the *wise* chorus which proclaims the truth from the heart of the world. This gives rise to that fantastical and seemingly distasteful figure of the wise and enthusiastic satyr who is at the same time 'the foolish man'[65] in contrast to his god; a copy of nature and its strongest impulses, indeed a symbol of them, and at the same time the proclaimer of her wisdom and art; musician, poet, dancer, seer of spirits, all in one person.

According to this insight and according to the traditional evidence, *Dionysos*, the true hero of the stage and centre of the vision, is initially, in the earliest period of the tragedy, not truly present, but rather is imagined as being present; i.e. originally the tragedy is only 'chorus' and not 'drama'. Later the attempt is made to show the god as real and to present the vision-ary figure, together with the transfiguring framework, as visible to every eye; at this point 'drama' in the narrower sense begins. Now the dithy-rambic chorus is given the task of infecting the mood of the audience with Dionysiac excitement to such a pitch that, when the tragic hero appears on the stage, they see, not some grotesquely masked human being, but rather a visionary figure, born, as it were, of their own ecstasy. If we think of Admetus,[66] lost in thought as he remembers his recently deceased wife Alcestis, and consuming himself entirely in mental contemplation of her – when, suddenly, the image of a woman, similar in form and with a similar walk, is led, veiled, towards him; if we think of his sudden, trembling rest-lessness, his stormy comparisons, his instinctive conviction – then we have an analogy for the feeling with which the spectator, in a state of Dionysiac excitement, saw approaching on the stage the god with whose suffering he has already become one. Involuntarily he transferred on to that masked figure the whole image of the god which he saw trembling magically before his soul, and he dissolved, so to speak, the reality of the figure into a ghostly unreality. This is the Apolline dream-state in which the day-world becomes shrouded, and a new, clearer, more comprehensible, more affecting world, but one which at the same time is more shadow-like, is born anew and pre-

---

65 In Tribschen Wagner had discussed with Nietzsche his project of turning the medieval epic by Wolfram von Eschenbach, *Parzival*, whose hero is precisely such a 'foolish man', into an opera. The opera was not completed until 1882.

66 Euripides, *Alcestis*, lines 860–1070.

sents itself, constantly changing, to our gaze. Accordingly, we recognize in tragedy a pervasive stylistic opposition: language, colour, mobility, dynamics, all of these diverge into distinct, entirely separated spheres of expression, into the Dionysiac lyric of the chorus on the one hand and the Apolline dream-world of the stage on the other. The Apolline appearances in which Dionysos objectifies himself are no longer an 'eternal sea, a changing weaving, a glowing life',[67] as the music of the chorus is; they are no longer those energies which were only felt and not yet concentrated in an image, in which the enthusiastic servant of Dionysos senses the closeness of his god; now the clarity and firmness of the epic shaping speak to him from the stage, now Dionysos no longer speaks in the form of energies but rather as an epic hero, almost in the language of Homer.

9

Everything that rises to the surface in dialogue, the Apolline part of Greek tragedy, appears simple, transparent, beautiful. In this sense the dialogue is a copy of the Hellene, whose nature is expressed in dance, because in dance the greatest strength is still only potential, although it is betrayed by the suppleness and luxuriance of movement. Thus the language of Sophocles' heroes surprises us by its Apolline definiteness and clarity, so that we feel as if we are looking straight into the innermost ground of its being, and are somewhat astonished that the road to this ground is so short. But if we once divert our gaze from the character of the hero as it rises to the surface and becomes visible – fundamentally, it is no more than an image of light (*Lichtbild*) projected on to a dark wall, i.e. appearance (*Erscheinung*) through and through[68] – if, rather, we penetrate to the myth which projects itself in these bright reflections, we suddenly experience a phenomenon which inverts a familiar optical one. When we turn away blinded after a strenuous attempt to look directly at the sun, we have dark, coloured patches before our eyes, as if their purpose were to heal them; conversely, those appearances of the Sophoclean hero in images of light, in other words, the Apolline quality of the mask, are the necessary result of gazing into the inner, terrible depths of nature – radiant patches, as it were, to heal a gaze seared by gruesome night. Only in this sense may we believe that we have grasped the serious and significant concept of 'Greek serenity' (*Heiterkeit*) correctly; admittedly, wherever one looks at present one

[67] Goethe, *Faust* I, 505ff.   [68] Plato, *Republic* 514a *et seq.*

comes across a misunderstood notion of this as 'cheerfulness', something identified with a condition of unendangered ease and comfort.

The most suffering figure of the Greek stage, the unfortunate *Oedipus*, was understood by Sophocles as the noble human being who is destined for error and misery despite his wisdom, but who in the end, through his enormous suffering, exerts on the world around him a magical, beneficent force which remains effective even after his death. The noble human being does not sin, so this profound poet wants to tell us; every law, all natural order, indeed the moral world, may be destroyed by his actions, yet by these very actions a higher, magical circle of effects is drawn which found a new world on the ruins of the old one that has been overthrown. This is what the poet, inasmuch as he is also a religious thinker, wishes to tell us; as a poet he first shows us a wonderfully tied trial-knot which the judge slowly undoes, strand by strand, to bring great harm upon himself; the genuinely Hellenic delight in this dialectical solution is so great that an air of sovereign serenity pervades the whole work, blunting all the sharp, horrifying preconditions of that trial. We encounter this same serenity in *Oedipus at Colonus*, but here it is elevated into infinite transfiguration; in this play the old man, stricken with an excess of suffering, and exposed, purely as a *suffering being*, to all that affects him, is contrasted with the unearthly serenity which comes down from the sphere of the gods as a sign to us that in his purely passive behaviour the hero achieves the highest form of activity, which has consequences reaching far beyond his own life, whereas all his conscious words and actions in his life hitherto have merely led to his passivity. Thus the trial-knot of the story of Oedipus, which strikes the mortal eye as inextricably tangled, is slowly unravelled – and we are overcome by the most profound human delight at this matching piece of divine dialectic. If our explanation has done justice to the poet, the question remains whether the content of the myth has been exhausted thereby; at this point it becomes plain that the poet's whole interpretation of the story is nothing other than one of those images of light held out to us by healing nature after we have gazed into the abyss. Oedipus, murderer of his father, husband of his mother, Oedipus the solver of the Sphinx's riddle! What does this trinity of fateful deeds tell us? There is an ancient popular belief, particularly in Persia, that a wise magician can only be born out of incest; the riddle-solving Oedipus who woos his mother immediately leads us to interpret this as meaning that some enormous offence against nature (such as incest in this case) must first have occurred to supply the cause whenever prophetic and magical energies break the spell of present and future, the rigid law of individuation, and indeed the actual magic of nature. How else could nature be forced to reveal its secrets, other than by victorious resistance to her, i.e. by some unnatural event? I see this insight expressed in that terrible trinity of Oedipus' fates: the same man who solves the riddle of nature – that of the double-natured sphinx – must also destroy the most sacred orders of nature by murdering his father and becoming his mother's husband. Wisdom, the myth seems to whisper to us, and Dionysiac wisdom in particular, is an unnatural abomination: whoever plunges nature into the abyss of destruction by what he knows must in turn experience the dissolution of nature in his own person. 'The sharp point of wisdom turns against the wise man; wisdom is an offence against nature': such are the terrible words the myth calls out to us. But, like a shaft of sunlight, the Hellenic poet touches the sublime and terrible Memnon's Column of myth[69] so that it suddenly begins to sound – in Sophoclean melodies!

I shall now contrast the glory of passivity with the glory of activity which shines around the *Prometheus* of Aeschylus. What the thinker Aeschylus had to tell us here, but what his symbolic poetic image only hints at, has been revealed to us by the youthful Goethe in the reckless words of his Prometheus:

> Here I sit, forming men
> In my own image,
> A race to be like me,
> To suffer and to weep,
> To know delight and joy
> And heed you not,
> Like me![70]

Raising himself to Titanic heights, man fights for and achieves his own culture, and he compels the gods to ally themselves with him because, in his very own wisdom, he holds existence and its limits in his hands.[71] But the most wonderful thing in that poem about Prometheus (which, in terms of its basic thought, is the true hymn of impiety) is its profound, Aeschylean tendency to *justice*: the limitless suffering of the bold

---

[69] The remnants of a monumental statue in Egypt were said to produce a musical tone when illuminated by the rays of the rising sun. *Cf* Pausanias, I.42.3; Tacitus, *Annals* 2.61.

[70] Goethe, *Prometheus*, lines 51ff.

[71] The German is ambiguous here. The last part of this sentence could also mean: 'he holds the existence of the gods and its – or their – limits in his hands'.

'individual' on the one hand, and the extreme plight of the gods, indeed a premonition of the twilight of the gods, on the other; the power of both these worlds of suffering to enforce reconciliation, metaphysical oneness – all this recalls in the strongest possible way the centre and principal tenet of the Aeschylean view of the world, which sees *moira*, as eternal justice, throned above gods and men. If the boldness of Aeschylus in placing the world of the Olympians on his scales of justice seems astonishing, we must remember that the deep-thinking Greek had an unshakably firm foundation for metaphysical thought in his Mysteries, so that all attacks of scepticism could be discharged on the Olympians. The Greek artist in particular had an obscure feeling that he and these gods were mutually dependent, a feeling symbolized precisely in Aeschylus' Prometheus. The Titanic artist found within himself the defiant belief that he could create human beings and destroy the Olympian gods at least, and that his higher wisdom enabled him to do so, for which, admittedly, he was forced to do penance by suffering eternally. The magnificent 'ability' (*Können*) of the great genius, for which even eternal suffering is too small a price to pay, the bitter pride of the *artist*: this is the content and the soul of Aeschylus' play, whereas Sophocles, in his *Oedipus*, begins the prelude to the victory-hymn of the *saint*. But even Aeschylus's interpretation of the myth does not plumb its astonishing, terrible depths; rather, the artist's delight in Becoming, the serenity of artistic creation in defiance of all catastrophes, is merely a bright image of clouds and sky reflected in a dark sea of sadness. Originally, the legend of Prometheus belonged to the entire community of Aryan peoples and documented their talent for the profound and the tragic; indeed, it is not unlikely that this myth is as significant for the Aryan character as the myth of the Fall is for the Semitic character, and that the relationship between the two myths is like that between brother and sister. The myth of Prometheus presupposes the unbounded value which naive humanity placed on *fire* as the true palladium[72] of every rising culture; but it struck those contemplative original men as a crime, a theft perpetrated on divine nature, to believe that man commanded fire freely, rather than receiving it as a gift from heaven, as a bolt of lightning which could start a blaze, or as the warming fire of the sun. Thus the very first philosophical problem presents a painful, irresolvable conflict between god and man, and pushes it like a mighty block of rock up against the threshold of every culture. Humanity achieves the best and highest of which it is capable by

---

[72] Here simply: 'prized possession'.

committing an offence and must in turn accept the consequences of this, namely the whole flood of suffering and tribulations which the offended heavenly powers *must* in turn visit upon the human race as it strives nobly towards higher things: a bitter thought, but one which, thanks to the *dignity* it accords to the offence, contrasts strangely with the Semitic myth of the Fall, where the origin of evil was seen to lie in curiosity, mendacious pretence, openness to seduction, lasciviousness, in short: in a whole series of predominantly feminine attributes. What distinguishes the Aryan conception is the sublime view that *active sin* is the true Promethean virtue; thereby we have also found the ethical foundation of pessimistic tragedy, its *justification* of the evil in human life, both in the sense of human guilt and in the sense of the suffering brought about by it. The curse in the nature of things, which the reflective Aryan is not inclined simply to explain away, the contradiction at the heart of the world, presents itself to him as a mixture of different worlds, e.g. a divine and a human one, each of which, taken individually, is in the right, but which, as one world existing alongside another, must suffer for the fact of its individuation. The heroic urge of the individual to reach out towards the general, the attempt to cross the fixed boundaries of individuation, and the desire to become the *one* world-being itself, all this leads him to suffer in his own person the primal contradiction hidden within the things of this world, i.e. he commits a great wrong and suffers. Thus great wrongdoing is understood as masculine by the Aryans, but as feminine by the Semites,[73] just as the original wrong was committed by a man and the original sin by a woman. These, incidentally, are the words of the warlocks' chorus:

> So what, if women on the whole
> Take many steps to reach the goal?
> Let them run as fast as they dare,
> With one good jump a man gets there.[74]

Anyone who understands the innermost kernel of the legend of Prometheus – namely that wrongdoing is of necessity imposed on the titanically striving individual – is bound also to sense the un-Apolline quality of this pessimistic view of things, for it is the will of Apollo to bring rest and calm to individual beings precisely by drawing boundaries between them, and by reminding them constantly, with his demands for self-knowledge and

---

[73] The noun translated as 'wrongdoing' (*der Frevel*) has masculine gender in German; 'sin' (*die Sünde*) has feminine.
[74] Goethe, *Faust*, I, 3982ff.

measure, that these are the most sacred laws in the world. But lest this Apolline tendency should cause form to freeze into Egyptian stiffness and coldness, lest the attempt to prescribe the course and extent of each individual wave should cause the movement of the whole lake to die away, the flood-tide of the Dionysiac would destroy periodically all the small circles in which the one-sidedly Apolline will attempted to confine Hellenic life. That sudden swell of the Dionysiac tide then lifts the separate little waves of individuals on to its back, just as the Titan Atlas, brother of Prometheus, lifted up the earth. This Titanic urge to become, as it were, the Atlas of all single beings, and to carry them on a broad back higher and higher, further and further, is the common feature shared by the Promethean and the Dionysiac. In this respect the Prometheus of Aeschylus is a Dionysiac mask, whereas the aforementioned deep strain of justice in Aeschylus reveals to those with eyes to see his paternal descent from Apollo, the god of individuation and of the boundaries of justice. The double essence of Aeschylus' Prometheus, his simultaneously Apolline and Dionysiac nature, could therefore be expressed like this: 'All that exists is just and unjust and is equally justified in both respects.'

That is your world. That you call a world.[75]

10

It is a matter of indisputable historical record that the only subject-matter of Greek tragedy, in its earliest form, was the sufferings of Dionysos, and that for a long time the only hero present on the stage was, accordingly, Dionysos. But one may also say with equal certainty that, right down to Euripides, Dionysos never ceased to be the tragic hero, and that all the famous figures of the Greek stage, Prometheus, Oedipus etc., are merely masks of that original hero, Dionysos. The fact that there is a deity behind all these masks is one of the essential reasons for the 'ideal' quality of those famous figures which has prompted so much astonishment. Someone or other (I do not know who) once remarked that all individuals, as individuals, are comic, and therefore un-tragic; from which one could conclude that the Greeks were quite *incapable* of tolerating any individuals on the tragic stage. And indeed this does appear to have been their feeling, just as the reason for the Platonic distinction between, and deprecation of, the 'idea' as opposed to the 'idol', or copied image, lay deep within the Hellenic

[75] Goethe, *Faust*, I, 409.

character. Using Plato's terminology, one would have to say something like this about the tragic figures of the Hellenic stage: the one, truly real Dionysos manifests himself in a multiplicity of figures, in the mask of a fighting hero and, as it were, entangled in the net of the individual will. In the way that he now speaks and acts, the god who appears resembles an erring, striving, suffering individual; and the fact that he *appears* at all with such epic definiteness and clarity, is the effect of Apollo, the interpreter of dreams, who interprets to the chorus its Dionysiac condition by means of this symbolic appearance. In truth, however, this hero is the suffering Dionysos of the Mysteries, the god who experiences the sufferings of individuation in his own person, of whom wonderful myths recount that he was torn to pieces by the Titans when he was a boy and is now venerated in this condition as Zagreus;[76] at the same time, it is indicated that his being torn into pieces, the genuinely Dionysiac *suffering*, is like a transformation into air, water, earth, and fire, so that we are to regard the state of individuation as the source and primal cause of all suffering, as something inherently to be rejected. From the smile of that Dionysos the Olympian gods were born, from his tears human beings. In this existence as a dismembered god, Dionysos has a double nature;[77] he is both cruel, savage demon and mild, gentle ruler. But what the epopts[78] hoped for was the rebirth of Dionysos, which we must now understand, by premonition, as the end of individuation; the epopts' roaring song of jubilation rang out to greet this third Dionysos. Only in the hope of this is there a gleam of joy on the countenance of a world torn apart and shattered into individuals; myth symbolizes this in the image of Demeter, sunk in eternal mourning, who knows no *happiness* until she is told that she can give birth to Dionysos *again*. In the views described here we already have all the constituent elements of a profound and pessimistic way of looking at the world and thus, at the same time, of *the doctrine of the Mysteries taught by tragedy*: the fundamental recognition that everything which exists is a unity; the view that individuation is the primal source of all evil; and art as the joyous hope

---

[76] A myth to the effect that Dionysos, under the name 'Zagreus', is torn apart and then reassembled occurs in some late Hellenistic sources. Whether this is a survival of an older (perhaps secret) doctrine about Dionysos, as Nietzsche assumes, or a late innovative embellishment of earlier traditions is, given the state of our knowledge, undecidable. Walter Burkert, one of the foremost contemporary scholars of ancient Greek religion, states that one cannot trace this myth back before the third century BC, but is generally sympathetic to 'indirect evidence' that it is older (Walter Burkert, *Greek Religion: Archaic and Classical*, trans. John Raffen (Oxford, Blackwell, 1985)).

[77] Euripides, *Bacchae* 859ff; Plutarch, *Antonius* 24.

[78] Devoted followers who have 'seen' their god.

that the spell of individuation can be broken, a premonition of unity restored.

We indicated earlier that the Homeric epic is the poetry of Olympian culture, in which it sang its own song of victory over the terrors of the struggle with the Titans. Now, under the overwhelming influence of tragic poetry, the Homeric myths are re-born to new life, and in this metempsychosis[79] they show that in the meantime Olympian culture, too, has been defeated by a yet deeper way of looking at the world. The defiant Titan Prometheus proclaimed to his Olympian torturer[80] that one day the greatest danger will threaten his rule if he does not make a timely alliance with Prometheus. In Aeschylus we see the terrified Zeus, fearful of his end, allying himself with the Titan. Thus the earlier age of the Titans is subsequently fetched out of Tartarus and brought back into the light. The philosophy of wild and naked nature gazes with the undisguised look of truth at the myths of the Homeric world as they go dancing past: they grow pale, they tremble before the lightning-like eye of this goddess – until the mighty fist of the Dionysiac artist forces them into the service of the new deity. Dionysiac truth takes over the entire territory of myth to symbolize *its own* insights, and it expresses these partly through the public cult of tragedy, and partly in secretly conducted dramatic mystery-festivals, but always under the old cloak of myth. What power was this, that could free Prometheus from his vultures and transform myth into a vehicle of Dionysiac wisdom? It was the Herculean strength of music which, having attained its supreme manifestation in tragedy, is able to interpret myth in a new and most profoundly significant way; we have already characterized this as the mightiest deed of which music was capable. For it is the fate of every myth to creep gradually into the narrow confines of an allegedly historical reality and to be treated by some later time as a unique fact with historical claims; and the Greeks themselves were already well down the road towards transforming their whole mythical, youthful dream, ingeniously and arbitrarily, into a historical-pragmatic *history of youth*. For this is usually how religions die. It happens when the mythical presuppositions of a religion become systematized as a finished sum of historical events under the severe, intellectual gaze of orthodox dogmatism, and people begin to defend anxiously the credibility of the myths while resisting every natural tendency within them to go on living and to throw out new shoots – in other words, when the feeling for myth dies and is replaced

---

[79] The transmigration of souls after death.   [80] Aeschylus, *Prometheus* 755ff.

by the claim of religion to have historical foundations. The re-born genius of Dionysiac music now took hold of this dying myth and under its hand it blossomed anew, in colours such as it had never shown before and with a perfume that awakened a longing premonition of a metaphysical world. After this last, brilliant show it collapses, its leaves wilt, and soon the mocking Lucians[81] of the ancient world chase after the discoloured, ravaged flowers scattered by all the winds that blow. In tragedy myth attains to its most profound content and most expressive form; it raises itself up once more, like a wounded hero, and all its excess of strength, together with the wise calm of the dying, burns in its eyes with a last, mighty gleam.

What did you want, wicked Euripides, when you sought to force this dying figure to do slave's work for you once more? He died at your violent hands; and now you needed a copy, a masked myth who, like Hercules' monkey,[82] could only use the old trappings to deck himself out prettily. And as myth died on you, the genius of music, too, died on you; however much you might plunder all the gardens of music with greedy hands, all you could manage was copied, masked music. And because you deserted Dionysos, Apollo, too, has deserted you; rouse all the passions from where they lie and cast a spell around them, sharpen and polish a sophistical dialectic for the speeches of your heroes – yet your heroes, too, have only copied, masked passions and they speak only copied, masked speeches.

11

Greek tragedy perished differently from all the other, older sister-arts: it died by suicide, as the result of an irresolvable conflict, which is to say tragically, while all the others died the most beautiful and peaceful deaths, fading away at a great age. If it accords with a happy state of nature to depart this life gently, leaving behind beautiful descendants, the end of those older branches of art exhibits just such a happy state of nature: they slip away slowly, and before their dying gaze there already stands their more beautiful offspring, raising his head impatiently and gesturing bravely. When Greek tragedy died, by contrast, there arose a vast emptiness which was felt deeply everywhere; just as Greek sailors from the time of Tiberius once heard, on a lonely island, the devastating cry, 'the great God Pan is

---

81 Ancient satirical writer (2nd century BC).
82 A monkey may clothe himself in the hero Hercules' characteristic garb, a lion-skin, but he still cannot lift Hercules' weapon, a heavy club.

dead'[83] so a call now rang like the painful sound of mourning throughout the Hellenic world: 'Tragedy is dead! And with it we have lost poetry itself! Away, away with you, withered, wasted epigones![84] Away to Hades, so that you may for once eat your fill of the crumbs left by those who once were masters!'

But when a new branch of art did blossom after all, one which revered tragedy as its predecessor and mistress, it was horribly plain that it did indeed bear the features of its mother, but only those which she had shown during her long death-struggle. It was *Euripides* who fought this death-struggle of tragedy; the later branch of art is known as the *New Attic Comedy*, in which tragedy lived on in degenerate form, as a monument to its own exceedingly laborious and violent demise.

Given this connection, one can understand the passionate affection which the poets of the New Comedy felt for Euripides; there is therefore nothing surprising about Philemon's desire to hang himself on the spot, simply in order to be able to visit Euripides in the Underworld[85] – provided he could be assured that the departed was still in his right mind. If one wishes to characterize very briefly, and without any claim to completeness, what Euripides had in common with Menander and Philemon, and what it was about him that struck them as being so exciting and exemplary, one simply needs to say that Euripides brought the *spectator* on to the stage. Anyone who has recognized from what stuff the Promethean tragedians before Euripides shaped their heroes, and how far they were from wanting to put on stage the faithful mask of reality, will also be aware that Euripides' aim was entirely different. Thanks to him people from everyday life pushed their way out of the audience and on to the stage; the mirror which once revealed only great and bold features now became painfully true to life, reproducing conscientiously even the lines which nature had drawn badly. In the hands of the new poets Odysseus, the typical Hellene of older art, now sank to the level of the Graeculus[86] figure who, as a good-natured and cunning domestic slave, is at the centre of dramatic interest from now on. What Euripides claims as his achievement in Aristophanes' *Frogs*, namely that his home-made recipes had freed dramatic art from its

---

[83] Plutarch, *de defac. orac.* 17.
[84] An epigone (i.e. one 'born later') is a weak imitator of the great spirits of the past.
[85] Important representative of New Comedy; Nietzsche gives a tendentious reading of some verses ascribed to him in ancient lives of Euripides.
[86] Literally 'little Greek' i.e. shifty character; stock figure of contempt in Roman literature: *cf.* Juvenal, 3.78.

pompous portliness, can be sensed above all in his tragic heroes.[87] Essentially, the spectator now heard and saw his double on the Euripidean stage, and was delighted that the latter knew how to speak so well. This delight was not the end of it; the people themselves took lessons in oratory from Euripides, something of which he boasts in his contest with Aeschylus, where he claims that, thanks to him, the people have learned to observe, to negotiate, and to draw conclusions artfully and with the most cunning sophistication. By radically changing public speech like this, it was he who made the New Comedy at all possible. For from now on it was no longer a secret how, and in which turns of phrase, everyday life could be represented on stage. Bourgeois mediocrity, on which Euripides built all his political hopes, now had its chance to speak, whereas previously the character of language had been determined by the demi-god in tragedy and by the drunken satyr or half-man in comedy. Thus Aristophanes' Euripides praises himself for the way he has represented general, familiar, everyday life and activity, things which everyone is capable of judging. If the broad mass now philosophizes, conducts trials, and administers land and property with unheard-of cleverness, then this was his achievement, the successful result of the wisdom he had injected into the people.

The New Comedy, for which Euripides, in a sense, had become the chorus-master, could now address itself to an enlightened and well-prepared mass, except that on this occasion it was the chorus of spectators who had to be trained. As soon as they were practised in singing in the Euripidean mode, a type of play resembling a game of chess came into existence, the New Comedy, where slyness and cunning are always triumphant. But Euripides, the chorus-master, was praised endlessly, indeed people would have killed themselves to learn more from him, if they had not known that the tragic poets were just as dead as tragedy. Along with tragedy, however, the Hellene had given up his belief in his immortality, not only his belief in an ideal past, but also his belief in an ideal future. The words of the famous epitaph, 'frivolous and capricious in old age',[88] also apply to the Hellenic world in its dotage. Its supreme deities are the present moment, wit, frivolity, caprice; the fifth estate, that of the slaves, now comes to power, at least as far as principles and convictions are concerned. If one can still speak of 'Greek serenity', then only as the cheerfulness of slaves who know no graver responsibility, no higher ambition, nothing in the past or future of higher value than the present. This

[87] Aristophanes, *Frogs* 937ff.   [88] Goethe, *Epigrammatic Epitaph*, line 7.

appearance of 'Greek cheerfulness' was what so outraged profound and fierce natures in the first four centuries of Christianity. It seemed to them that this womanish flight from all that was grave and frightening, this cowardly contentment with comfortable pleasure, was not simply despicable, but was the true anti-Christian attitude of mind. Their influence ensured that this pink glow of cheerfulness continued to colour the prevailing view of the ancient Greek world, with almost unconquerable stubbornness, for centuries, as if there had never been a sixth century, with its birth of tragedy, its Mysteries, its Pythagoras and Heraclitus, as if indeed the works of art of the great period simply did not exist. Yet they are all, taken severally, quite inexplicable as products of this kind of senile and slavish enjoyment of life and cheerfulness, and they all point to a completely different way of looking at the world as the ground of their being.

The assertion that Euripides brought the spectator on to the stage and thus made him capable of judging drama for the first time might make it seem as if the older tragic art never got beyond a false relationship to the spectator, and one might be tempted to praise, as an advance beyond Sophocles, the radicalism of Euripides' attempt to match the work of art to the public. Yet 'public' is merely a word which in no way denotes a uniform and constant entity. Why should the artist be obliged to accommodate himself to a force which is strong only by virtue of its numbers? And if his talent and intentions make him feel superior to each individual spectator, why should he feel more respect for the joint expression of all these inferior capabilities than for the most talented individual spectator?[89] In truth, no Greek artist ever treated his public more audaciously and complacently than Euripides did throughout his whole long life. Euripides was the man who, even as the masses were falling at his feet, openly and with sublime defiance insulted his own tendency, that very tendency with which he had gained victory over the masses. If this genius had even the slightest respect for the pandemonium of the public, he would have collapsed under the hammer-blows of his failures long before he had reached the middle of his career. Clearly, then, our comment that Euripides brought the spectator on to the stage in order to make him capable of judgment was merely provisional, and we now need to search more deeply to understand his tendency. Moreover, everyone knows that Aeschylus and Sophocles enjoyed the unqualified approval of the public throughout their lives, and indeed well beyond, so that there can be no question of a wrong

[89] *Cf.* Plato, *Symposium* 194a7ff.

relationship between the work of art and the public as far as Euripides' predecessors are concerned. What, then, can have driven this richly talented artist, with his constant compulsion to create, so violently off a road above which shone the sun of the greatest poets' names and the unclouded heaven of popular favour? What strange consideration for the spectator led him towards the spectator? How could too-great respect for his public cause him to treat his public – disrespectfully?

The solution to the above puzzle is this: as a poet, Euripides may very well have felt himself superior to the mass, but not to two of his spectators. He brought the mass on to the stage, but he revered these two spectators as the only masters and judges capable of judging all his art. Following their admonitions and instructions, he transferred into the souls of his heroes on stage the whole world of feelings, passions, and experiences which hitherto had assembled as an invisible chorus on the spectators' benches for every festive performance; he yielded to their demands when he searched for new words and a new tone for these new characters; and he heard in their voices alone the only valid verdicts on his creations, but also the encouraging promise of victory whenever he found himself condemned, yet again, by the justice of the public.

One of these two spectators is Euripides himself, Euripides *the thinker*, not the poet. One might say of him, as of Lessing,[90] that if the extraordinary wealth of his critical talent did not actually generate a productive artistic side-shoot, it did at least fructify his productivity constantly. Euripides had sat in the theatre with this talent, with all the clarity and agility of his critical thinking, and he had strained every sinew to recognize feature after feature, line after line, in the masterpieces of his predecessors, as if studying paintings darkened by the passage of time. And here he encountered something which can come as no surprise to anyone who has been initiated into the deeper secrets of Aschylean tragedy: he perceived something incommensurable in every feature and every line, a certain deceiving definiteness, and at the same time a puzzling depth, indeed infinity, in the background. Even the clearest figure still trailed a comet's tail after it which seemed to point into the unknown, into that which cannot be illuminated. The same twilight covered the structure of the drama, particularly the

[90] Gotthold Ephraim Lessing (1729–81), one of the major figures of the German Enlightenment, was a literary critic, aesthetician, and theological controversialist of the first rank who also wrote four major plays. Despite the historical importance and the aesthetic merits of these plays, which are not inconsiderable, Lessing was himself aware that his primary gifts were those of the critic, not the creative artist.

significance of the chorus. And how dubious the solution of the ethical problems seemed to him! How questionable the treatment of the myths! How uneven the distribution of happiness and unhappiness! Even in the language of the older tragedy there was much that he found objectionable, or at least puzzling; in particular he found too much pomp for simple circumstances, too many tropes and enormities for the plainness of the characters. So he sat there in the theatre, brooding restlessly, and confessed to himself, as a spectator, that he did not understand his great predecessors. But if he held reason to be the real root of all enjoyment and creation, he was bound to ask and look around to see whether there was no one else who thought as he did and admitted to themselves, as he did, that this incommensurability existed. But most people, and among them the best of individuals, had only a mistrustful smile for him; yet no one could explain to him why, despite his scruples and objections, the great masters were, after all, in the right. It was in this agonized state that he found *the other spectator* who did not understand tragedy and therefore had no respect for it. In league with this man he could dare, from his isolated position, to embark on an enormous campaign against the works of art of Aeschylus and Sophocles – not in the form of polemics, but as a dramatic poet who opposes *his* idea of tragedy to the traditional one.

12

Before we name this other spectator, let us pause here for a moment to recall the impression, described above, of something dichotomous and incommensurable in the essence of Aeschylean tragedy itself. Let us think of our own puzzlement about the *chorus* and the *tragic hero* of that tragedy, both of which we were unable to reconcile either with our habits or with the historical tradition – until, that is, we rediscovered this very same doubleness in the origin and essence of Greek tragedy, as the expression of two interwoven artistic drives, *the Apolline and the Dionysiac*.

What we now see revealed, indeed brilliantly illuminated, is the tendency of Euripides, which was to expel the original and all-powerful Dionysiac element from tragedy and to re-build tragedy in a new and pure form on the foundations of a non-Dionysiac art, morality, and view of the world.

In the evening of his life Euripides confronted his contemporaries very forcefully with a question, cast in the form of a myth, about the value and significance of this tendency. Can the Dionysiac be permitted to exist at all? Should it not be eradicated forcibly from Hellenic soil? It certainly should, the poet tells us, if this were at all possible, but the god Dionysos is too powerful; even the most rational and thoughtful of his opponents, such as Pentheus in the *Bacchae*,[91] becomes enchanted by him unexpectedly and later runs into his fate because of this enchantment. The judgment of the two old men, Cadmus and Tiresias, seems also to be the judgment of the aged poet, namely that the thoughtfulness of even the cleverest individuals cannot overthrow the old traditions of the people, the eternally self-procreating veneration of Dionysos; indeed, in the face of such wonderful forces, it is proper to evince at least some diplomatically cautious sympathy, although it is still possible that the god will take offence at such lukewarm participation, and will finally transform the diplomat – as happens to Cadmus in this case – into a dragon. We are told this by a poet who has resisted Dionysos with heroic strength throughout a long life – only to end his career with a glorification of his opponent and a suicide, like someone suffering from vertigo who finally throws himself off a tower simply in order to escape the terrible dizziness he can tolerate no longer. That tragedy is a protest against the feasibility of his own tendency; but alas, it had already been put into practice! The miracle had occurred; by the time the poet recanted, his tendency was already victorious. Dionysos had already been chased from the tragic stage, and, what is more, by a daemonic power speaking out of the mouth of Euripides. In a certain sense Euripides, too, was merely a mask; the deity who spoke out of him was not Dionysos, nor Apollo, but an altogether newborn daemon called *Socrates*. This is the new opposition: the Dionysiac versus the Socratic, and the work of art that once was Greek tragedy was destroyed by it. Although Euripides may try to comfort us with his recantation, he fails; the most glorious temple lies in ruins; what use to us is the lament of the destroyer or his confession that it was the most beautiful of temples? And even the fact that Euripides was punished by being transformed into a dragon by every judge of art throughout the ages – who could be satisfied with such a miserable compensation?

Let us now take a closer look at this *Socratic* tendency with which Euripides opposed and defeated Aeschylean tragedy.

The question we must ask ourselves is this: if we imagine it as having

---

[91] The enchantment of Pentheus: *Bacchae* 915ff; the judgment of Cadmus and Tiresias: *Bacchae* 201ff; Cadmus as dragon: *Bacchae* 1330f

been executed in the most ideal manner possible, what could possibly have been the goal of Euripides' aim of putting drama on to entirely non-Dionysiac foundations? What form of drama was left, if it was not to be born from the womb of music, in that mysterious twilight of the Dionysiac? The *dramatized epos* alone remained, an area of Apolline art in which the effect of the *tragic* is of course unattainable. What matters here is not the substance of the events depicted; indeed I would assert that it would have been impossible for Goethe, in his projected *Nausicaa*,[92] to make the suicide of that idyllic creature, which was to occupy the fifth act, tragically moving; the power of the epic–Apolline is so extraordinary that, thanks to the delight in semblance and release through semblance which it imparts, it casts a spell over even the most terrifying things before our very eyes. The poet of the dramatized epic is just as incapable as the epic rhapsode of merging completely with his images: he remains a calm, unmoved gaze which sees the images *before* it with eyes wide open. In this dramatized epic the actor remains fundamentally a rhapsode; the consecrated aura of inward dreaming lies over all his actions, so that he is never fully an actor.

Now what is the relationship between this ideal of the Apolline drama and Euripidean drama? The relation is like that between the solemn rhapsode of ancient times and the younger rhapsode who describes his own character thus in Plato's *Ion*: 'If I say something sad my eyes fill with tears; but if what I say is terrible and horrifying, the hairs on my head stand on end from dread, and my heart pounds.'[93] There is not a trace left here of that epic condition of losing oneself in semblance, of the dispassionate coolness of the true actor who, at the very height of his activity, is nothing but semblance and delight in semblance. Euripides is the actor with the pounding heart, with his hair standing on end; he draws up his plan as a Socratic thinker; he executes it as a passionate actor. Neither in the planning nor in the execution is he a pure artist. Thus Euripidean drama is simultaneously fiery and cool, equally capable of freezing and burning; it is impossible for it to achieve the Apolline effect of epic poetry, but on the other hand it has liberated itself as far as possible from the Dionysiac elements, and it now needs new means of stimulation to have any effect at all, means which are

---

[92] In the *Odyssey* (Book VI) Nausicaa, daughter of the king of the Phaeacians, is doing the washing on the beach when she discovers the naked Odysseus, who has been cast up there after a shipwreck during the night. She fantasizes about marrying him, but he eventually leaves to return to Ithaca. In 1786–7 Goethe mentions plans for a 'tragedy' on this topic and writes a few fragments of verse, but he never executed the project.

[93] Plato, *Ion* 535c5ff.

no longer part of the two artistic drives, the Apolline and the Dionysiac. These stimulants are cool, paradoxical *thoughts* – in place of Apolline visions – and fiery *affects* – in place of Dionysiac ecstasies – and, what is more, thoughts and affects most realistically imitated, not ones which have been dipped in the ether of art.

We have come to see that Euripides had no success at all in putting drama on to purely Apolline foundations, and that his non-Dionysiac tendency got lost in a naturalistic and un-artistic one. We can therefore now get closer to the nature of *aesthetic Socratism*, whose supreme law runs roughly like this: 'In order to be beautiful, everything must be reasonable' – a sentence formed in parallel to Socrates' dictum that 'Only he who knows is virtuous.'[94] With this canon in his hand Euripides measured every single element – language, characters, dramatic construction, choral music – and rectified it in accordance with this principle. What we criticize so frequently as a poetic flaw and a step backwards in Euripides' work, as compared with Sophoclean tragedy, is mostly the product of that penetrating critical process, that bold application of reason. The Euripidean *prologue* will serve to illustrate the productivity of his rationalist method. Nothing can be more contrary to our stage technique than the prologue in Euripides' drama. That a single person on stage should explain at the beginning of a play who he is, what precedes the action, what has happened so far, indeed what will happen in the course of the play – all this would be described by a modern writer for the stage as a capricious and inexcusable renunciation of the effect of suspense. Everyone knows what is going to happen, so who will want to wait to see it actually happen (since the relationship is anything but the exciting one of a prophetic dream to the ensuing reality)? Euripides thought quite differently about this. The effect of tragedy never rested on epic suspense, on teasing people and making them uncertain about what will happen now or later, but rather on those great rhetorical and lyrical scenes in which the passion and dialectic of the protagonist swelled into a broad and mighty stream. Everything was a preparation for pathos, not for action; and anything that was not a preparation for pathos was held to be objectionable. The greatest obstacle to the listener's enjoyable self-abandonment to such scenes would be some missing link, some gap in the texture of the story preceding the action; as long as the listener has to work out what this or that person signifies, what the preconditions are for this or that conflict of inclinations and intentions,

---

[94] Aristotle, *Eudemian Ethics* 1216c.

it is not yet possible for him to immerse himself completely in the suffering and activity of the main characters, or to share breathlessly in their fears and sufferings. Aeschylean–Sophoclean tragedy used the most ingenious artistic means to place all the threads needed to understand events in the spectator's hands in the opening scenes and, to some extent, by chance. This feature demonstrates the value of the kind of noble artistry which masks, as it were, things which are formally *necessary*, so as to make them appear fortuitous. Nevertheless, Euripides believed he had noticed that the spectators were peculiarly restive during those first scenes as they tried to work out the story so far, so that the poetic beauties and the pathos of the exposition were lost on them. This is why he places the prologue before the exposition and places it in the mouth of a character who can be trusted: often a deity had to guarantee the course of the tragedy to the public, as it were, and remove all doubts about the reality of the myth; in a similar way Descartes could only prove the reality of the empirical world by an appeal to the truthfulness of god and his inability to lie.[95] Euripides makes use of the same divine truthfulness again, at the end of his drama, in order to reassure the public about the future of his heroes; this is the task of the infamous *deus ex machina*. Between the epic retrospect and the prospect beyond the end of the action lies the dramatic-lyrical present, the 'drama' proper.

As a poet, Euripides is thus the echo of his conscious perceptions, and this is precisely what gives him such a remarkable place in the history of Greek art. With regard to his critical-productive work, he must often have felt as though his task was to give dramatic life to the beginning of Anaxagoras'[96] work, which opens with the words: 'In the beginning everything was together; then reason came and created order.'[97] And if Anaxagoras with his *nous*[98] appeared among the philosophers like the first 'sober' man in a company of drunks, Euripides may well have applied the same image to his relationship to the other tragic poets. As long as the *nous*, the sole orderer and ruler of the world, remained shut out from artistic creation, everything was together in a chaotic, primal soup; this is how Euripides must have judged things; this is why he, the first sober man, was bound to condemn the 'drunken' poets. What Sophocles said about

---

[95] Descartes, *Meditations* IV and VI.

[96] Pre-Socratic philosopher who spent most of his active life in Athens. He was prosecuted for impiety because he allegedly claimed that the sun was not a god, but a lump of molten stone.

[97] Aristotle, *Metaphysics* 984b15ff.

[98] An approximate translation of this word is 'reason' or 'mind'.

Aeschylus, namely that he did the right thing, although he did it unconsciously,[99] was certainly not meant in Euripides' sense, who would only have allowed that what Aeschylus created was wrong *because* he created unconsciously. The divine Plato, too, is usually being ironical when he speaks of the poet's creative ability, except when it takes the form of conscious insight, and he equates it with the gift of soothsaying and interpreting dreams; the poet, he says, is unable to compose poetry until he has lost consciousness and reason no longer dwells within him.[100] Like Plato, Euripides undertook to show the world the opposite of the 'unreasoning' poet; as I have said, his aesthetic principle, 'Everything must be conscious in order to be beautiful', is a parallel to Socrates' assertion that, 'Everything must be conscious in order to be good.' Accordingly, we may regard Euripides as the poet of aesthetic Socratism. Socrates, however, was that *second spectator* who did not understand the older tragedy and therefore did not respect it; in league with Socrates, Euripides dared to be the herald of a new kind of artistic creation. If this caused the older tragedy to perish, then aesthetic Socratism is the murderous principle; but insofar as the fight was directed against the Dionysiac nature of the older art, we may identify Socrates as the opponent of Dionysos, the new Orpheus who rises up against Dionysos and who, although fated to be torn apart by the maenads of the Athenian court of justice, nevertheless forces the great and mighty god himself to flee. As before, when he fled from Lykurgos, King of the Edonians,[101] Dionysos now sought refuge in the depths of the sea, namely in the mystical waters of a secret cult which gradually spread across the entire world.

13

It did not escape their contemporaries in the ancient world that the tendencies of Socrates and Euripides were closely related. The most eloquent expression of their good nose for things was the legend circulating in Athens that Socrates was in the habit of helping Euripides compose his poetry.[102] When it came to listing the present seducers of the people whose influence was responsible for the fact that the old, sturdy, Marathonian toughness of body and soul was falling victim increasingly to a dubious

[99] Reported by Athenaeus, 10.428f.
[100] *Cf. Apology* 22bf, *Ion* 533e–534d, *Phaedrus* 244a–245a.
[101] The story is told at *Iliad* 6.134ff.
[102] *Cf.* Diogenes Laertius, II.18.

enlightenment, and that physical and spiritual energies were atrophying progressively, the supporters of the 'good old days'[103] would mention both names in one breath. It is in this tone, half outraged, half scornful, that Aristophanic comedy usually spoke of these men, to the consternation of those moderns who would gladly have abandoned Euripides, but who could not get over their surprise that Socrates should figure in Aristophanes' plays as the first and leading *Sophist*, as the mirror and quintessence of everything the Sophists were trying to do; the only comfort they could find was in pillorying Aristophanes himself as a dissolute, mendacious Alcibiades of poetry.[104] Without defending at this point the deep instincts of Aristophanes against such attacks I shall continue to demonstrate, on the basis of what the Ancients felt, the close affinity between Socrates and Euripides. In this connection it should be mentioned explicitly that Socrates, as an opponent of the tragic art, refrained from attending the tragedy, and would only join the spectators when a new play by Euripides was being performed. Best known of all is the close association of the two names in a saying of the Delphic oracle which described Socrates as the wisest of men, but also judged that the second prize in the contest of wisdom should go to Euripides.[105]

The third name in this ranking was Sophocles, the man who could boast that, in contrast to Aeschylus, he did what was right and, what was more, he did so because he *knew* what was right. Clearly, what distinguishes these three men, taken together, as the three 'knowing ones' of their time, is the degree of clarity of this *knowledge*.

The sharpest words in favour of that new, unheard-of esteem for knowledge and insight were those spoken by Socrates when he said that he was the only man of his acquaintance who confessed to *knowing nothing*; on his critical wanderings through Athens, by contrast, when he called on the greatest politicians, orators, poets, and artists, he encountered the same illusion of knowledge everywhere.[106] He registered with astonishment the fact that all those famous men lacked even a secure and correct under-

---

103 *Cf.* Aristophanes, *Clouds* 961ff., 1353ff.
104 Aristocratic Athenian associate of Socrates notorious for his extravagant mode of life and for changing sides during the Peloponnesian War.
105 One of Socrates' students, Chaerephon, is said to have asked the oracle of Delphi whether anyone was wiser than Socrates We have reports of three slightly different answers. Nietzsche here refers to what is perhaps the least well documented of these answers: 'Sophocles is wise, Euripides is wiser, but of all men Socrates is wisest.' *Cf.* J. Fontenrose, *The Delphic Oracle* (University of California Press, 1978), p.245.
106 Plato, *Apology* 20d ff.

standing of their profession, and performed it only by instinct. 'Only by instinct': the phrase goes to the heart and centre of the Socratic tendency. With these words Socratism condemns existing art and existing ethics in equal measure; wherever it directs its probing gaze, it sees a lack of insight and the power of delusion, and it concludes from this lack that what exists is inwardly wrong and objectionable. Socrates believed that he was obliged to correct existence, starting from this single point; he, the individual, the forerunner of a completely different culture, art, and morality, steps with a look of disrespect and superiority into a world where we would count ourselves supremely happy if we could even touch the hem of its cloak in awe.

This is the enormous scruple which befalls us whenever we contemplate Socrates, and which goads us on, time after time, to understand the meaning and intention of this, the most questionable phenomenon in Antiquity. Who is this individual who may dare to negate the nature of the Greeks which, whether as Homer, Pindar, or Aeschylus, as Phidias, as Pericles, as Pythia and Dionysos, as the deepest abyss or the highest peak, is certain of our astonished worship? What daemonic force is this that may dare to spill this magic potion in the dust? What demi-god is this, to whom the chorus of the noblest spirits of mankind must call out:

> Woe! Woe!
> You have destroyed
> This lovely world
> With mighty fist;
> It falls, it shatters[107]

We are offered a key to the essence of Socrates by that wonderful phenomenon known as the 'daimonion of Socrates'.[108] In particular situations, when his enormous mind began to sway uncertainly, he was able to get a firm hold on things again thanks to a divine voice which made itself heard at such moments. Whenever it appears, this voice always *warns* him to *desist*. In this utterly abnormal nature the wisdom of instinct only manifests itself in order to *block* conscious understanding from time to time. Whereas in the case of all productive people instinct is precisely the creative-affirmative force and consciousness makes critical and warning gestures, in the case of Socrates, by contrast, instinct becomes the critic and consciousness the creator – a true monstrosity *per defectum*![109] To be more

---

[107] Goethe, *Faust*, I, 1607ff.   [108] Plato, *Euthyphro* 3b5, *Apology* 31c8, 40a.
[109] 'by virtue of lacking something'.

precise, what we observe here is a monstrous lack of any capacity for mysticism, so that Socrates could be described as the specific *non-mystic*, in whom logical nature is just as over-developed, thanks to some super-foetation,[110] as instinctive wisdom is in the mystic. On the other hand, the logical drive which appeared in Socrates was completely incapable of turning against itself; in its unfettered flow it reveals a power of nature such as we encounter, to our awed surprise, only in the very greatest instinctual forces. Anyone who, reading Plato's writings, has felt even a breath of that divine naïveté and certainty in the direction of Socrates' life will also have felt that the enormous drive-wheel of logical Socratism is in motion *behind* Socrates, as it were, and that in order to see it one must look through Socrates as if through a shadow. That he himself had an intimation of this relationship is expressed in the dignified seriousness with which he asserted his divine calling everywhere, and did so even before his judges. Fundamentally it was just as impossible to disprove this claim as it was to approve of his disintegrative influence on the instincts. Given this irre-solvable conflict, once he had been summoned before the forum of the Greek state, the only appropriate form of punishment was banishment; they could have sent him across the border as something thoroughly enig-matic, unclassifiable, as an indissoluble mystery, and posterity would have had no right to accuse the Athenians of a shameful deed. The fact that he was condemned, not just to banishment but to death, is something that Socrates himself, with complete clarity and without the natural dread of death, seems to have accomplished; he went to his death with the same calm as he had shown when, according to Plato's account, he left the sym-posium[111] as the last drinker in the grey of the dawn to begin a new day, while his sleeping companions remained behind, on the benches and on the ground, to dream of Socrates, the true eroticist. The *dying Socrates* became the new, hitherto unknown ideal of noble Greek youth; more than any of them, it was the typical Hellenic youth, Plato, who threw himself down before this image with all the passionate devotion of his enthusiastic soul.

14

Let us now imagine Socrates' one great Cyclopian eye turned on tragedy, an eye in which the lovely madness of artistic enthusiasm never glowed, let

---

[110] Excessive fertility.   [111] Plato, *Symposium* 223b to end.

us remember how that eye was debarred from ever looking with pleasure into the abysses of the Dionysiac; what was this eye actually bound to see in the 'sublime and renowned' art of tragedy, as Plato called it?[112] Something quite unreasonable, with causes which apparently lacked effects and effects which apparently lacked causes, while the whole was so varied and multifarious that it was bound to be repugnant to a reflective disposition, but also dangerous tinder for sensitive and easily aroused souls. We know that the only genre of poetry Socrates understood was the *Aesopian fable*,[113] and no doubt he did so with the same smiling condescension with which good, honest Gellert sings the praises of poetry in the fable of the Bee and the Hen:

> In me it is made very plain
> That parables are told in vain
> To those who have but little brain.[114]

But the art of tragedy did not seem to Socrates even to 'tell the truth', quite apart from the fact that it addresses itself to those who 'have but little brain',[115] in other words not to the philosopher – a double reason to stay clear of it. Like Plato, he thought it belonged to the flattering arts, which represent only what is pleasant and not what is useful, and he therefore demanded that his disciples should desist and keep themselves strictly away from such un-philosophical stimulants; so successful was he that the first thing the youthful tragedian Plato did was to burn his poetry so that he could become a pupil of Socrates. But where irrepressible predispositions fought against the Socratic maxims, the strength of these maxims, allied with the force of that enormous character, was still great enough to force poetry itself into new and hitherto unknown positions.

The above-named Plato is an example of this; although his condemnation of tragedy certainly did not lag behind that of his master in its naive cynicism, downright artistic necessity nevertheless compelled him to create a form of art which was inwardly related to the existing forms of art he had rejected. Above all, Plato's main objection to the older type of art, namely that it was the imitation of an illusory image and thus belonged to an even lower sphere than the empirical world,[116] could not be allowed to be levelled against the new work of art; we therefore see Plato attempting

---

[112] Plato, *Gorgias* 502b.   [113] *Cf.* Plato, *Phaedo* 60c1ff; also Diogenes Laertius, under 'Socrates'.
[114] An eighteenth-century didactic poet; *cf. Werke (Behrend)* I, 93.
[115] *Cf.* Plato, *Symposium* 194a7ff.   [116] Plato, *Republic* 596a5ff.

to go beyond reality and to represent the idea underlying that pseudo-reality. In this way the thinker Plato had arrived by a roundabout route at the very spot where he had always been at home as a poet – and from where Sophocles and the entire older type of art protested solemnly against the accusation levelled against them. If tragedy had absorbed all previous artistic genres, the same can be said, in an eccentric sense, of the Platonic dialogue, which was created by mixing all available styles and forms together so that it hovers somewhere midway between narrative, lyric, and drama, between prose and poetry, thus breaking the strict older law about the unity of linguistic form. The *cynical*[117] writers went even further down this road, for with their stylistic patchwork and alternations between prosaic and metrical forms they also achieved a literary image of the 'mad Socrates'[118] whom they usually represented in real life. One could say that the Platonic dialogue was the boat on which the older forms of poetry, together with all her children, sought refuge after their shipwreck; crowded together in a narrow space, and anxiously submissive to the one helmsman, Socrates, they now sailed into a new world which never tired of gazing at this fantastic spectacle. Plato really did bequeath the model of a new art-form to all posterity, the model of the *novel*, which can be defined as an infinitely intensified Aesopian fable where poetry has the same rank in relation to dialectic philosophy as, for centuries, philosophy had in relation to theology, namely that of *ancilla*.[119] This was the new position into which Plato forced poetry under pressure from the daemonic Socrates.

Here art becomes overgrown with *philosophical thought* which forces it to cling tightly to the trunk of dialectics. The *Apolline* tendency has disguised itself as logical schematism; we have already observed a corresponding tendency in Euripides, along with the translation of the *Dionysiac* into naturalistic affects. Socrates, the dialectical hero in Platonic drama, recalls the related nature of the Euripidean hero who must defend his actions with reasons and counter-reasons and thereby is often in danger of losing our tragic sympathy; for who could fail to notice the *optimistic* element in the essence of dialectics, which celebrates jubilantly

---

117 The Cynic philosopher Menippus of Gadara who lived in the first half of the third century (BC) wrote works in which prose and verse (in different metres) were mixed, thereby violating what had up to that time been considered a central stylistic principle. None of Menippus' works has survived, but they were an important model for Lucian: *see* above footnote 81.

118 Diogenes Laertius reports (VI.54) that when Plato was asked what kind of man Diogenes the Cynic was, he replied: 'A Socrates gone mad.'

119 Literally 'hand-maid' i.e. a subordinate auxiliary discipline.

at each conclusion reached, and which can only breathe where there is cool clarity and consciousness? Having once penetrated tragedy, this optimistic element was bound to spread gradually across its Dionysiac regions and drive it, of necessity, to self-destruction by taking a death-leap into domestic tragedy. One only needs to consider the consequences of these Socratic statements:[120] 'Virtue is knowledge; sin is only committed out of ignorance; the virtuous man is a happy man'; in these three basic forms of optimism lies the death of tragedy. For the virtuous hero must now be a dialectician; there must now be a necessary, visible connection between virtue and knowledge, faith and morality; the solution by transcendental justice in the plays of Aeschylus is now debased to the shallow and impertinent principle of 'poetic justice', with its usual *deus ex machina*.

How does the *chorus*, and generally the whole musical-Dionysiac foundation of tragedy, now appear in relation to this new Socratic-optimistic world on stage? It now appears to be something fortuitous, a reminiscence of the origins of tragedy, and one which could probably be dispensed with – whereas we have recognized that the only way the chorus can be understood at all is as the *cause* of tragedy and the tragic. There is already some embarrassment about the chorus evident in Sophocles – an important sign that the Dionysiac ground of tragedy is already beginning to give way. He no longer dares to entrust a main share of the effect to the chorus; instead, he restricts its territory so much that it almost seems coordinated with the actors, as if it had been lifted on to the stage from the orchestra; the effect of this is of course to destroy its essence entirely, even if Aristotle did give his approval to this conception of the chorus.[121] That change in the position of the chorus, which Sophocles recommended at least in practice and, according to tradition, even in writing, is the first step towards the *annihilation* of the chorus which occurs in a frighteningly rapid sequence of phases in Euripides, Agathon and the New Comedy. The optimistic dialectic drives *music* out of tragedy under the lash of its syllogisms; i.e. it destroys the essence of tragedy which can only be interpreted as a manifestation and transformation into images of Dionysiac states, as the visible symbolization of music, as the dream-world of Dionysiac intoxication.

Thus, if we have to assume that an anti-Dionysiac tendency was already at work even before Socrates and was only expressed by him with unheard-of grandeur, we must also ask ourselves what a phenomenon like Socrates points to, for the Platonic dialogues do not permit us to view him solely as

[120] *Cf.* Plato, *Protagoras* 352c etc.   [121] *Poetics* 1456a25.

a disintegrative, negative force. Although it is certain that the first effect which the Socratic drive aimed to achieve was the disintegration of Dionysiac tragedy, a profound experience in Socrates' own life compels us to ask whether the relationship between Socrates and art is *necessarily* and exclusively antithetical, and whether the birth of an 'artistic Socrates' is something inherently contradictory.

Just occasionally that despotic logician felt there was something missing in his relation to art, an emptiness, a half-reproach, a duty which he had perhaps failed to perform. As he tells his friends in prison, the same figure kept appearing to him in dream time after time, and it always said the same thing: 'Socrates, make music!'[122] Until his very last days he put his mind at rest with the thought that his philosophizing was the highest art of the Muses, and that he could not really believe a deity would remind him of 'common, popular music'. Finally, in prison, he agrees to play the music for which he has so little respect, so as to unburden his conscience completely. In this state of mind he composes a proemium[123] to Apollo and versifies some Aesopian fables. Whatever urged these exercises on him was something similar to his warning voice; it was his Apolline insight that, like some barbarian king, he did not understand the noble image of some god and, in his ignorance, was in danger of committing a sin against a deity. The words spoken by the figure who appeared to Socrates in dream are the only hint of any scruples in him about the limits of logical nature; perhaps, he must have told himself, things which I do not understand are not automatically unreasonable. Perhaps there is a kingdom of wisdom from which the logician is banished? Perhaps art may even be a necessary correlative and supplement of science?

15

As these last, prophetic, questions indicate, it now has to be said that Socrates' influence has spread out across all posterity to this very day, and indeed into the whole future, like a shadow growing ever longer in the evening sun, obliging men, time after time, to create *art* anew – art, understood in its widest, deepest and already metaphysical sense – and that his influence, being unending itself, also guarantees the infinity of art.

Before this could be recognized, before the innermost dependence of all art on the Greeks – the Greeks from Homer down to Socrates – was

---

[122] Plato, *Phaedo* 60e5ff.   [123] In this case this means a short hymn to a god.

demonstrated convincingly, we had to experience these Greeks in the same way as the Athenians experienced Socrates. Almost every age and stage of culture has attempted at some point to free itself, with deep feelings of anger, from the Greeks, because, in comparison with them, all one's own achievements, although apparently completely original and quite sincerely admired, suddenly seemed to lose colour and life and to shrivel into an unsuccessful copy or even a caricature. Thus heartfelt rage breaks out time after time against that presumptuous little people who dared to declare, for all time, that everything which did not have its home and origin there was 'barbaric': who are these people, one asks, who have only ephemeral historical splendour to show for themselves, ridiculously narrow institutions, questionable moral toughness, who are even marked out by ugly vices, but who nevertheless lay claim to the kind of dignity and special position amongst the nations which are owed to the genius amongst the mass? Unfortunately, no one was lucky enough to find the cup of hemlock with which they could simply do away with a creature like this, for all the inner poison generated by envy, calumny, and fury did not suffice to destroy such self-sufficient magnificence. Thus people feel shame and fear in the face of the Greeks – unless there be one individual who reveres truth above all else and is therefore able to admit even this truth to himself: that the Greeks are chariot-drivers who hold the reins of our culture, and every other culture, in their hands, yet the chariot and the horses are almost always made of too-puny stuff and unequal to the glory of their drivers, who then regard it as a joke to drive such a vehicle into the abyss – and then jump across it themselves with the leap of Achilles.

To show that even Socrates deserves the dignity of this kind of leading position, one only needs to recognize in him the archetype of a form of existence unknown before him, the archetype of *theoretical man*; our next task is to understand the significance and goal of this human type. Like the artist, theoretical man, too, finds infinite contentment in the world as it exists, and, like the artist, he is protected by his contentment against the practical ethic of pessimism and its Lynkeus-eyes[124] which only gleam in the dark. Whenever truth is unveiled, the ecstatic eyes of the artist remain fixed on what still remains veiled, even after the unveiling; similarly, theoretical man enjoys and satisfies himself with the discarded veil, and his desire finds its highest goal in a process of unveiling which he achieves by

[124] Lynkeus was a somewhat obscure ancient mythological figure who became proverbial for his sharp-sightedness. He appears in Goethe's *Faust* II.

his own efforts and which is always successful. Science would not exist if it were concerned only with that *one*, naked goddess and with nothing else besides. For if this were the case its disciples would be bound to feel that they were like those people who want to dig a hole right through the earth, each of whom recognizes that, even if he exerts all his might his whole life through, he will only be able to dig down through a very tiny piece of the vast depths, and that this piece is being filled in again, before his very eyes, by the work of his neighbour, so that a third person would apparently be well advised to go off and choose a new place for his own attempts at boring a hole. If one person now proves convincingly that the goal in the Antipodes cannot be reached, who will want to carry on labouring down in the old depths, unless in the meantime he has become content with finding precious stones or discovering the laws of nature? This is why Lessing, the most honest of theoretical men, dared to state openly that searching for the truth meant more to him than truth itself;[125] thereby the fundamental secret of science is revealed, much to the astonishment, indeed annoyance, of the scientifically minded. Admittedly, alongside this isolated recognition (which represents an excess of honesty, if not of arrogance), one also finds a profound *delusion* which first appeared in the person of Socrates, namely the imperturbable belief that thought, as it follows the thread of causality, reaches down into the deepest abysses of being, and that it is capable, not simply of understanding existence, but even of *correcting* it. This sublime metaphysical illusion is an instinct which belongs inseparably to science, and leads it to its limits time after time, at which point it must transform itself into *art; which is actually, given this mechanism, what it has been aiming at all along*.

Taking this thought to light our way, let us now look at Socrates: he then appears to us as the first man who was capable, not just of living by the instinct of science, but also, and this is much more, of dying by it. This is why the image of the *dying Socrates*, of a man liberated from fear of death by reasons and knowledge, is the heraldic shield over the portals of science, reminding everyone of its purpose, which is to make existence appear comprehensible and thus justified; and if reasons are insufficient to achieve that end, then it must ultimately be served by *myth* – which I have just defined as the necessary consequence, indeed intention, of science.

Consider for a moment how, after Socrates, the mystagogue of science, one school of philosophy follows another, like wave upon wave; how an

---

125 In *Eine Duplik* (1778): 'A Rejoinder'.

unimaginable, universal greed for knowledge, stretching across most of the cultured world, and presenting itself as the true task for anyone of higher abilities, led science on to the high seas, from which it could never again be driven completely; and how for the first time, thanks to this universality, a common network of thought was stretched over the whole globe, with prospects of encompassing even the laws of the entire solar system; when one considers all this, along with the astonishingly high pyramid of knowledge we have at present, one cannot do other than regard Socrates as the vortex and turning-point of so-called world history. For if one were to imagine that the quite incalculable sum of energy which has been expended on behalf of this tendency in the world had *not* been placed at the service of understanding, but applied instead to the practical, i.e. egotistical goals of individuals and nations, then man's instinctive lust for life would probably have been so weakened amidst general wars of extinction and unceasing migrations that, with suicide having become habitual, the individual would be bound to feel the last remnant of a sense of duty when, like some inhabitant of the Fijian islands, he throttles his parents as their son, and his friend as a friend – a practical pessimism which could generate a horrifying ethic of genocide out of pity; a pessimism, incidentally, which exists, and has existed, throughout the entire world, wherever art has not appeared in one form or other, especially as religion or science, to heal and to ward off the breath of that pestilence.

In the face of this practical pessimism, Socrates is the archetype of the theoretical optimist whose belief that the nature of things can be discovered leads him to attribute to knowledge and understanding the power of a panacea, and who understands error to be inherently evil. To penetrate to the ground of things and to separate true knowledge from illusion and error was considered by Socratic man to be the noblest, indeed the only truly human vocation, just as, from Socrates onwards, the mechanism of concepts, judgments and conclusions was prized, above all other abilities, as the highest activity and most admirable gift of nature. Even the most sublime moral deeds, the stirrings of pity, sacrifice, heroism, and that elusive placidity of the soul which the Apolline Greek called *sophrosyne*,[126] were derived by Socrates and his like-minded successors (down to the present) from the dialectic of knowledge, and were therefore declared to be teachable. Anyone who has experienced the intense pleasure of a Socratic insight, and felt it spread out in ever-widening circles as it

[126] Traditionally translated as 'temperance'.

attempted to encompass the entire world of appearances, will forever feel that there can be no sharper goad to life than the desire to complete the conquest and weave the net impenetrably close. To anyone in this state of mind, Plato's Socrates seems to be the teacher of a quite new form of 'Greek serenity' and bliss in existence, one which seeks to discharge itself in actions and mostly achieves this discharge by having a maieutic[127] and educative effect on noble youths, in the hope of eventually fathering a genius.

At present, however, science, spurred on by its powerful delusion, is hurrying unstoppably to its limits, where the optimism hidden in the essence of logic will founder and break up. For there is an infinite number of points on the periphery of the circle of science, and while we have no way of foreseeing how the circle could ever be completed, a noble and gifted man inevitably encounters, before the mid-point of his existence, boundary points on the periphery like this, where he stares into that which cannot be illuminated. When, to his horror, he sees how logic curls up around itself at these limits and finally bites its own tail, then a new form of knowledge breaks through, *tragic knowledge*, which, simply to be endured, needs art for protection and as medicine.

If we now, with eyes strengthened and refreshed by the Greeks, look at the highest spheres of the world around us, we can see the insatiable greed of optimistic knowledge, of which Socrates appeared to be the exemplar, turning suddenly into tragic resignation and a need for art; admittedly, that same greed, on its lower levels, is bound to express hostility towards art, and feel disgust at Dionysiac-tragic art in particular, as is illustrated by Socratism's opposition to Aeschylean tragedy.

Now we knock, with emotions stirred, at the gates of the present and the future: will that 'transformation' lead to ever new configurations of genius and especially of the *music-making Socrates*? Will the net of art which is spread over existence, whether it goes under the name of science or of religion, be woven ever stronger and finer, or is it destined to be torn to shreds in the restlessly barbaric turmoil known as 'the present'? Concerned, but not comfortless, we stand aside for a little, as contemplative spirits who are permitted to witness these enormous struggles and transitions. Alas! The magic of these struggles is such, that he who sees them must also take part in them!

---

[127] In Plato's *Theaetetus* (149af, 210) Socrates compares himself to a midwife, who, herself barren, can help others give birth to thoughts.

16

By elaborating this historical example we have tried to make one thing clear: it is certain that tragedy perishes with the disappearance of the spirit of music, and it is just as certain that this spirit alone can give birth to tragedy. To take the edge off this unusual assertion and, at the same time, to reveal the origin of this insight of ours, we must now look with clear eyes at analogous phenomena in the present; we must enter into the thick of the battles being waged between insatiable, optimistic knowledge and the tragic need for art in the highest spheres of the world today. In doing so, I shall disregard all the other hostile drives which are at work against art, and specifically against tragedy, in every age, and which at present are spreading their influence so triumphantly that, for example, of all the theatrical arts only farce and ballet are growing rampant and bearing blooms which perhaps do not smell sweet to everyone. I shall speak only of the *most illustrious opposition* to the tragic view of the world, by which I mean science, optimistic to its deepest core, with its ancestor Socrates at the head of it. Thereafter I intend to name the forces which seem to me to guarantee a *rebirth of tragedy* – and some other blissful hopes for the German character!

Before plunging into the thick of these battles, let us first put on the armour of the insights we have gained so far. In contrast to all those who are determined to derive the arts from a single principle, as the necessary source of life for every work of art, I have kept my gaze fixed on those two artistic deities of the Greeks, Apollo and Dionysos, in whom I discern the living and visible representatives of *two* art-worlds which differ in their deepest essence and highest goals. Apollo stands before me as the transfiguring genius of the *principium individuationis*, through whom alone release and redemption in semblance can truly be attained, whereas under the mystical, jubilant shout of Dionysos the spell of individuation is broken, and the path to the Mothers of Being,[128] to the innermost core of things, is laid open. This enormous opposition, which opens up as a gaping gulf between plastic, Apolline, art and the Dionysiac art of music, was revealed to one, and one alone, of the great thinkers so forcibly that, even without being guided by the symbolism of the Hellenic gods, he

---

[128] In the second part of *Faust* the hero wishes to summon up Helen of Troy from the dead. To do so, he is told, he must descend to 'the mothers' as the mythical sources of the power to bring things to life (*Faust* II, 6212–93).

attributed to music a different character and origin from all other arts, because music is not, as all the others are, a copy of appearances, but a direct copy of the Will itself, so that it represents *the metaphysical in relation to all that is physical in the world*, the thing-in-itself in relation to all appearances. In confirmation of its eternal truth, Richard Wagner has put his own stamp on this insight, the most important in all aesthetics (and the insight with which aesthetics, in any serious sense, begins), when he writes, in his 'Beethoven', that music is to be assessed by quite different aesthetic criteria from those which apply to all image-making arts, and not at all by the category of beauty; and this, he asserts, is the case, despite the fact that an erroneous aesthetics, following the example of misguided and degenerate art and basing itself on a concept of beauty which is valid in the world of image-making, has been in the habit of demanding from music the same effect as is demanded of the arts of image-making, namely that it should arouse *pleasure in beautiful forms*. After I had grasped this enormous opposition, I felt strongly compelled to get closer to the essence of Greek tragedy and thus to the most profound revelation of the Hellenic genius; for only now did I feel that I had the magic at my command which would enable me to get beyond the phraseology of our usual aesthetics, and to conjure up the original problem of tragedy in physical form before my very soul. Thereby I was granted such a surprising and strange look into the nature of the Hellenic that I could not avoid the impression that our classical-Hellenic scholarship, for all its proud gestures, had so far known no better, in the main, than to ruminate contentedly on externals and shadow-plays.

We might perhaps touch on that original problem with this question: what aesthetic effect is created when the inherently separate artistic powers of the Apolline and the Dionysiac become active alongside one another? Or, more briefly, how does music relate to image and concept? Schopenhauer, whom Richard Wagner praises for the supreme clarity and transparency of his presentation on this particular point, deals with it most fully in the following passage, which I shall now reproduce in full:

As a result of all this, we can regard the phenomenal world, or nature, and music as two different expressions of the same thing; and this thing itself is therefore the only medium of their analogy, a knowledge of which is required if we are to understand that analogy. Accordingly, music, if regarded as an expression of the world, is in the highest degree a universal language that is related to the universality of concepts much as these are related to the particular things. Yet its universality is by no means that empty universality of abstraction, but is of quite a different kind; it is united with thorough and unmistakable distinctness. In this respect it is like geometrical figures and numbers, which are the universal forms of all possible objects of experience and are *a priori* applicable to them all, and yet are not abstract, but perceptible and thoroughly definite. All possible efforts, stirrings, and manifestations of the will, all the events that occur within man himself and are included by the reasoning faculty in the wide, negative concept of feeling, can be expressed by the infinite number of possible melodies, but always in the universality of mere form without the material, always only according to the in-itself, not to the phenomenon, as it were the innermost soul of the phenomenon without the body. This close relation that music has to the true nature of all things can also explain the fact that, when music suitable to any scene, action, event, or environment is played, it seems to disclose to us its most secret meaning, and appears to be the most accurate and distinct commentary on it. Moreover, to the man who gives himself up entirely to the impression of a symphony, it is as if he saw all the possible events of life and of the world passing by within himself. Yet if he reflects, he cannot assert any likeness between that piece of music and the things that passed through his mind. For, as we have said, music differs from all the other arts by the fact that it is not a copy of the phenomenon, or, more exactly, of the will's adequate objectivity, but is directly a copy of the will itself, and therefore expresses the metaphysical to everything physical in the world, the thing-in-itself to every phenomenon. Accordingly, we could just as well call the world embodied music as embodied will; this is the reason why music makes every picture, indeed every scene from real life and from the world, at once appear in enhanced significance, and this is, of course, all the greater, the more analogous its melody is to the inner spirit of the given phenomenon. It is due to this that we are able to set a poem to music as a song, or a perceptive presentation as a pantomime, or both as opera. Such individual pictures of human life, set to the universal language of music, are never bound to it or correspond to it with absolute necessity, but stand to it only in the relation of an example, chosen at random, to a universal concept. They express in the distinctness of reality what music asserts in the universality of mere form. For, to a certain extent, melodies are, like universal concepts, an abstraction from reality. This reality, and hence the world of particular things, furnishes what is perceptive, special, and individual, the particular case, both to the universality of the concepts and to that of the melodies. These two universalities, however, are in a certain respect opposed to each other, since the concepts contain only the forms, first of all abstracted from perception, so to speak the stripped-off outer shell of things; hence they are quite properly *abstracta.* Music, on the other hand, gives the innermost kernel preceding all form, or the heart of things. This relation could very well be expressed in the language of the scholastics by saying that the concepts are the *universalia post rem*,[129] but music gives the *universalia ante rem*, and reality the *universalia in re*. Even other examples, just as arbitrarily chosen, of the universal expressed in a poem could correspond in the same degree to the general significance of the melody assigned to this poem; and so the same composition is suitable to many verses; hence also the *vaudeville*. But that generally a relation between a composition and a perceptive expression is possible is due, as we have said, to the fact that the two are simply quite different expressions of the same inner nature of the world. Now when in the particular case such a relation actually exists, thus when the composer has known how to express in the universal language of music the stirrings of will that constitute the kernel of an event, then the melody of the song, the music of the opera, is expressive. But the analogy discovered by the composer between these two must have come from the immediate knowledge of the inner nature of the world unknown to his faculty of reason; it cannot be an imitation brought about with conscious intention by means of concepts. Otherwise the music does not express the inner nature of the will itself, but merely imitates its phenomenon inadequately. All really imitative music does this. (*World as Will and Representation*, I, p.309)

Thus, according to Schopenhauer, we understand music, the language of the Will, directly, and feel our fantasy stimulated to create an analogous example that will give shape and body to this spirit-world which speaks to us and which, although invisible, is so full of movement and life. On the other hand, image and concept acquire a heightened significance under the influence of the kind of music which truly corresponds to them. Thus the art of Dionysos customarily exerts two kinds of influence on the Apolline capacity for art: music stimulates us to *contemplate symbolically* Dionysiac universality, and it causes the symbolic image to emerge with the *highest degree of significance*. From these facts, which are inherently intelligible and not inaccessible to deeper examination, I conclude that music is able to give birth to *myth*, i.e. to the most significant example, and in particular to *tragic myth*, myth which speaks of Dionysiac knowledge in symbols. I have used

---

[129] A topic of considerable interest in the Middle Ages was the nature of 'universals', i.e. such things as cat-hood, carnivorousness, animality, etc., and the relation of such universals to the individual objects in our world which instantiated them. Roughly speaking three approaches were distinguished: (a) the universals exist *prior to* the individuals, i.e. there is a 'cat-hood' which exists in some logical (or temporal) sense 'before' any individual cat does. Those who held this view were said to claim that universals existed *ante rem* (i.e. 'before the thing'); often they also held that individual instances were in some sense 'less real' than the universals they instantiate; (b) the universals exist only *after* the individuals so that 'cat-hood' in some sense depends on the antecedent existence of individual cats, perhaps in that it is simply a concept abstracted from a perception of them. Those who held this view were said to claim that universals existed *post rem* (i.e. 'after the thing'); often they also held that a universal was nothing but a name and lacked reality; (c) the universals do exist but *in* the individual objects – i.e. *in re* ('in the thing').

the phenomenon of the lyric poet to show how, in him, music struggles to inform us about its nature in Apolline images; if we now reflect that music, raised to its highest power, is also bound to seek the highest form of expression in images, it must seem possible that music also knows how to find symbolic expression for its true, Dionysiac wisdom; and where else are we to look for this expression, if not in tragedy and more generally in the concept of the *tragic*?

The tragic cannot be derived in any honest way from the nature of art as commonly understood, that is, according to the single category of semblance and beauty; only the spirit of music allows us to understand why we feel joy at the destruction of the individual. For individual instances of such destruction merely illustrate the eternal phenomenon of Dionysiac art, which expresses the omnipotent Will behind the *principium individuationis*, as it were, life going on eternally beyond all appearance and despite all destruction. Our metaphysical delight in the tragic translates instinctive, unconscious Dionysiac wisdom into the language of images: we take pleasure in the negation of the hero, the supreme appearance of the Will, because he is, after all, mere appearance, and because the eternal life of the Will is not affected by his annihilation. Tragedy calls out: 'We believe in eternal life', whereas music is the immediate idea of this life. The plastic arts have a quite different goal: here Apollo overcomes the individual's suffering by his luminous glorification of the *eternity of appearance*; here beauty gains victory over the suffering inherent in life; in a certain sense, a lie is told which causes pain to disappear from the features of nature. In Dionysiac art and its tragic symbolism this self-same nature speaks to us in its true, undisguised voice: 'Be as I am! – the primal mother, eternally creative beneath the surface of incessantly changing appearances, eternally forcing life into existence, forever satisfying myself with these changing appearances!'

17

Dionysiac art, too, wants to convince us of the eternal lust and delight of existence; but we are to seek this delight, not in appearances but behind them. We are to recognize that everything which comes into being must be prepared for painful destruction; we are forced to gaze into the terrors of individual existence – and yet we are not to freeze in horror: its metaphysical solace tears us momentarily out of the turmoil of changing figures.

For brief moments we are truly the primordial being itself and we feel its unbounded greed and lust for being; the struggle, the agony, the destruction of appearances, all this now seems to us to be necessary, given the uncountable excess of forms of existence thrusting and pushing themselves into life, given the exuberant fertility of the world-Will; we are pierced by the furious sting of these pains at the very moment when, as it were, we become one with the immeasurable, primordial delight in existence and receive an intimation, in Dionysiac ecstasy, that this delight is indestructible and eternal. Despite fear and pity, we are happily alive, not as individuals, but as the *one* living being, with whose procreative lust we have become one.

The genesis of Greek tragedy now tells us with great clarity and definiteness how the tragic work of art of the Greeks was truly born from the spirit of music; we believe that, with this thought, we have done justice for the first time to the original and quite astonishing significance of the chorus. At the same time, we have to admit that the meaning of the tragic myth, as we have stated it, never became transparent and conceptually clear to the Greek poets, far less to the Greek philosophers; to a certain extent, their heroes speak more superficially than they act; myth is certainly not objectified adequately in the spoken word. The structure of the scenes and the vivid images reveal a deeper wisdom than the poet himself can put into words and concepts; the same thing can be seen in Shakespeare, whose Hamlet, for example, similarly speaks more superficially than he acts, so that the aforementioned lesson of *Hamlet* cannot be drawn from the words of the play, but from intense contemplation of, and reflection on, the whole. In the case of Greek tragedy, which we admittedly only find in the form of a word-drama, I have even indicated that the incongruity of myth and word could easily mislead us into thinking that it is shallower and more insignificant than it really is, and therefore into supposing that it had a more superficial effect than it must have had in reality, according to the testimony of the ancients, for it is so easy to forget that what the word-poet failed to achieve, namely the highest spiritualization and idealization of myth, he could accomplish successfully at any moment as a creative musician. Admittedly, we have to reconstruct the overpowering effect of the music almost by scholarly means, in order to receive something of that incomparable solace which must be inherent in true tragedy. But only if we were Greeks would we have felt the overpowering effect of music to be precisely this; whereas, when we listen to fully evolved Greek music and compare it to the much richer music with which we are now familiar, we believe that we are hearing only the youthful song of musical genius, struck up with a shy feeling of strength. As the Egyptian priests said, the Greeks are eternal children,[130] and in the tragic art, too, they are mere children who do not know what sublime toy has been created – and smashed – by their hands.

That struggle of the spirit of music to be revealed in image and myth, a struggle which grows in intensity from the beginnings of the lyric up to Attic tragedy, suddenly breaks off, having just unfolded its riches, and disappears, as it were, from the face of Hellenic art, whereas the Dionysiac view of the world which was born out of this struggle lives on in the Mysteries and, while undergoing the strangest metamorphoses and degenerate mutations, never ceases to attract more serious natures. Will it perhaps, at some time in the future, re-emerge from its mystical depths as art?

What concerns us here is the question of whether the opposing power on which tragedy foundered will for ever remain strong enough to prevent the re-awakening of tragedy and the tragic view of the world. If ancient tragedy was thrown off course by the dialectical drive towards knowledge and the optimism of science, one should conclude from this fact that there is an eternal struggle between the *theoretical* and the *tragic views of the world*. Only when the spirit of science has been carried to its limits and its claim to universal validity negated by the demonstration of these limits might one hope for a rebirth of tragedy; the symbol which we would propose for this cultural form is that of the *music-making Socrates* in the sense discussed above. In making this contrast, what I understand by the spirit of science is the belief, which first came to light in the person of Socrates, that the depths of nature can be fathomed and that knowledge can heal all ills.

Anyone who recalls the immediate effects produced by this restlessly advancing spirit of science will recognize at once how *myth* was destroyed by it, and how this destruction drove poetry from its natural, ideal soil, so that it became homeless from that point onwards. If we are correct in ascribing to music the power to give birth to myth once more, we must also expect to see the spirit of science advancing on a hostile course towards the myth-creating force of music. This occurs during the evolution of the *new Attic dithyramb*, where the music no longer expressed the inner essence, the Will itself, but simply reproduced appearances inadequately,

[130] Plato, *Timaeus* 22b4.

in an imitation mediated by concepts; truly musical natures then turned away from this inwardly degenerate music with the same feeling of revulsion as they felt for Socrates' tendency to murder art. Aristophanes' sure instinct certainly grasped things correctly when he expressed the same hatred for Socrates himself, the tragedy of Euripides, and the music of the new exponents of the dithyramb, for he scented the characteristics of a degenerate culture in all three phenomena. Thanks to the new dithyramb, a sacrilege was committed which turned music into a mere counterfeit of some phenomenon, e.g. of a battle or a storm at sea, and thus robbed it entirely of its myth-making power. For if music seeks to excite our pleasure merely by compelling us to seek out external analogies between events in life or nature and certain rhythmical figures or characteristic musical sounds, if our understanding is to be satisfied by recognizing these analogies, then we are dragged down into a mood in which it is impossible to be receptive to the mythical; for myth needs to be felt keenly as a unique example of something universal and true which gazes out into infinity. In true Dionysiac music we find just such a general mirror of the world-Will; a vivid event refracted in this mirror expands immediately, we feel, into a copy of an eternal truth. Conversely, a vivid event of this kind is immediately stripped of any mythical character by the tone-painting of the new dithyramb; now music has become a miserable copy of a phenomenon, and is thus infinitely poorer than the phenomenon; as far as our feelings are concerned, this poverty even reduces the phenomenon itself, so that, for example, a battle imitated by such music amounts to no more than the noise of marching, the sounds of signals etc., and our fantasy is arrested precisely by these superficial details. Tone-painting is thus the antithesis of the myth-creating energy of true music, for it makes the phenomenal world even poorer than it is, whereas Dionysiac music enriches and expands the individual phenomenon, making it into an image of the world. It was a great victory for the un-Dionysiac spirit when, during the evolution of the new dithyramb, it alienated music from itself and reduced it to the status of a slave of appearances. Euripides, who must be described as a thoroughly un-musical nature in a higher sense, is passionately attached to the new dithyrambic music for precisely this reason, and he makes free with all its showy effects and manners with all the liberality of a robber.

Elsewhere we can see the force of this un-Dionysiac spirit directed actively against myth if we look at the excessive growth in the *presentation of character* and of psychological refinement in tragedy from Sophocles onwards. Character is no longer meant to be capable of being expanded into an eternal type; on the contrary, artificial subsidiary features, shading and the fine definition of every line, are all meant to give such an impression of individuality that the spectator no longer senses the myth at all, but only the great fidelity to nature and the imitative skills of the artist. Here too we may observe the victory of the phenomenal over the universal, and pleasure being taken in the individual anatomical specimen, as it were; already we are breathing the air of a theoretical world where scientific understanding is more highly prized than the artistic reflection of a universal rule. The trend towards the characteristic advances rapidly; whereas Sophocles still paints whole characters, harnessing myth to expound them subtly, Euripides is already at the stage of painting only individual characteristics which can be expressed in powerful passions; in the New Attic Comedy there are only masks with a *single* expression: frivolous old people, cheated pimps, cunning slaves, all tirelessly repeated. Where has the myth-shaping spirit of music gone now? All that remains of music is either music to excite the emotions or to prompt memory, i.e. either a stimulant for blunt and jaded nerves or tone-painting. The former hardly cares about the text to which it is set; even in Euripides verbal expression is already beginning to become quite slovenly when the heroes or choruses start to sing; how far are things likely to have gone amongst his shameless successors?

But the clearest sign of the new, un-Dionysiac spirit can be seen in the *endings* of the new dramas. In the old tragedy the audience experienced metaphysical solace, without which it is quite impossible to explain man's pleasure in tragedy; the sounds of reconciliation from another world can perhaps be heard at their purest in *Oedipus at Colonus*. Now that the spirit of music had flown from tragedy, it is, in the strictest sense, dead, for from what other source was that metaphysical solace to come? Thus people looked for an earthly resolution of the tragic dissonance: after he had been sufficiently tortured by fate, the hero gained a well-earned reward in the form of a handsome marriage, or in being honoured by the gods. The hero had become a gladiator who was occasionally granted his freedom after he had been thoroughly flailed and was covered in wounds. The *deus ex machina* has taken the place of metaphysical solace. I do not say that the tragic view of the world was destroyed everywhere and utterly by the advancing spirit of the un-Dionysiac; we only know that it had to flee from art and into the underworld, as it were, where it degenerated into a secret cult. But almost everywhere in Hellenic life havoc was wreaked by the withering breath of that spirit which manifests itself in the kind of 'Greek cheerfulness' discussed above, as senile, unproductive pleasure in existence; this cheerfulness is the very opposite of the glorious 'naïveté' of the older Greeks as this should be understood, according to the characterization above, namely as the flower of Apolline culture growing from the depths of a gloomy abyss, as a victory which the Hellenic will gains over suffering and the wisdom of suffering through the image of beauty shown in its mirror. The noblest form of that other, Alexandrian type of 'Greek cheerfulness' is the cheerfulness of *theoretical man* which exhibits the same characteristics as I have just derived from the spirit of the un-Dionysiac: it fights against Dionysiac wisdom and art; it strives to dissolve myth; it puts in the place of metaphysical solace a form of earthly harmony, indeed its very own *deus ex machina*, namely the god of machines and smelting furnaces, i.e. the energies of the spirits of nature, understood and applied in the service of higher egotism; it believes in correcting the world through knowledge, in life led by science; and it is truly capable of confining the individual within the smallest circle of solvable tasks, in the midst of which he cheerfully says to life: 'I will you: you are worth understanding.'

18

It is an eternal phenomenon: by means of an illusion spread over things, the greedy Will always finds some way of detaining its creatures in life and forcing them to carry on living. One person is held fast by the Socratic pleasure in understanding and by the delusion that he can thereby heal the eternal wound of existence; another is ensnared by art's seductive veil of beauty fluttering before his eyes; a third by the metaphysical solace that eternal life flows on indestructibly beneath the turmoil of appearances – to say nothing of the commoner and almost more powerful illusions which the Will constantly holds in readiness. Indeed, these three levels of illusion are only for those equipped with nobler natures, who generally feel the burden and heaviness of being with more profound aversion and who have to be tricked by exquisite stimulants into ignoring their aversion. Everything we call culture consists of such stimulants; depending on the proportions of the mixture, we have a culture which is predominantly *Socratic* or *artistic* or *tragic*; or, if historical illustrations are permitted, a culture is either Alexandrian or Hellenic or Buddhistic.

Our whole modern world is caught in the net of Alexandrian culture, and the highest ideal it knows is *theoretical man*, equipped with the highest powers of understanding and working in the service of science, whose archetype and progenitor is Socrates. The original aim of all our means of education is to achieve this ideal; every other form of existence has to fight its way up alongside it, as something permitted but not intended. It is almost terrifying to think that for a long time the man of culture was to be found here only in the guise of the man of learning; even our poetic arts had to evolve from learned imitations, and the main effect of rhyme still shows that our poetic form originated in experiments with a non-native and, in the true sense of the word, learned language. How incomprehensible the true Greek must find *Faust*, the modern man of culture, although he is inherently understandable – Faust, who storms unsatisfied through all the faculties, who has devoted himself to magic and the devil out of the drive for knowledge; we only have to compare him with Socrates to realize that modern man is beginning to sense the limits of the Socratic lust for knowledge, and that he longs to reach some shore and get off the vast, barren sea of knowledge. When Goethe says to Eckermann, speaking of Napoleon, 'Yes, my good friend, actions, too, are a form of productivity',[131] he reminds us, with graceful naïveté, that non-theoretical man is something incredible and astonishing to modern man, so that the wisdom of a Goethe is needed in order to re-discover the fact that even such a surprising form of existence is understandable, indeed forgivable.

We should not now disguise from ourselves what lies hidden in the womb of this Socratic culture: an optimism which imagines itself to be limitless! We should not now take fright when the fruits of this optimism ripen, when the acid of this kind of culture trickles down to the very lowest levels of our society so that it gradually begins to tremble from burgeoning surges and desires, when the belief in the earthly happiness of all, when the belief that such a general culture of knowledge is possible, gradually transforms itself into the menacing demand for such Alexandrian happiness on earth, into the invocation of a Euripidean *deus ex machina*! It should be noted that Alexandrian culture needs a slave-class in order to exist in the long term; as it views existence optimistically, however, it denies the necessity of such a class and is therefore heading towards horrifying extinction when the effects of its fine words of seduction and pacification, such as 'human dignity' and 'the dignity of labour', are

---

[131] Conversation of 11 March 1828.

exhausted. There is nothing more terrible than a class of barbaric slaves which has learned to regard its existence as an injustice and which sets out to take revenge, not just for itself but for all future generations. Who will dare, when faced with such menacing storms, to appeal with confident courage to our pale and tired religions which have themselves degenerated, down to their very foundations, into religions of the learned, so that myth, the necessary precondition of every religion, is already crippled everywhere, and the spirit of optimism which we have just described as the seed of our society's destruction has seized power even in this area.

The catastrophe slumbering in the womb of theoretical culture is gradually beginning to frighten modern man; in other words, he is beginning to suspect the consequences of his own existence; he therefore dips into his store of experiences for some means of warding off the danger, although he does not really believe in them. Meanwhile great natures with a bent for general problems have applied the tools of science itself, with incredible deliberation, to prove that all understanding, by its very nature, is limited and conditional, thereby rejecting decisively the claim of science to universal validity and universal goals. Thanks to this demonstration it has been recognized for the first time that it is an arrogant delusion to believe that we can penetrate to the innermost essence of things by following the chain of causality. The hardest-fought victory of all was won by the enormous courage and wisdom of *Kant* and *Schopenhauer*, a victory over the optimism which lies hidden in the nature of logic and which in turn is the hidden foundation of our culture. Whereas this optimism once believed in our ability to grasp and solve, with the help of the seemingly reliable *aeternae veritates*,[132] all the puzzles of the universe, and treated space, time, and causality as entirely unconditional laws of the most general validity, Kant showed that these things actually only served to raise mere appearance, the work of maya, to the status of the sole and supreme reality and to put this in the place of the innermost and true essence of things, thereby making it impossible really to understand this essence – putting the dreamer even more deeply to sleep, as Schopenhauer put it (*World as Will and Representation*, I, p.498). This insight marks the beginning of a culture which I now dare to describe as a tragic culture. Its most important feature lies in putting wisdom in place of science as the highest goal. This wisdom is not deceived by the seductive distractions of the sciences; instead it turns its unmoved gaze on the total image of the world, and in this image it seeks

132 Eternal truths.

to embrace eternal suffering with sympathetic feelings of love, acknowledging that suffering to be its own. Let us imagine a rising generation with this fearless gaze, with this heroic attraction to what is monstrous (*ungeheuer*), let us imagine the bold stride of these dragon-killers, the proud recklessness with which they turn their backs on all the enfeebled doctrines of scientific optimism so that they may 'live resolutely',[133] wholly and fully; would not the tragic man of this culture, given that he has trained himself for what is grave and terrifying, be bound to desire a new form of art, the art of metaphysical solace, in fact to desire tragedy as his very own Helen, and to call out along with Faust:

> And shall I not, with all my longing's vigour,
> Draw into life that peerless, lovely figure?[134]

Now that Socratic culture has been profoundly shaken from two directions and can only hold the sceptre of its infallibility with trembling hands, first because it fears its own consequences (which it is gradually beginning to suspect), and secondly because it no longer has the same naive confidence and conviction that its foundations are eternally valid, it is a sad spectacle to watch the dance of its thought throwing itself longingly into the arms of ever-new figures, only to let go of them again with a sudden shudder, as when Mephistopheles shakes off the seductive Lamiae.[135] It is, after all, the mark of that 'fracture' which everyone agrees is the original ill of modern culture, that theoretical man should take fright at his own consequences, and, in his discontent, no longer dares to entrust himself to the terrible, icy stream of existence; anxiously, he runs up and down along the shore. He no longer wants anything in its entirety, complete with all the natural cruelty of things; this is how enfeebled and softened he has become by the optimistic way of looking at things. Furthermore, he feels that a culture built on the principle of science must perish when it begins to become *illogical*, i.e. to turn and flee from its own consequences. Our art exhibits this general crisis: in vain do the artists imitate all the great productive periods and natures, in vain is the whole of 'world literature' piled up around modern man for his solace, in vain is he placed amongst all the artistic styles and artists of all times, so that he may give them names – as Adam gave names to the beasts; despite all this, he remains eternally hungry, a 'critic' without desire or energy, Alexandrian man who is basically a librarian and proof-reader, sacrificing his sight miserably to book-dust and errors.

---

[133] Goethe, *General Confession*.   [134] Goethe, *Faust*, II, 7438ff.   [135] Goethe, *Faust*, II, 7697ff.

19

Nothing can define the innermost substance of this Socratic culture more sharply than the *culture of the opera*,[136] for in this area our culture has given evidence of its will and understanding with unique naïveté – something which must surprise us, if we set the genesis of opera and the facts of its evolution alongside the eternal truths of the Apolline and the Dionysiac. Let me first remind you of the emergence of the *stilo rappresentativo*[137] and the recitative. Is it credible that this utterly externalized operatic music, incapable as it is of all piety, could have been conceived and cherished – as the rebirth of all true music, so to speak – by an age that was blessed with enthusiasm, from which the ineffably sublime and sacred music of Palestrina had just emerged? Who, on the other hand, would wish to blame only the amusement-hungry luxury of certain circles in Florence and the vanity of their dramatic singers for the stormy spread of pleasure in opera? The part played by some *extra-artistic tendency* in the nature of recitative is the only explanation I can find for the fact that, alongside the vaulted architecture of Palestrina's harmonies, which the entire Christian Middle Ages had helped to build, this passion for a half-musical manner of declamation awakened at the same time and even in the very same people.

In order to satisfy the listener's wish to hear the words clearly amidst the singing, the singer speaks more than he sings and he intensifies the pathetic expression of the words by this kind of half-singing; by intensifying the pathos in this way he makes it easier to understand the words and overcomes the remaining half of the music. The real danger which now threatens him is that he may allow the music to become dominant at the wrong time, whereby both the pathos of the delivery and the clarity of the words are bound to be destroyed immediately; at the same time he constantly feels the drive to discharge himself in music and present his voice in a virtuoso manner. Here he is helped by the 'poet' who knows how to provide him with sufficient opportunities for lyrical interjections, repetitions of words or *sententia* etc., passages which permit the singer to relax in the purely musical element and pay no heed to the words. This alternation between affectively emphatic, but only half-sung, declamation, and fully sung interjection, which lies at the heart of the *stilo rappresentativo*, the rapid shifts between attempts to affect the listener's understanding and

---

[136] 'Opera' of course, means the traditional pre-Wagnerian opera, not Wagner's own 'music-dramas'.
[137] This should actually be *stile rappresentativo*: early sixteenth-century form of recitative.

imagination on the one hand and his musical ground on the other, is something so utterly unnatural and, at the same time, inwardly so at odds with the artistic drives of the Apolline and the Dionysiac, that one is bound to conclude that the origin of recitative lies outside all artistic instincts. According to this description, we must define the recitative as a mixture of the epic and the lyrical modes of presentation, and indeed a mixture which, far from being internally stable (since this could not result from such utterly disparate things), is the most external, mosaic-like conglomeration, the like of which is not to be found in the whole of nature or experience. *However, this was not the opinion of those who invented the recitative;* they, and their age, believed indeed that the *stilo rappresentativo* had solved the secret of ancient music and that this alone explained the enormous effect of Orpheus, Amphion,[138] and indeed of Greek tragedy. The new style was held to be the rediscovery of the most effective kind of music, that of Ancient Greece; indeed, given the general and wholly popular belief that the Homeric world was the *world in its original state*, people at that time could give themselves over to the dream that they had descended once more to the paradisiac beginnings of humankind when music, too, must necessarily have possessed that incomparable purity, power, and innocence of which the poets spoke so touchingly in their Arcadian tales. Here we can see down to the very heart of that truly modern genre, opera: a form of art is forced into existence here by a powerful need, but a need of a non-aesthetic kind: the longing for the idyll, the belief that at the very beginning of time mankind was both artistic and good. Recitative was thought to be the rediscovered language of those original humans, and opera to be the rediscovered land of that idyllic or heroic good being who follows a natural artistic drive in all his actions; who, whenever he speaks, at least sings a little; and who promptly bursts into full song at the slightest stirring of emotion. It no longer matters to us that the Humanists of the period used this newly created image of the paradisiac artist to oppose the church's old view of mankind as being inherently corrupt and lost, so that opera must be understood as the opposing dogma of the good human being (which also meant, however, that they had simultaneously discovered a source of solace against the pessimism which, given the terrifying uncertainty of all the conditions of their existence, affected serious minds at the time most powerfully). We only need to recognize that the true magic, and thus also the genesis, of this new form of art, lay in satisfying an entirely

---

[138] Legendary inventor of the lyre.

un-aesthetic need, in the optimistic glorification of mankind as such, in the view that primal man was both good and artistic by nature – an operatic principle which gradually transformed itself into the threatening and terrible *demand* which we, faced by the socialist movements of the present, can no longer ignore. 'Man in his original goodness' demands his rights; what a paradisiac prospect!

Next to this I shall now place another, equally clear confirmation of my view that opera is built on the same principles as our Alexandrian culture. Opera is born of theoretical man, of the layman as critic, not of the artist – one of the most astonishing facts in the history of all the arts. Genuinely un-artistic listeners demanded that they should be able, above all, to understand the words, so that a rebirth of music could only be expected through the discovery of some form of singing in which the words of the text governed the counterpoint as a master governs his servant. For, just as the spirit was so much nobler than the body, the word was supposedly nobler than the accompanying system of harmony. When opera was just beginning the connection between music, image, and word was discussed on the basis of the crudely unmusical opinions of these laymen; and it was in the circles of aristocratic laypeople in Florence, and among the poets and singers whom they patronized, that the first experiments based on this aesthetic were made. A man with no artistic capability generates for himself a form of art precisely by being the un-artistic man *per se*. Because he has no inkling of the Dionysiac depths of music, he transforms for himself the enjoyment of music into the reason-governed rhetoric of passion in sound and word in the *stilo rappresentativo*, and into the sensuous pleasure afforded by the arts of singing; because he is incapable of seeing a vision, he presses the theatrical technician and stage-decorator into his service; because he cannot grasp the true essence of the artist, he conjures up before his mind's eye 'original man, the artist' in accordance with the demands of his own taste, i.e. a man who sings when he is passionate and who speaks in verse. He dreams himself into a far-off time when passion sufficed to create song and poetry – as if the affects had ever been capable of creating anything artistic. The precondition of opera is an erroneous belief about the artistic process, or more precisely the idyllic belief that every man of feeling is actually an artist. In line with this belief, opera is the expression in art of the lay mentality which dictates its laws with the cheerful optimism of theoretical man.

If we wanted to unite conceptually the two sets of ideas which were described above as having contributed to the genesis of the opera, we would have to speak of the *idyllic tendency of opera*, and Schiller's explanation and vocabulary would be all we required in order to do so.[139] Schiller states that nature and the ideal are either objects of mourning, when the former is represented as lost and the latter as unattained; or both are objects of joy, when they are imagined as real. The first condition produces the elegy in the narrower sense, the second the idyll in the widest sense. At this point we must immediately draw attention to a characteristic shared by both of the ideas which contributed to the genesis of opera, namely that in opera the ideal is not felt to be unattained and nature is not felt to be lost. According to this sentiment, there was once a time at the beginning of time when man lay in the bosom of nature and, in this natural state, had achieved the ideal of humanity in a unity of paradisiac goodness and artistry; we are all supposedly descended from this perfect original human being, indeed we are all still its faithful likeness; it was just that we needed to cast off certain things, voluntarily rid ourselves of excessive learning and excessive cultural opulence, in order to recognize ourselves in the image of that original being. The educated man of the Renaissance allowed himself to be accompanied back to an idyllic reality, to just such a consonance of nature and the ideal, by his operatic imitation of Greek tragedy; he used this tragedy, as Dante used Virgil, to be led to the gates of Paradise. From this point onwards he made his own way, proceeding from an imitation of the Greeks' highest form of art to the 'bringing back of all things', to a re-creation of the original artistic world of mankind. What confident good nature these reckless ventures in the very womb of theoretical culture displayed! One can only explain this as the result of a comforting faith that 'man *per se*' is the eternally virtuous operatic hero, the eternally singing or flute-playing shepherd who, if ever he were truly to lose himself for a time, was always bound to re-discover eventually that this was indeed his true nature; it can only be explained as the fruit of the optimism which arises during this period, like some sweetly seductive column of perfume, from the depths of the Socratic view of the world.

Thus what the features of opera express is not at all the elegiac pain caused by eternal loss but rather the cheerfulness of eternal re-discovery, comfortable delight in an idyllic reality which one can at least imagine to be real at any time; admittedly one does perhaps guess occasionally that this supposed reality is nothing but a fantastic, ridiculous dalliance which is

[139] In his *On Naive and Sentimental Poetry.*

bound to elicit the exclamation, 'Away with the phantom!' from anyone capable of measuring it against the fearful gravity of nature as it truly is, or of comparing it with the actual, original scenes from the beginnings of mankind. Nevertheless it would be an illusion to believe that one could simply shoo away the flirtatious creature that is opera with a loud shout, as if it were a ghost. Anyone who wants to destroy opera must take up arms against that Alexandrian cheerfulness which expresses its favourite idea so naively in opera, an idea which indeed finds its true artistic form in opera. But what can art itself expect from a form of art which does not originate in the aesthetic sphere, but rather has stolen into the territory of art from a semi-moral sphere, and which can only occasionally disguise the fact of its hybrid origins? From which juices does this parasitic creature called opera nourish itself, if not from those of true art? Are we not driven to assume that its idyllic seductions, its Alexandrian arts of flattery, will cause the supreme and truly serious task of art to degenerate into an empty, amusing distraction – that task being to free the eye from gazing into the horrors of the night and, with the healing balm of semblance, save the subject from the vain exertions of the will? What will become of the eternal truths of the Dionysiac and the Apolline where there is such a mixture of styles as I have shown to lie at the heart of the *stilo rappresentativo?* – where music is regarded as the servant and the libretto as master, where music is compared to the body and the words to the soul? – where the highest that is aimed for will be periphrastic tone-painting at best, just as it once was in the new Attic dithyramb? – where music is deprived of its true dignity, which consists in being a Dionysiac mirror of the world, so that all that remains to music, as the slave of the world of appearances, is to imitate the forms of the world of appearances and to excite external pleasure in the play of line and proportion. On close scrutiny, this fateful influence of opera on music can be seen to be virtually identical with the entire development of modern music; the optimism lurking in the genesis of opera and at the heart of the culture it represents has succeeded in divesting music with frightening speed of its Dionysiac purpose in the world and in imposing on it the character of a pleasurable play with form. The only thing to which this change could perhaps be compared is the metamorphosis of Aeschylean man into the blithe spirit of the Alexandrian world.

However, if, with the example we have sketched here, we are right in linking the disappearance of the Dionysiac spirit with the very striking but hitherto unexplained degeneration of the Hellenic world – what hopes must stir in us when we are assured by the most reliable auspices that *the reverse process, the gradual awakening of the Dionysiac spirit,* is taking place in the world in which we live! It is not possible for Hercules' divine spirit to remain flaccid for ever in luxuriant slavery to Omphale.[140] From the Dionysiac ground of the German spirit a power has risen up which has nothing in common with the original conditions of Socratic culture and which can neither be explained nor excused by these conditions; rather, this culture feels it to be something terrifying and inexplicable, something overpowering and hostile, namely *German music,* as we see it in the mighty, brilliant course it has run from Bach to Beethoven, from Beethoven to Wagner. What can the knowledge-lusting Socratism of today hope to do with this daemon as it emerges from unfathomable depths? Neither the jagged arabesques of operatic melody nor the arithmetic abacus of the fugue and the dialectic of counterpoint will yield the formula with whose thrice-powerful light one could make this daemon subject to one's will and compel it to speak. What a spectacle our aestheticians present as they lash about, with movements that are to be judged neither by the standard of eternal beauty nor of the sublime, attempting to catch in a net made from a 'beauty' of their own devising the genius of music as it disports itself with incomprehensible vitality before their eyes. One only needs to examine closely and in person these patrons of music with their untiring cries of 'Beauty! Beauty!', and ask oneself if they give the impression of being Nature's most favoured children, of having been nurtured and cosseted in the womb of the beautiful, or whether they are not in fact seeking a deceitful cover for their own coarseness, or an aesthetic pretext for their own sober-sided, impoverished sensibility; I am thinking, for example, of Otto Jahn.[141] But the liar and hypocrite should beware of German music, for it alone, in the midst of our entire culture, is the uniquely unsullied, pure and purifying spirit of fire which, as the great Heraclitus of Ephesus taught, is the point of origin and return for the double orbit of all things;[142] all those things which we now call culture, education, civilization must some day appear before the judge Dionysos whom no man can deceive.

Let us recall, then, how Kant and Schopenhauer made it possible for the

[140] Mythological queen who was said to have kept Hercules as a slave for a period of time.
[141] An anti-Wagnerian classical philologist who was party to an academic quarrel with Nietzsche's teacher and patron Ritschl at the University of Bonn.
[142] Notoriously obscure sixth-century philosopher who believed that everything in the world was in constant flux and any stability was the result of a (hidden) unity of opposites. The view reported here was said to be another part of his doctrine.

spirit of *German philosophy*, which springs from similar sources, to destroy scientific Socratism's contented pleasure in existence by demonstrating its limits, and how this demonstration ushered in an incomparably deeper and more serious consideration of ethical questions and art, one which can be defined as the conceptual formulation of *Dionysiac wisdom*. In what direction does this mysterious unity of German music and German philosophy point, if not towards a new form of existence, the content of which can only be guessed at from Hellenic analogies? For that we, standing as we do at the watershed of two different forms of existence, should still find something of inestimable value in the example of the Greeks is a consequence of the fact that their example contains the very same transitions and struggles in classically instructive form; the difference is that we are experiencing, by analogy, the main epochs of the Hellenic world in *reverse* order, as it were, so that now, for example, we appear to be moving *back* from the Alexandrian age and *towards* the period of tragedy. At the same time we feel that the birth of a tragic age means the return of the German spirit to itself, a blissful reunion with its own being after the German spirit, which had been living in hopeless formal barbarism, had been tyrannized for too long by forms introduced from outside by a vast invading force. Now, at long last, having returned to the original spring of its being, that spirit can dare to walk, bold and free, before all other peoples, without the leading-reins of Latin civilization; provided, of course, that the German spirit goes on learning, unceasingly, from the Greeks, for the ability to learn from this people is in itself a matter of lofty fame and distinguishing rarity. And when was our need of these supreme teachers greater than now, as we are experiencing the *rebirth of tragedy* and yet are in danger of not knowing whence it comes, nor of being able to discern where it wants to go?

20

Some day the attempt might be made to weigh up, under the gaze of an impartial judge, at what period and through which men the German spirit had striven most vigorously to learn from the Greeks; and if we may confidently assume that this unique praise must be accorded to the noblest struggles for self-cultivation[143] of Goethe, Schiller, and

---

[143] This rendering of *Bildung* as 'self-cultivation' is taken from H. Bruford, *The German Tradition of Self-Cultivation* (Cambridge University Press, 1975). No English term will adequately render *Bildung*, which remains strongly connected to its root, *bilden*, meaning to shape or form. At times, however, one is forced to render it as 'education'.

Winckelmann,[144] we would also have to add that, since those days and the immediate effects of their struggle, the striving to reach the Greeks and to achieve self-cultivation by the same route has become, for incomprehensible reasons, weaker and weaker. If we are not to despair utterly of the German spirit, ought we not to conclude from this that those warriors, too, might have failed in some central area to penetrate to the essential core of Hellenism and to create a lasting bond of love between German and Greek culture? Some unconscious recognition of this failure might perhaps have awakened faint-hearted doubt even amongst the more serious-minded as to whether, following in the wake of such predecessors, they would ever advance any further along the road to self-cultivation than their predecessors had done, or indeed whether they would ever reach the goal at all. This is why, since that time, we have seen a most worrying decline in judgments about the educational value of the Greeks; one hears expressions of pitying superiority issuing from various camps, intellectual and non-intellectual alike; elsewhere completely ineffectual fine words are wasted in flirting with 'Greek harmony', 'Greek beauty', 'Greek cheerfulness'. Precisely in those circles whose dignity could consist in drawing inexhaustibly from the Greek stream to the benefit of German education, precisely the teachers in our institutions of higher education, have learned better than most how to reach a quick and comfortable accommodation with the Greeks, even to the extent of abandoning sceptically the Hellenic ideal and completely perverting the true aim of all classical studies. In those circles one either exhausts oneself in the attempt to become a reliable corrector of old texts or a natural historian studying language in microscopic detail, or one perhaps seeks to appropriate Greek antiquity, alongside other antiquities, 'historically', but at any rate adopting the method and the haughty demeanour of today's cultured historiographers. If, accordingly, the real educational energy of our institutions of higher education is at present probably at a lower, weaker ebb than it has ever been, if the 'journalist', the paper slave of every day, has won the battle, as far as any concern for education goes, over the teachers in higher education, so that all that remains to the latter is to undergo the final metamorphosis, as others have done before them, and to adopt the diction of the journalist, moving with the 'easy elegance' of that group, like some carefree, educated butterfly – with what embarrassed confusion must those with such an education in a

---

[144] Eighteenth-century German antiquarian who was important in stimulating the revival of interest in ancient art as a model for all time.

present such as this stare at the phenomenon of the re-awakening of the Dionysiac spirit and the rebirth of tragedy, something which could only be understood, by analogy, from the deepest ground of the hitherto uncomprehended genius of the Hellenes. There is no other period in art in which so-called education and true art have confronted each other with such feelings of estrangement and aversion as the one we now see before our very eyes. We understand why such debilitated education hates true art, for it fears that it will be destroyed by it. But might not the entire Socratic–Alexandrian type of culture have reached the end of its life, now that it has culminated in such a delicate but feeble topmost shoot as present-day education? If such heroes as Goethe and Schiller were not granted the ability to break open the enchanted gateway leading into the Hellenic magic mountain, if the furthest reach of their most courageous struggle was that wistful gaze which Goethe's Iphigeneia sends homewards across the sea from the barbaric land of the Taurians,[145] what was left to the epigones of such heroes to hope for, if the gate did not open of its own accord, suddenly, in a quite different place, as yet untouched by all the previous exertions of culture – to the mystical sound of the re-awakened music of tragedy?

Let no one seek to diminish our belief in the impending rebirth of Hellenic Antiquity, for this alone allows us to hope for a renewal and purification of the German spirit through the fire-magic of music.[146] What else could one say to awaken any comforting expectation for the future amidst the growing sterility and exhaustion of present-day culture? We look around in vain for just one root bearing vigorous branches, for a single patch of fertile and healthy soil; wherever we look, we see only dust, sand, petrification, things dying from thirst. Anyone who feels quite alone and without comfort in this situation could choose no better symbol than the Knight with Death and the Devil as Dürer drew it for us, the armoured knight with the hard, steely gaze who, alone with just his horse and dog, knows how to find his way along a path of terror, unperturbed by his dread companions and yet bereft of all hope. One such Knight after the manner of Dürer was our own Schopenhauer; he lacked all hope, but he wanted the truth. His like does not exist.

But how suddenly the wilderness of our tired culture, which we have just painted in such gloomy colours, can be transformed, when it is touched

---

[145] Goethe, *Iphigenie auf Tauris* (*Iphigeneia among the Taurians*), act I, scene I.
[146] Allusion to the 'magic fire music' in act III of Wagner's *Die Walküre* (*The Valkyrie*).

by Dionysiac magic! A storm seizes everything that is worn out, rotten, broken, and withered, wraps it in a whirling cloud of red dust and carries it like an eagle into the sky. Our eyes gaze in confusion after what has disappeared, for what they see is like something that has emerged from a pit into golden light, so full and green, so luxuriantly alive, so immeasurable and filled with longing. Tragedy sits in the midst of this superabundance of life, suffering, and delight, in sublime ecstasy, listening to a distant, melancholy singing which tells of the Mothers of Being, whose names are delusion, will, woe. Yes, my friends, believe as I do in Dionysiac life and in the rebirth of tragedy. The time of Socratic man is past. Put on wreaths of ivy, take up the *thyrsus* and do not be surprised if tigers and panthers lie down, purring and curling round your legs. Now you must only dare to be tragic human beings, for you will be released and redeemed. You will accompany the festive procession of Dionysos from India to Greece! Put on your armour for a hard fight, but believe in the miracles of your god!

21

Slipping from this tone of exhortation back into the mood which befits the contemplative spirit, I repeat that only from the Greeks can one learn what an almost miraculous, sudden awakening of tragedy means for the innermost vital ground of a people. The people of the tragic Mysteries is the very same people which fought the Persian wars; conversely, the people which fought those wars needs tragedy, of necessity, as a restorative draught. Who would have expected another such vigorous outpouring of the simplest political feeling, of the most natural instincts for the homeland, of the original male lust for struggle, from this of all peoples, after it had been excited to its very core for several generations by the strongest convulsions of the Dionysiac daemon? After all, wherever there is a significant outbreak of Dionysiac fervour, the attendant liberation from the shackles of the individual always makes itself felt, first and foremost, in a dwindling of the political instincts, to the point of indifference even or indeed hostility; on the other hand, it is equally true that the state-founding Apollo is also the genius of the *principium individuationis* and that the state and the sense of homeland cannot survive without the affirmation of the individual personality. The orgiastic experience leads a people in just one direction, along the road towards Indian Buddhism which, if its longing for nothingness is to be borne at all, requires those rare, ecstatic states with their elevation above space, time, and the individual, while these in their turn demand a philosophy which teaches one how to overcome the indescribable apathy of the intervening moods by means of a representation. By the same token, where the political impulses reign supreme, a people is bound, just as inevitably, to embark on a course towards the most extreme worldliness which finds its most grandiose, but also most terrifying, expression in the Roman *imperium*.

Placed between India and Rome, and under pressure to make a seductive choice, the Greeks succeeded in inventing a new, third form in classical purity, one which they themselves would not make use of for any length of time, it is true, but one which, for that very reason, would survive for all time. For the saying that the favourites of the gods die young applies to all things, but it is just as certain that they then live with the gods for ever. One should not expect the noblest material of all to have the enduring toughness of leather; the coarse durability which was characteristic of the Roman national instinct, for example, probably does not belong to the necessary attributes of perfection. If we ask, however, what healing substance made it possible for the Greeks during their great period, despite the extraordinary strength of their Dionysiac and political impulses, to avoid exhausting themselves either in ecstatic brooding or in a debilitating chase after worldly power and honour, but to achieve instead that magnificent blend, like that of a noble wine, which both fires the spirit and induces a mood of contemplation, we must remember the enormous power of *tragedy* to stimulate, purify, and discharge the entire life of the people. We shall never comprehend the supreme value of tragedy until, like the Greeks, we experience it as the essence of all prophylactic healing energies, as a mediator between the strongest and inherently most fateful qualities of a people.

Tragedy absorbs the supreme, orgiastic qualities of music, so that in Greek culture, as in our own, it effectively brings music to fulfilment, but then allies it with the tragic myth and the tragic hero who, like some mighty Titan, lifts the whole Dionysiac world on to his back, relieving us of its burden; at the same time, by means of this same tragic myth and in the person of the tragic hero, tragedy can release us from the greedy urge for this existence and remind us with warning hand that there is another being and a higher delight, for which the fighting hero is preparing himself, prophetically, not by his victories but by his destruction. Between the universal validity of its music and the listener who is receptive to the

Dionysiac, tragedy places a sublime symbolic likeness – myth – and awakens in the listener the illusion that music is merely a supreme presentational device to enliven the plastic world of myth. Trusting in this noble deception, music can move its limbs in Dionysiac dance and abandon itself without scruple to an orgiastic feeling of freedom in which it could not dare indulge itself, purely as music, without this deception. Myth shields us from music, but it also grants music its supreme freedom for the first time. In return music bestows on myth a moving and convincing metaphysical significance to which word and image alone, without that unique source of help, could never attain; above all, it is thanks to music that the tragic spectator is overcome by that certain foreknowledge of a supreme delight reached by a path leading through destruction and negation, so that the spectator believes he is hearing the innermost abyss of things speaking audibly to him.

If my last sentences have only been able to express this difficult idea in a preliminary manner which few will find immediately comprehensible, I may not desist, at this point above all, from urging my friends to make another attempt and asking them to consider a single example from our shared experience, in order to prepare them for an understanding of the general principle. In citing this example, I cannot appeal to those who use the images of the events on stage and the words and passions of the *dramatis personae* in order thereby to get closer to a feeling for the music; for people like this do not have music as their mother-tongue and, despite all such assistance, they can only go as far as the entrance hall of musical perception, without ever reaching its innermost sanctum; some of them (such as Gervinus)[147] do not even reach the entrance hall by this route. Rather, I can appeal only to those who have a direct affinity with music, who were born of its womb, so to speak, and who relate to things almost exclusively via unconscious musical relationships. I now ask these true musicians whether they can conceive of any person capable of perceiving the third act of *Tristan and Isolde* purely as a vast symphonic movement, with no assistance from words or images, and who would not then suffocate as their soul attempted, convulsively, to spread its wings. How could anyone fail to be shattered immediately, having once put their ear to the heart of the universal Will, so to speak, and felt the raging desire for existence pour forth into all the arteries of the world as a thundering torrent or as the finest spray

---

[147] Extraordinarily prolific historian of literature at the University of Göttingen. Nietzsche disliked his work both because of its rather pedestrian rationalism and because of Gervinus' liberal political views.

of a stream? Is such a person, trapped within the miserable glass vessel of human individuality, supposed to be able to bear listening to countless calls of lust and woe re-echoing from the 'wide space of the world's night',[148] without fleeing, unstoppably, with the strains of this shepherd's dance of metaphysics in his ears, towards his first and original home? If, however, it is possible to perceive such a work as a whole, without the negation of individual existence, if such a creation can be brought into being without destroying its creator – where does the solution to such a contradiction lie?

At this point the tragic myth and the tragic hero interpose themselves between the music and our most intense musical excitement, basically as a mere likeness of those most universal facts of which music alone can speak directly. But if we felt as purely Dionysiac beings, then myth, as symbol, would simply be left on one side, unaffecting and unregarded, and would not distract us for even a moment from listening to the echoes of the *universalia ante rem*.[149] This is where the power of the *Apolline*, bent on restoring the almost shattered individual, bursts forth, bringing the healing balm of a blissful deception; suddenly we believe we are hearing only Tristan as he asks himself, motionless and numbed, 'the old melody; why does it awaken me?'[150] And what had seemed to us earlier like some hollow sigh from the centre of being now tells us only how 'barren and empty is the sea'.[151] And where we had imagined we were expiring, breathless, in the convulsive reaching-out of all feelings, and that there was little which still tied us to this existence, now we hear and see only the hero, mortally wounded and yet not dying, with his despairing cry: 'Yearning! Yearning! Dying, to yearn; for yearning not to die'.[152] And where earlier the jubilant sound of the horn[153] had rent our heart in two, almost as the most intense agony of all, after such an excess and superabundance of consuming agonies, there now stands between us and 'jubilation *per se*' Kurwenal, whooping with delight, facing the ship that bears Isolde. Powerfully though compassion may reach into us and seize hold of our feelings, in a sense compassion saves us from the primal suffering of the world, just as the symbolic image of myth saves us from looking directly at the highest idea of the world – and just as thoughts and words save us from the unchecked outpouring of the unconscious Will. Thanks to that magnificent

---

[148] Wagner, *Tristan*, act III, bars 310ff.   [149] *Cf.* footnote 128 above.
[150] Wagner, *Tristan*, act III, bars 159ff.   [151] Ibid., bars 140ff.   [152] Ibid., bars 703ff.
[153] In act III of Wagner's *Tristan* the sighting of the ship bringing Isolde to the castle of the dying Tristan is announced by the English horn (starting at bar 999), after which Tristan's henchman Kurwenal breaks out into jubilation.

Apolline illusion, it seems to us that the very realm of sound itself confronts us here like a visible, tangible world, as if the music gives shape and form to the fate of Tristan and Isolde alone, as in the most delicate and most expressive of materials.

Thus the Apolline tears us away from Dionysiac generality and causes us to take delight in individuals; it attaches the compassion which has been awakened in us to these individuals; through them it satisfies the sense of beauty which thirsts after great and sublime forms; it parades images of life before our eyes and stimulates us to comprehend in thought the core of life contained within them. With the enormous force of image, concept, ethical doctrine and sympathetic excitement, the Apolline wrenches man out of his orgiastic self-destruction, deceives him about the generality of the Dionysiac event, and induces in him the delusion that he is seeing a single image of the world (e.g. *Tristan and Isolde*), and is simply meant to *see* it better and with greater inward involvement *thanks to the music*. What can be beyond the healing magic power of Apollo, if it can even deceive us into believing that the Dionysiac could really be a servant of the Apolline, intensifying its effects, or indeed that music is essentially an art for the presentation of an Apolline content?

Thanks to the pre-established harmony which exists between fully realized drama and its music, drama achieves a supreme degree of visual intensity which is unattainable by spoken drama. Just as all the living figures on the stage are simplified in the lines of the music (which move independently), so that they acquire the clarity of an undulating line, we in turn hear the coexistence of these lines in the changes of harmony which sympathize in the most delicate way possible with the movements of the action; consequently the relations between things become directly audible in a sensuously perceptible and by no means abstract manner, just as we can recognize that the essence of a character and of a melodic line is only expressed in pure form in these relationships. While music forces us to see more, and in a more intensely inward manner than usual, and to see the events on stage spread out before us like some delicate tissue, our spiritualized eye, gazing into the interior of things, sees the world of the stage both as infinitely enlarged and as illumined from within. What could the poet of the word hope to offer that is analogous to this, as he strives vainly, with the much more imperfect mechanism of word and concept, to achieve that inward enlargement of the visible world of the stage and its illumination from within? Although musical tragedy also makes use of the word, it can also set alongside it the depths from which the word is born, and clarify for us, from within, the genesis of the word.

But the process we have just described could also, and with equal certainty, be said to be merely a magnificent semblance, namely the abovementioned Apolline *deception*, the intended effect of which is to relieve us of the pressing, excessive burden of the Dionysiac. Fundamentally, the relationship of music to drama is the exact reverse of this: music is the true idea of the world, drama only a reflection of that idea, an isolated, shadowy image of it. That identity between the melodic line and the living figure, between harmony and the figure's relations to other characters, is true in an opposite sense to the impression we might gain from watching musical tragedy. However vividly we may move a figure, enliven it and illuminate it from within, it always remains a mere appearance, from which no bridge could lead across into true reality, into the heart of the world. But music speaks from the depths of this heart; countless appearances like this could pass before the same music, yet they would never exhaust its essence, but would for ever remain mere externalized copies of it. It is true that the popular and entirely false opposition of soul and body, far from explaining the difficult relationship of music to drama, only confuses it utterly; but for some unknown reason the unphilosophical coarseness of that opposition seems to have become an article of faith gladly confessed by our aestheticians in particular, whereas they have not learned, or not wished to learn, for equally unknown reasons, anything about the opposition between appearance and thing-in-itself.

If the result of our analysis has been that in tragedy the Apolline, thanks to its deception, wins a complete victory over the primal, Dionysiac element of music, and uses the latter for its own purposes, in order to lend the greatest possible clarity to the drama, we must now add one very important qualification, namely that the Apolline deception is punctured and destroyed where it matters most of all. If drama, with the help of music, spreads out all its movements and figures before us with such inwardly illuminated clarity, as if we were seeing a tissue being woven on a rising and falling loom, it also produces, taken as a whole, an effect which goes *beyond all the effects of Apolline art*. In the total effect of tragedy the Dionysiac gains the upper hand once more; it closes with a sound which could never issue from the realm of Apolline art. Thereby Apolline deception is revealed for what it is: a persistent veiling, for the duration of the tragedy, of the true Dionysiac effect, an effect so powerful, however, that it finally drives the

Apolline drama itself into a sphere where it begins to speak with Dionysiac wisdom and where it negates itself and its Apolline visibility. Thus the difficult relationship of the Apolline and the Dionysiac in tragedy truly could be symbolized by a bond of brotherhood between the two deities: Dionysos speaks the language of Apollo, but finally it is Apollo who speaks that of Dionysos. At which point the supreme goal of tragedy, and indeed of all art, is attained.

22

I would ask my attentive friend to call to mind his experience of the pure and unalloyed effect of a true musical tragedy. I believe I have described the phenomenon of this effect, in both its aspects, in a way which will enable him to interpret his own experiences. That is to say, he will recall how, watching the myth as it moved before him, he felt himself elevated to a kind of omniscience, as if the visual power of his eyes were not merely a power to attend to surfaces, but as if it were capable of penetrating to the interior, as if, with the help of music, he were now able to see before him, in sensuously visible form, so to speak, the undulations of the Will, the conflict of motives, the swelling current of passions, and as if he could dive down into the most delicate secrets of unconscious stirrings. He is conscious that those drives within him which are directed towards visibility and transfiguration are now at their highest pitch of intensity, yet he feels just as definitely that this long series of Apolline artistic effects does *not* engender that static, contented, will-less contemplation which the art of the sculptor and the epic poet (i.e. the true Apolline artists) induces in him, namely the justification of the world of *individuatio* attained through contemplation, which is the pinnacle and essence of Apolline art. He sees the transfigured world of the stage, and yet he negates it. He sees before him the tragic hero with all the clarity and beauty of the epic, and yet he takes delight in his destruction. He comprehends events on the stage to their innermost core, and yet he gladly flees into the incomprehensible. He feels the actions of the hero to be justified, and yet he feels even more elated when these actions destroy the man who performs them. He shivers in horror at the sufferings which will befall the hero, and yet they give him a premonition of a higher, far more overwhelming delight. He sees more and deeper than ever before, and yet he wishes he were blind. Where are we to find the origin of this wondrous self-division, this breaking and bending-back of the point of Apollo, if not in *Dionysiac* magic which, while apparently stimulating the Apolline impulses to their highest pitch, is nevertheless able to force the exuberance of Apolline energy into its service? *The tragic myth* can only be understood as the transformation of Dionysiac wisdom into images by means of Apolline artistry; it leads the world of appearances to its limits where it negates itself and seeks to flee back into the womb of the one, true reality; at which point it seems to sing, with Isolde, its metaphysical swan-song:

> In the surging swell
> Where joys abound,
> In perfumed wavelets'
> Trembling sound,
> In the world's soft breathing
> Whisp'ring round -
> To drown thus - sink down thus
> - all thought gone - delight alone![154]

Thus the experiences of the truly aesthetic listener reveal to us the tragic artist himself as someone who, like some abundant deity of *individuatio*, creates his figures (which means that his work could hardly be said to be the 'imitation of nature'), but whose enormous Dionysiac drive then consumes this entire world of appearances, thereby allowing us to sense, behind that world and through its destruction, a supreme, artistic, primal joy in the womb of the Primordial Unity. Admittedly, our aestheticians have nothing to report about this return to home and origin, about the brotherly bond between the two deities of art in tragedy, nor about the combination of Apolline and Dionysiac excitement felt by the listener; on the other hand, they never tire of characterizing the true essence of tragedy as the struggle of the hero with fate, the triumph of a universal moral order, or the discharge of affects induced by tragedy; such persistence makes me think that they may not be susceptible to aesthetic stimulation at all, and that, when they are listening to tragedy, they can perhaps only be considered as moral beings. Since the time of Aristotle, no one has yet given an explanation of the effect of tragedy which would permit the conclusion that artistic states were involved, or that the audience was engaged in aesthetic activity. One voice tells us that pity and fear are to be driven by these grave events to the point of discharge and hence relief,[155] another

---

[154] Last lines of Wagner's *Tristan.*   [155] Aristotle, *Poetics* 1449b21ff.

that we are to feel elevated and inspired by the victory of good and noble principles when we see the hero being sacrificed in the name of a moral view of the world;[156] while I fully believe that precisely this and only this is the effect which tragedy has on very many people, the clear conclusion to be drawn from this fact is that all of them, along with the aestheticians who interpret things for them, have never heard that tragedy is a supreme *art*. The pathological discharge which Aristotle calls catharsis, and which leaves the philologists uncertain whether to count it amongst the moral or medical phenomena, is reminiscent of a curious premonition of Goethe's. He says, 'I have never succeeded in treating any tragic situation artistically without some lively pathological interest, and I have therefore chosen to avoid them rather than seek them out. Could it be yet another of the merits of the ancients that even subjects of the most intense pathos were merely aesthetic play for them, since in our case truth to nature must be involved if a work of this kind is to be produced?'[157] Now, after our magnificent discoveries, we can give a positive answer to this very profound final question, since we have indeed been astonished to experience, precisely in musical tragedy, subjects of the most intense pathos as being no more than aesthetic play after all; this is why we may be allowed to believe that only now can the primal phenomenon of the tragic be described with some success. Anyone who can still speak only about the kinds of surrogate effect which derive from extra-aesthetic spheres, and who does not feel himself raised above the pathological-moral process, can now only despair of his own aesthetic nature; against which we would recommend, as a harmless substitute, the interpretation of Shakespeare after the manner of Gervinus and the assiduous search for 'poetic justice'.

Thus, along with the rebirth of tragedy, the *aesthetic listener* too is reborn, whose place in the theatre has been occupied up till now by a strange *quid pro quo*, with expectations that were part moral, part scholarly, namely the 'critic'. Hitherto everything in his sphere was artificial and covered with just a thin veneer of life. The performing artist no longer knew where to begin with this kind of listener and his critical demeanour, so that both he and the dramatist or operatic composer who inspired him searched restlessly for the last traces of life in this creature who was demanding, barren, and utterly incapable of enjoyment. Yet hitherto the

---

[156] Schiller's *Über den Grund des Vergnügens an tragischen Gegenständen* (*On the Reason for our Pleasure in Tragic Subjects*).

[157] *Letter to Schiller*, 19 December 1797.

public consisted of just such 'critics'; the student, the schoolboy, even the most harmless female creature, had all been prepared unknowingly by their education and by journals to perceive a work of art in the same way. Given such a public, the nobler natures among the artists aimed at stimulating moral-religious energies, and the invocation of the 'universal moral order' stepped in as a substitute for the mighty artistic magic which should really have delighted the true listener. Or the dramatist would present a grand, or at least exciting, tendency taken from current political or social events so vividly that the listener could forget his critical exhaustion and abandon himself to affects similar to those felt at times of patriotic or martial sentiment, or declaimed from the rostrum in parliament, or invoked when crime and vice are being denounced; this alienation from the true aims of art was bound to lead here and there to an outright cult of tendentiousness. But at this point something happened which has always happened wherever art has become artificial, namely the breathtakingly rapid degradation of those tendencies, so that, for example, the tendency to use the theatre as an institution of popular moral education, an idea taken seriously in Schiller's time,[158] is already numbered amongst the implausible relics of an outdated and abandoned culture. While the critic was seizing power in the theatre and concert hall, the journalist in schools, and the press in society, art degenerated to an object of entertainment of the lowest kind, and aesthetic criticism was used to bind together a vain, distracted, selfish, and furthermore meagre and unoriginal sociability, the meaning of which is supplied by Schopenhauer's parable of the hedgehogs;[159] in consequence, there has never been a time when art was chattered about so much and valued so little. But can one still share the company of anyone who is capable of conversing about Beethoven and Shakespeare? Let each answer this question according to his own feeling; at all events his answer will demonstrate what he understands by 'cultivation', always supposing that he even attempts to answer the question and has not already fallen silent from sheer surprise.

On the other hand, there are those whom nature has equipped with nobler and more delicate faculties, and who, even if they had gradually

---

[158] *Cf.* Schiller's *Die Schaubühne als eine moralische Anstalt betrachtet* (*On the Theatre, Regarded as a Moral Institution*).

[159] *Parerga et Paralipomena* § 396. A 'parable' about human sociability. Consider a group of hedgehogs on a cold day who try to keep a middle distance from each other: close enough to keep warm but not so close that they prick each other. This appropriate middle distance defines what counts as 'good manners' in that society. An individual, Schopenhauer concludes, who has too much 'inner warmth' should keep away from human society so as neither to offend nor be offended.

evolved into critical barbarians in the manner described above, could speak of a quite unexpected and wholly incomprehensible effect produced in them by, for example, a successful performance of *Lohengrin*; except that they lacked a hand to take hold of them, to warn and interpret, so that even the incomprehensibly different and utterly incomparable feeling which had shaken them to the core at the time remained something isolated and then was extinguished again, like some mysterious planet which had shone only briefly. At that time they had an intimation of what it is to be an aesthetic listener.

23

Anyone who wishes to examine just how closely he is related to the true aesthetic listener, or whether he belongs to the community of Socratic, critical human beings, should ask himself honestly what he feels when he receives the *miracle* presented on the stage: whether he feels an affront to his sense of history and his attention to strict psychological causality, whether he makes a benevolent concession to the miracle, as it were, admitting it as a phenomenon which was understandable in childhood but from which he is now alienated, or whether he suffers anything else at this moment. This will enable him to estimate the extent to which he is at all equipped to understand the *myth*, the contracted image of the world, which, as an abbreviation of appearances, cannot dispense with the miracle. It is probable, however, that almost everyone, on close examination, will feel himself to have been so corrupted by the critical-historical spirit of our education that he can only make himself believe in the former existence of myth by taking a scholarly approach and by means of mediating abstractions. Without myth, however, all cultures lose their healthy, creative, natural energy; only a horizon surrounded by myths encloses and unifies a cultural movement. Only by myth can all the energies of fantasy and Apolline dream be saved from aimless meandering. The images of myth must be the unnoticed but omnipresent, daemonic guardians under whose tutelage the young soul grows up and by whose signs the grown man interprets his life and his struggles; even the state knows of no more powerful unwritten laws than the mythical fundament which guarantees its connection with religion and its emergence from mythical representations.

Now place beside this type of mythical culture abstract man, without guidance from myth, abstract education, abstract morality, abstract law, the abstract state; consider the rule-less wandering of artistic fantasy, unbridled by an indigenous myth; think of a culture which has no secure and sacred place of origin and which is condemned to exhaust every possibility and to seek meagre nourishment from all other cultures; that is the present, the result of Socratism's determination to destroy myth. Now mythless man stands there, surrounded by every past there has ever been, eternally hungry, scraping and digging in a search for roots, even if he has to dig for them in the most distant antiquities. The enormous historical need of dissatisfied modern culture, the accumulation of countless other cultures, the consuming desire for knowledge – what does all this point to, if not to the loss of myth, the loss of a mythical home, a mythical, maternal womb? The reader should ask himself whether the feverish and uncanny agitation of this culture is anything other than the greedy grabbing and chasing after nourishment of the hungry – and who would care to give anything more to such a culture, since it cannot be satisfied by anything it devours, and since even the most nourishing, health-giving food, when touched by it, is usually transformed into 'history and criticism'?

One would be bound to despair of our German character, too, if it had already become so inextricably entangled in its culture, indeed entirely at one with it, as is horrifyingly evident in the case of civilized France; the very thing which was France's great advantage for a long time, and the cause of its vast superiority, namely the identity of people and culture, should now, as we contemplate the consequences, make us thank our good fortune that this questionable culture of ours still has nothing in common with the noble core of our national character. Instead, all our hopes reach out longingly towards the perception that beneath this restlessly agitated cultural life and senseless education there lies hidden a magnificent, inwardly healthy, ancient strength, which admittedly only stirs powerfully in momentous times and then returns to dreaming of some future awakening. The German Reformation grew up out of the depths of this abyss, and in its chorale there could be heard for the first time the future melody of German music. This chorale of Luther's sounded so profound, courageous, and soulful, so joyously good and tender, the first, enticing call of the Dionysiac, breaking forth from a tangled thicket at the approach of spring. It was answered by competing echoes from that consecrated yet exuberant procession of Dionysiac enthusiasts to whom we owe German music – and to which we shall owe the *rebirth of the German myth*!

I know that I must now lead the friend who is following these arguments sympathetically to a high place of lonely contemplation where he will have but a few companions, and I call out to encourage him that we must hold fast to our radiant leaders, the Greeks. So far we have borrowed from them two divine images to purify our aesthetic understanding, each of which governs a separate kingdom of art, while Greek tragedy has given us some sense of their mutual interaction and intensification. We saw the demise of Greek tragedy as resulting inevitably from a curious tearing-apart of these two primal artistic drives, a process which was consonant with the degeneration and transformation of the national character of the Greeks, prompting us to consider earnestly just how necessarily and closely intertwined are the foundations of art and nation, myth and morality, tragedy and state. The demise of tragedy was at the same time the demise of myth. Until that point the Greeks had been compelled to connect everything they experienced, immediately and involuntarily, to their myths, indeed they could only understand their experiences through this connection; thereby even the most immediate present was bound to appear to them straight away *sub specie aeterni* and, in a certain sense, as timeless. But, like art, the state also plunged into this current of timelessness in order to find respite there from the burden and greed of the moment. And a people – or, for that matter, a human being – only has value to the extent that it is able to put the stamp of the eternal on its experiences; for in doing so it sheds, one might say, its worldliness and reveals its unconscious, inner conviction that time is relative and that the true meaning of life is metaphysical. The opposite of this occurs when a people begins to understand itself historically and to demolish the metaphysical buttresses surrounding it; this is usually accompanied by a decided growth in worldliness and a break with the unconscious metaphysics of its previous existence, with all the ethical consequences this entails. Above all Greek art and, particularly, Greek tragedy delayed the destruction of myth; these things had to be destroyed at the same time as myth in order that the Greeks might live, detached from the soil of home, unbridled in the wilderness of thought, morals, and action. Even then that metaphysical drive still attempts to create for itself a kind of transfiguration, albeit in a much weaker form, in the Socratism of science; but at lower levels this same drive led only to a feverish search which gradually lost its way in a pandemonium of myths and superstitions garnered from everywhere and thrown into a disorderly heap; in the midst of all this the Hellene still sat with unstilled heart, until he learned how to mask this fever with Greek cheerfulness and Greek frivolity, as Graeculus, or to anaesthetize himself with some obscure oriental superstition or other.

It is quite obvious that, ever since the re-awakening of Alexandrian-Roman antiquity in the fifteenth century, we have been approaching this same condition after a long interlude which is hard to describe. On the heights we find the same excessive lust for knowledge, the same unsatisfied delight in discovery, the same enormous growth in worldliness, and alongside these things a homeless roaming-about, a greedy scramble to grab a place at the tables of others, frivolous deification of the present, or a dull, numbed turning away from it, all of this *sub specie saeculi* – of the 'here and now'; these same symptoms all suggest that at the heart of this culture there is the same lack: the destruction of myth. It hardly seems possible to transplant a foreign myth to a new place with lasting success without doing irreparable damage to the tree in the process; occasionally the tree is perhaps strong and healthy enough to reject the foreign element after a terrible struggle, but usually it becomes sickly and withers away or exhausts itself in sickly, rampant growth. We hold the pure and vigorous core of the German character in such esteem that we dare to expect that it will eventually reject those foreign elements which have been forcibly grafted on to it, and we consider it possible that the German spirit will take stock of itself once again. Some of us will perhaps tend to believe that this spirit must begin its struggle by rejecting the Latin influence, for which they might see some outward preparation and encouragement in the victorious courage and bloody glory of the recent war, but the inner necessity for such change must be sought in the zealous ambition always to be worthy of the great champions who have fought this fight before – of Luther and all our great artists and poets. But let no one believe that he can fight such fights without gods of the hearth, without a mythical home, without a 'bringing back' of all things German! And if the German should look around with faint heart for a leader to take him back to his long-lost home, whose paths and highways he hardly remembers, then let him but listen to the blissfully enticing call of the Dionysiac bird which is on the wing, hovering above his head, and which wants to show him the way.[160]

24

We had cause to draw attention to one of the peculiar artistic effects of the musical tragedy, namely an Apolline *deception*, by means of which we are to be saved from direct oneness with Dionysiac music, while our musical

[160] The forest-bird in Wagner's *Siegfried* leads Siegfried to the rock on which Brünnhilde is sleeping.

excitement can discharge itself in an Apolline realm and in response to an interposed, visible, middle world. At the same time we believe we have observed how this discharge causes the middle world of events on stage, indeed the drama generally, to become visible and comprehensible from within to a degree that is unattainable in all other forms of Apolline art; consequently we were obliged to recognize this moment when the Apolline soars upward, as it were, borne on the wings of music, as the supreme intensification of its energies, and thus to see in the brotherly bond between Apollo and Dionysos the pinnacle of both the Apolline and the Dionysiac artistic intentions.

Of course, the Apolline light-image, particularly when illuminated from within by music, did not achieve the peculiar effect produced by the weaker degrees of Apolline art; although imbued with greater soulfulness and clarity, the drama could not rival the ability of epic poetry or animated marble to compel the contemplating eye to take such calm delight in the world of *individuatio*. We looked at drama and penetrated with piercing gaze into the inner movements of its world of motives – and yet it seemed as if only a symbolic image were passing before our eyes, the deepest meaning of which we thought we could almost grasp, and which we wanted to pull aside, like a curtain, in order to gaze on the primal image behind it. Even the brightest clarity of the image was not enough for us, for this seemed to conceal something as much as it revealed it; and while its symbolic revelation seemed to invite us to tear the veil, to uncover the secrets in the background, its very illumination and complete visibility cast a spell on the eye, barring it from penetrating further.

Anyone who has not had this experience of being compelled to look and, at the same time, of being filled with a desire to go beyond looking, will have difficulty in imagining how clearly and definitely these two processes are felt to coexist when one is contemplating the tragic myth; on the other hand, the truly aesthetic spectator will confirm my observation that the co-existence of these two things is the most remarkable of the peculiar effects of tragedy. If one translates this phenomenon of the aesthetic spectator into an analogous process in the tragic artist, one will have understood the genesis of the *tragic myth*. This shares with the Apolline sphere of art the same utter delight in semblance and in looking at it, and at the same time it negates this delight and finds yet higher satisfaction in the destruction of the visible world of semblance. In the first instance, the content of the tragic myth is an epic event with its glorification of the fighting hero; yet from what source does that inherently mysterious feature of tragedy come (particularly when a people is full of the most youthful, vigorous life) – its preference for presenting ever anew and in countless forms the suffering in the hero's fate, the most painful, repeated overcoming of obstacles, the most agonizing conflicts of motives, in short, the illustration of Silenus' wisdom or, to put it in aesthetic terms, the ugly and disharmonious – if not from the perception of some higher delight in all these things?

For the fact that such tragic things really do happen in life would in no way explain the origins of a form of art, unless art did not simply imitate the reality of nature but rather supplied a metaphysical supplement to the reality of nature, and was set alongside the latter as a way of overcoming it. Inasmuch as it belongs to art at all, the tragic myth participates fully in the aim of all art, which is to effect a metaphysical transfiguration; but what does it transfigure when it presents the world of appearances in the image of the suffering hero? Certainly not the 'reality' of this world of appearances, for it says to us: 'Take a look! Take a close look! This is your life! This is the hour-hand on the clock of your existence!'

And we are supposed to believe that myth shows us this life in order thereby to transfigure it before our eyes? But if this is not the case, what gives rise to our aesthetic delight when we let even these images pass before our eyes? My question concerns aesthetic delight, but I am fully aware that many of these images can sometimes also generate moral pleasure, in the form of pity, say, or ethical triumph. Anyone seeking to derive the effect of the tragic from these moral sources alone, however, as was the normal practice in aesthetics for far too long, should not believe that this does anything to benefit art, since the first demand of art must be for purity in its own realm. In order to explain tragic myth, the very first requirement is to seek the kind of delight that is peculiar to it in the purely aesthetic sphere, without reaching across into the territory of pity, fear, or the morally sublime. How can things which are ugly and disharmonious, the content of tragic myth, induce aesthetic delight?

At this point we need to take a bold run-up and vault into a metaphysics of art, as I repeat my earlier sentence that only as an aesthetic phenomenon do existence and the world appear justified; which means that tragic myth in particular must convince us that even the ugly and disharmonious is an artistic game which the Will, in the eternal fullness of its delight, plays with itself. Yet this difficult, primal phenomenon of Dionysiac art can be grasped in a uniquely intelligible and direct way in the wonderful significance of *musical dissonance*; as indeed music generally is the only thing which, when set alongside the world, can illustrate what is meant by the justification of the world as an aesthetic phenomenon. The pleasure engendered by the tragic myth comes from the same homeland as our pleasurable sensation of dissonance in music. The Dionysiac, with the primal pleasure it perceives even in pain, is the common womb from which both music and the tragic myth are born.

Could it not be that, with the assistance of musical dissonance, we have eased significantly the difficult problem of the effect of tragedy? After all, we do now understand the meaning of our desire to look, and yet to long to go beyond looking when we are watching tragedy; when applied to our response to the artistic use of dissonance, this state of mind would have to be described in similar terms: we want to listen, but at the same time we long to go beyond listening. That striving towards infinity, that wing-beat of longing even as we feel supreme delight in a clearly perceived reality, these things indicate that in both these states of mind we are to recognize a Dionysiac phenomenon, one which reveals to us the playful construction and demolition of the world of individuality as an outpouring of primal pleasure and delight, a process quite similar to Heraclitus the Obscure's comparison of the force that shapes the world to a playing child who sets down stones here, there, and the next place, and who builds up piles of sand only to knock them down again.[161]

Thus, in order to judge the Dionysiac capacity of a people correctly, it is necessary for us to consider the evidence not simply of their music but also of their tragic myth. Given the intimate relationship between music and myth, one would expect that the atrophy of the one would be connected to the degeneration and depravation of the other, if indeed it is true that any weakening of myth generally expresses a waning of the capacity for the Dionysiac. One only needs to glance at the development of the German character to be left in no doubt on both counts: we saw that the nature of Socratic optimism, something which is as unartistic as it is parasitic on life, was revealed in equal measure both in opera and in the abstract character of our mythless existence, in an art which had sunk to the level of mere entertainment as much as in a life guided by concepts. We took some comfort, however, from certain signs that, despite all this, the German spirit has remained whole, in magnificent health, depth, and Dionysiac strength, resting and dreaming in an inaccessible abyss like a knight who has sunk

---

[161] This is fragment 52 in the standard numbering (that of the Diels–Kranz edition).

into slumber; now the Dionysiac song rises from this abyss to tell us that, at this very moment, this German knight still dreams his ancient Dionysiac myth in blissfully grave visions. Let no one believe that the German spirit has lost its mythical home for ever, if it can still understand so clearly the voices of the birds which tell of its homeland. One day it will find itself awake, with all the morning freshness that comes from a vast sleep; then it will slay dragons, destroy the treacherous dwarfs, and awaken Brünnhilde – and not even Wotan's spear itself will be able to bar its path![162]

My friends, you who believe in the music of Dionysos, you also know what tragedy means for us. In it we have the tragic myth, reborn from music – and in this you may hope for all things and forget that which is most painful! But for all of us the most painful thing is that long period of indignity when the German genius lived in the service of treacherous dwarfs, estranged from hearth and home. You understand what my words mean – just as you will also understand, finally, my hopes.

25

Music and tragic myth both express, in the same way, the Dionysiac capacity of a people, and they cannot be separated from one another. Both originate in an artistic realm which lies beyond the Apolline; both transfigure a region where dissonance and the terrible image of the world fade away in chords of delight; both play with the goad of disinclination, trusting to their immeasurably powerful arts of magic; both justify by their play the existence of even the 'worst of all worlds'. Here the Dionysiac shows itself, in comparison with the Apolline, to be the eternal and original power of art which summons the entire world of appearances into existence, in the midst of which a new, transfiguring semblance is needed to hold fast within life the animated world of individuation. If you could imagine dissonance assuming human form – and what else is man? – this dissonance would need, to be able to live, a magnificent illusion which would spread a veil of beauty over its own nature. This is the true artistic aim of Apollo, in whose name we gather together all those countless illusions of beautiful semblance which, at every moment, make existence at all worth living at every moment and thereby urge us on to experience the next.

At the same time, only as much of that foundation of all existence, that Dionysiac underground of the world, can be permitted to enter an

---

[162] *Cf.* Wagner's *Siegfried*.

individual's consciousness as can be overcome, in its turn, by the Apolline power of transfiguration, so that both of these artistic drives are required to unfold their energies in strict, reciprocal proportion, according to the law of eternal justice. Where the Dionysiac powers rise up with such unbounded vigour as we are seeing at present, Apollo, too, must already have descended amongst us, concealed in a cloud, and his most abundant effects of beauty will surely be seen by a generation which comes after us.

That there is a need for this effect is a feeling which each of us would grasp intuitively, if he were ever to feel himself translated, even just in dream, back into the life of an ancient Hellene. As he wandered beneath rows of high, Ionic columns, gazing upwards to a horizon cut off by pure and noble lines, seeing beside him reflections of his own, transfigured form in luminous marble, surrounded by human beings who walk solemnly or move delicately, with harmonious sounds and a rhythmical language of gestures – would such a person, with all this beauty streaming in on him from all sides, not be bound to call out, as he raised a hand to Apollo: 'Blessed people of Hellas! How great must Dionysos be amongst you, if the God of Delos considers such acts of magic are needed to heal your dithyrambic madness!' It is likely, however, that an aged Athenian would reply to a visitor in this mood, looking up at him with the sublime eye of Aeschylus: 'But say also this, curious stranger: how much did this people have to suffer in order that it might become so beautiful! But now follow me to the tragedy and sacrifice along with me in the temple of both deities!'

The Dionysiac World View

I

The Greeks, who simultaneously declare and conceal the mystery of their view of the world in their gods, established as the double source of their art two deities, Apollo and Dionysos. In the realm of art these names represent stylistic opposites which exist side by side and in almost perpetual conflict with one another, and which only once, at the moment when the Hellenic 'Will' blossomed, appeared fused together in the work of art that is Attic tragedy. For there are two states in which human beings attain to the feeling of delight in existence, namely in *dream* and in *intoxication*. Every human being is fully an artist when creating the worlds of dream, and the lovely semblance of dream is the father of all the arts of image-making, including, as we shall see, an important half of poetry. We dream with pleasure as we understand the *figure* directly; all forms speak to us; nothing is indifferent or unnecessary. Yet even while this dream-reality is most alive, we nevertheless retain a pervasive sense that it is *semblance*; only when this ceases to be the case do the pathological effects set in whereby dream no longer enlivens and the healing natural energy of its states ceases. Within that boundary, however, it is not just the pleasant and friendly images in us which we seek out with that complete sense of comprehension; things which are grave, sad, gloomy, and dark are contemplated with just as much pleasure, always provided that here too the veil of semblance is in fluttering movement and does not completely cover up the basic forms of the real. Thus, whereas in dream the individual human being plays with the real, the art of the image-maker (in the wider sense) is a *playing with dream*. As a block of marble the statue is something very real, but the reality of the statue *as a dream figure* is the living person of the god. As long as the statue hovers as an image of fantasy before the eyes of the artist, he is still playing with the real; when he translates this image into marble, he is playing with dream.

Now, in what sense could *Apollo* be made into a god *of art?* Only inasmuch as he is the god of dream-representations. He is the 'luminous one' through and through; at his deepest root he is a god of the sun and light who reveals himself in brilliance. 'Beauty' is his element, eternal youth his companion. But the lovely semblance of the world of dreams is his realm too; the higher truth, the perfection of these dream-states in contrast to the only partially intelligible reality of the daylight world, raise him to the status of a prophetic god, but equally certainly to that of an artistic god. The god of lovely semblance must be the god of true knowledge as well. But the image of Apollo must also include that delicate line which the dream image must not overstep if its effect is not to become pathological, in which case the semblance does not simply deceive but also cheats; it must include that measured limitation, that freedom from wilder impulses, that wise calm of the image-making god. His eye must be 'sun-like' and calm; even when it is angry and shows displeasure, the consecrated aura of lovely semblance surrounds it.

Dionysiac art, by contrast, is based on play with intoxication, with the state of ecstasy. There are two principal forces which bring naive, natural man to the self-oblivion of intense intoxication: the drive of spring and narcotic drink. Their effects are symbolized in the figure of Dionysos. In both states the *principium individuationis* is disrupted, subjectivity disappears entirely before the erupting force of the general element in human life, indeed of the general element in nature. Not only do the festivals of Dionysos forge a bond between human beings, they also reconcile human beings and nature. Freely the earth brings its gifts, the fiercest beasts approach one another in peace; the flower-decked chariot of Dionysos is drawn by panthers and tigers. All the caste-like divisions which necessity and arbitrary power have established between men disappear; the slave is a free-man, the aristocrat and the man of lowly birth unite in the same Bacchic choruses. In ever-swelling bands the gospel of 'universal harmony' rolls on from place to place; as they sing and dance, human beings express their membership of a higher, more ideal community; they have forgotten how to walk and speak. Yet it is more than this: they feel themselves to have been transformed by magic, and they really have become something different. Just as the animals now talk and the earth gives milk and honey, something supernatural now sounds out from within man. He feels himself to be a god; that which had previously lived only in his imagination he now feels in his own person. What does he now care for images and statues? Man is no longer an artist, he has become a work of art; man himself now moves with the same ecstasy and sublimity with which, in dream, he once saw the gods walk. The artistic force of nature, not that of an individual artist, reveals itself here; a nobler clay, a more precious marble is kneaded and chiselled here: the human being. This human being whom the artist Dionysos has formed stands in the same relation to nature as a statue does to the Apolline artist.

If intoxication is nature playing with human beings, the Dionysiac artist's creation is a playing with intoxication. If one has not experienced it for oneself this state can only be understood by analogy; it is rather like dreaming and at the same time being aware that the dream is a dream. Thus the attendant of Dionysos must be in a state of intoxication and at the same time he must lie in ambush, observing himself from behind. Dionysiac art manifests itself, not in the alternation of clear-mindedness and intoxication, but in their co-existence.

This co-existence marks the high point of Hellenic culture; originally, only Apollo is a Hellenic god of art, and it was his power which so moderated Dionysos when he came storming in from Asia that the most beautiful brotherly bond could come about. Nowhere can the incredible idealism of the Hellenic race be grasped more readily than here: a cult of nature which, amongst the peoples of Asia, had meant the crudest unleashing of the lower drives, a panhetaeric[1] animality which sundered all social ties for a certain period of time, was transformed amongst the Hellenes into a festival of universal redemption, a day of transfiguration. All the sublime drives of their character were revealed in this idealization of orgy.

Yet never was the Hellenic world in greater danger than during the stormy approach of the new god. Conversely, the wisdom of the Delphic god never showed itself in a more beautiful light. Reluctantly at first, he laid the finest of webs about his powerful antagonist so that the latter could hardly tell that he was wandering about in semi-captivity. When the Delphic priesthood perceived that the new cult had a profound effect on the processes of social regeneration, and promoted it in line with their political and religious intention; when the Apolline artist, with thoughtful moderation, learned from the revolutionary art of the rites of Bacchus; and, finally, when, in the ordering of the Delphic cult, sovereignty over the year

1 'Panhetaerism' is a state of universal sexual promiscuousness.

was shared between Apollo and Dionysos, both gods emerged victorious, as it were, from their contest: an act of reconciliation on the battlefield. Anyone who wants to see clearly just how powerfully the Apolline element held down the irrational, supernatural quality of the Dionysiac element, should consider that in the older period of music the *genos dithyrambikon* was also the *hesuchastikon*.[2] The more vigorously the Apolline spirit of art now flourished, the more freely did his brother-god Dionysos develop; in the same period as the first of them was attaining to the full, one might say immobile, vision of beauty, at the time of Phidias,[3] the other was interpreting the mysteries and terrors of the world in tragedy and giving voice in the music of tragedy to the innermost thought of nature: the weaving of the 'Will' in and above all appearances.

If music, too, is Apolline art, this applies, strictly speaking, only to rhythm, the *image-creating* energy of which was developed to represent Apolline states; the music of Apollo is architecture in sound, and, what is more, in the merely hinted-at sounds characteristic of the *cithara*. Cautiously it holds at a distance precisely that element which defines the character of Dionysiac music (and thus of music generally), the power of musical sound to shake us to the core and the quite incomparable world of harmony. The Greeks had the finest feeling for harmony, as their strict characterization of the *modes* obliges us to conclude, although the need for an *elaborated*, truly audible harmony was much weaker amongst them than it is in the modern world. In the sequence of harmonies, and even in their abbreviated form, so-called melody, the 'Will' reveals itself directly, without previously having embodied itself in a phenomenon. Every individual can, as it were, serve as a likeness, as an individual instance of a general rule; conversely, however, the Dionysiac artist presents the essence of everything that appears in a way that is immediately intelligible, for he has command over the chaos of the Will before it has assumed individual shape, and from it he can bring a new world into being at each creative moment, but *also the old world* with which we are already familiar as phenomenon. In this latter sense he is a tragic musician.

Nature expresses itself with its highest energy in Dionysiac intoxication, in the tumultuous, wild chase across all the scales of the soul under the influence of narcotic stimulants or when the drives of spring are unleashed; it binds individual creatures together again, and it makes them feel that

[2] 'The dithyrambic kind [of poetry] . . . is restful/calming'.
[3] Sculptor, active in Athens *c.* 460–430 BC.

they are one with each other, so that the *principium individuationis* appears, so to speak, to be a perpetual state of weakness of the Will. The more degenerate the Will is, the more everything fragments into individual elements; the more selfish and arbitrary the development of the individual, the weaker is the organism which it serves. This is why there erupts in those states what one might call a sentimental (*sentimentalisch*) tendency in the Will, a 'sigh of the creature' for what is lost; out of highest joy there comes a cry of horror, the yearning sounds of lament at some irredeemable loss. Abundant nature celebrates its saturnalian festivals and its rites of death at one and the same time. The affects of its priests are most wondrously mixed, pain awakens delight, rejoicing wrings sounds of agony from the breast. The god *ho lysios*[4] has transformed everything, redeemed and released everything from itself. The singing and the expressive gestures of a mass stimulated in this manner, and in whom nature acquired a voice and movement, was something new and unheard-of in the Homeric-Greek world; it struck the Greeks as something Oriental which they first had to tame with their enormous rhythmic and image-making energy, and which they did indeed tame, just as they tamed the Egyptian temple-style at the same time. It was the Apolline people who laid the chains of beauty on over-mighty instinct, who yoked and harnessed nature's most dangerous elements, her wildest beasts. The idealistic power of the Hellenic character is seen at its most admirable when one compares its spiritualization of the festival of Dionysos with what emerged from the same origin amongst other peoples. Similar festivals are very ancient and their existence is demonstrable everywhere, most notably in Babylon where they are known as the *sacaea*. Here, during five-day-long festivals, every political and social bond was torn apart; but the centre of the cult lay in the absence of all sexual discipline, in the destruction of all family life by unrestrained hetaerism. The very antithesis of this is to be found in the image of the Greek festivals of Dionysos, as drawn by Euripides in his *Bacchae*,[5] an image which radiates the same loveliness, the same transfiguring musical intoxication as Skopas and Praxiteles[6] embodied in their statues. A messenger describes how he had withdrawn with his herds to the very peaks of the mountains during the midday heat; this is the right moment and the right place to see the unseen; Pan is now asleep, the sky is now the unmoving background of a glory, the day now *blossoms*. On an alpine meadow the messenger notices three choruses of women lying in scattered

---

[4] Cult name of Dionysos: 'he who gives release'. [5] vv. 692ff. [6] Fourth-century sculptors.

groups on the ground and in decorous pose; many women stand leaning against pine trees; all slumber. Suddenly the mother of Pentheus breaks out in jubilation, sleep is banished, all leap to their feet, a model of noble comportment; the young girls and the women let their locks fall to their shoulders, the doe-skin is put in order if its ribbons and bows have become loosened during sleep. They gird themselves about with snakes which lick their cheeks confidingly, some women take young wolves and deer in their arms and suckle them. All adorn themselves with garlands of ivy; when the *thyrsus* is struck against a rock water bubbles forth, and when the earth is struck with a staff a fountain of wine rises up. Sweet honey drops from the twigs, and when someone touches the earth with just the tips of their fingers snow-white milk springs forth. This is an utterly enchanted world, nature celebrates its festival of reconciliation with mankind. The myth recounts that Apollo joined Dionysos together again after he had been dismembered. This is the image of Dionysos created anew by Apollo and saved from his Asiatic dismemberment.

2

The Greek gods, in the perfection with which they already appear in Homer, are certainly not to be understood as having been born of calamity and need; it is certain that such creatures were not conceived by a heart shaken by fear; it was not to turn away from life that a genial fantasy projected their images into the blue. What speaks out of them is a religion of life, not one of duty or asceticism or spirituality. All these figures breathe the triumph of existence, a luxuriant vitality accompanies their cult. They do not make demands; all that exists is deified in them, regardless of whether it is good or evil. Measured against the gravity, the sanctity and severity of other religions, Greek religion is in danger of being under-estimated as a playful fantasy – unless one includes in one's representation of it an often overlooked trait of most profound wisdom, so that the Epicurean life of the gods suddenly appears to be a creation of that incomparable artist-people, indeed almost as its supreme creation. It is the philosophy of the *people* which the captive wood-god unveils to mortals: 'The best is not to be, the second best to die soon.' It is this same philosophy which forms the background of that pantheon. The Greeks knew the terrors and horrors of existence, but they covered them with a veil in order to be able to live: a cross hidden behind roses, to adopt Goethe's symbol.[7] That luminous Olympian company only came to rule so that the sombre sway of *moira*, which determined Achilles' early death and the horrifying marriage of Oedipus, should be hidden by the radiant figures of Zeus, Apollo, Hermes, etc. If someone had removed the artistic *semblance* of that *middle world*, the Greeks would have had to follow the wisdom of the wood-god, the companion of *Dionysos*. It was out of this *necessity* that the artistic genius of this people created these gods. For this reason, theodicy was never a Hellenic problem; they took care never to attribute the existence of the world, and hence responsibility for the way it is, to the gods. The gods, too, are subject to *ananke*;[8] this is a confession of the rarest wisdom. To view its own existence in a transfiguring mirror and to protect itself with this mirror against the Medusa – this was the genial strategy adopted by the Hellenic 'Will' in order to be able to live at all. For how else could that infinitely sensitive people with such brilliant talent for *suffering* have been able to bear life, if *that self-same life* had not been revealed to them in their gods, suffused with a higher glory! The same drive which summons art into being in order to perfect existence, to augment it and seduce men into continuing to live, also led to the creation of the Olympian world, a world of beauty, calm and pleasure.

Under the influence of such a religion life is understood in the Homeric world as that which is inherently desirable: life beneath the sunshine of such gods. The *pain* of Homeric man related to departure from this existence, above all to imminent departure. If a lament is heard at all, it sings again of short-lived Achilles, of the rapid succession of the generations of mankind, of the passing of the heroic age. It is not unworthy of the greatest hero to long to go on living, even as a day-labourer. The 'Will' never expressed itself more plainly than in the Hellenes, whose very lament is still a song of praise. For this reason modern man feels a longing for that time when he believes he can hear nature and mankind in complete harmony; for this reason the Hellenic is the solution for all those who need to look about them for radiant models for the conscious affirmation of their will; for this reason, finally, the concept of 'Greek cheerfulness' has emerged at the hands of pleasure-seeking writers, so that, with an utter lack of respect, a slovenly life of self-indulgence dares to excuse, indeed honour itself, with the word 'Greek'.

In all of these representations, ranging from the noblest to the most

---

[7] Goethe, *Die Geheimnisse. Ein Fragment* (1789) (*The Secrets. A Fragment*); cf. *The Birth of Tragedy* § 3.
[8] Necessity.

common and misguided, the Greeks are understood in too crude and simple a manner and, to a certain extent, shaped in accordance with the image of unambiguous and, so to speak, one-sided nations (e.g. the Romans). After all, it ought to be suspected that some need for artistic semblance will be present even in the world view of a people which habitually turns everything it touches into gold. And we do indeed find, as we have indicated, an enormous illusion in this world view, the same illusion as nature regularly employs to achieve its goals. The true goal is obscured by a deluding image; we stretch out our hands towards the image, and nature achieves its goal by means of this deception. In the Greeks the Will wished to gaze on a vision of itself transfigured in a work of art; in order that the Will might glorify itself, its creatures too had to feel themselves to be worthy of glorification; they had to recognize a reflection of themselves in a higher sphere, elevated to the ideal, as it were, without feeling that the perfected world of their vision was an imperative or a reproach. This is the sphere of beauty in which they see their mirror images, the Olympians. With this weapon the Hellenic 'Will' fought against the talent for *suffering* and for the wisdom of suffering that is the correlative of artistic talent. Out of this struggle, and as a monument to its *victory*, tragedy was born.

The *intoxication* of *suffering* and the *beautiful dream* have different pantheons. By virtue of the omnipotence of its character, the former penetrates to the innermost thoughts of nature, it recognizes the fearful drive to exist and at the same time the perpetual death of everything that comes into existence; the gods which this intoxication creates are good and evil, they resemble chance, they startle us by the sudden emergence of a plan in their actions, they are pitiless and without delight in beauty. They are related to truth and approximate to concepts; rarely and only with difficulty do they become concentrated in figures. Looking at them turns the viewer to stone; how is one to live with them? Yet it is not intended that one should; that is their lesson.

If this pantheon cannot be concealed completely, like some punishable secret, the human gaze must be distracted from it by placing next to it the radiant, dream-born world of the Olympians; this is why the intensity of their colours, the sensuousness of their figures, grows ever greater, the more powerfully truth or its symbol makes its presence felt. Never was the struggle between truth and beauty greater than when the worship of Dionysos invaded Greece; here nature unveiled itself and spoke of its secret with terrifying clarity, in *musical sound*, in the face of which seductive semblance almost lost its power. The source of this spring lay in Asia, but in Greece it had to become a river because here, for the first time, it encountered something which Asia had never offered, the most easily aroused sensibility and capacity for suffering, paired with the lightest mental alertness and clear-sightedness. How did Apollo save the Hellenes? The new arrival was drawn over into the world of beautiful semblance, into the world of the Olympians; many of the honours due to the most highly respected deities, to Zeus and Apollo, for example, were sacrificed to him. Never was more fuss made of a stranger; on the other hand, he was a fearful stranger (*hostis* in every sense of the word),[9] powerful enough to demolish the house of his host. A great revolution began in all forms of life: Dionysos penetrated into every area, including that of art.

The gaze, the beautiful, semblance: these things delimit the territory of Apolline art. It is the transfigured world of the eye which is artistically creative in dream, when our eyes are closed. *Epic poetry*, too, seeks to put us into this state of dreaming; our open eyes are to see nothing while we feast our gaze on the inner images which the bard seeks to induce us to produce by means of his concepts. The effect of the plastic arts is achieved here in a roundabout way. By means of carved marble the sculptor leads us to the *living* god he has seen in a dreamlike vision, so that the figure that hovers as the real *telos*[10] before the mind's eye becomes clear to both the sculptor and the viewer, and the former causes the latter to recreate his vision retrospectively via the *mediating figure* of the statue. The epic poet, too, sees the same living figure and wants to let others see it, but he no longer places a statue between himself and others; rather he tells in a story how that figure demonstrates its life, in movement, tone, word and action; he forces us to trace a mass of effects back to their cause; he requires us to engage in artistic composition. He has reached his goal when we see clearly before us the figure or group or image, when he has conveyed to us that dreamlike state in which he himself first engendered those representations. The demand of epic poetry that we should create in a *plastic* manner proves just how absolute the difference is between lyric and epic poetry, since lyric poetry never has the formation of images as its goal. The only common ground they share is something material, the word, which is even more general than the concept; when we speak of poetry we do not thereby have a category which is coordinated with the plastic arts and music, but rather a conglutination of two totally different artistic means, one of which

---

[9] Means both 'stranger' and 'enemy'.   [10] Goal, objective, aim.

signifies a way towards plastic art, the other a way towards music, but both of which are only *ways* to the creation of art, not arts themselves. In this sense painting and sculpture are, of course, also only artistic means; true art is the ability to create images, regardless of whether this is a creation in advance or in retrospect. It is on this quality – a general human quality – that the *cultural significance* of art rests. The artist, as one who uses artistic means to induce others to produce art, cannot at the same time be the absorbing organ of artistic activity.

The image-worship of Apolline *culture*, whether expressed in temples, in statues, or in the Homeric epic, had its sublime goal in the ethical demand for *measure* which runs parallel to the aesthetic demand for beauty. It is only possible to demand measure where measure and limits are held to be *knowable*. In order to be able to respect one's limits, one has to know what they are; hence the Apolline warning *gnothi seauton*.[11] But the only mirror in which the Greek could see himself, i.e. know himself, was the world of the Olympian gods; in this, however, he recognized the very core of his own nature, veiled by the beautiful semblance of dream. The new pantheon (in contrast to the overthrown world of the Titans) moved beneath the yoke of the measure of beauty; the limit which the Greeks had to observe was that of beautiful semblance. The innermost purpose of a culture directed towards semblance and measure can only be the veiling of truth; the warning *meden agan*[12] was called out to the tireless researcher labouring in the service of *truth*, just as it was to the over-mighty Titan. In Prometheus the Greeks were shown an example of the pernicious effect which the excessive promotion of human knowledge has both on what is promoted and on those who promote it. Anyone who wishes to prove himself and his wisdom before this god must, like Hesiod, *metron echein sophies*.[13]

It was into a world built up and artificially protected like this that the ecstatic tones of the festival of Dionysos now penetrated, tones in which all the *excess* of pleasure and suffering and knowledge in nature revealed itself at one and the same time. Here everything which, up to this point, had been acknowledged as a limit, as a definition of measure, proved to be an artificially created illusion: 'excess' unveiled itself as the truth. For the first time there roared out the daemonically fascinating song of the people in all the

---

[11] 'Know thyself': one of the two mottoes carved over the entrance to Apollo's oracle at Delphi.

[12] 'Not too much': the other of the two mottoes at Apollo's oracle in Delphi; *cf.* also above, *The Birth of Tragedy* § 4.

[13] 'To keep the measure of wisdom', from an epigram by Pindar on Hesiod (Pindarus I in *Epigrammatica Graeca* ed. Page, Oxford, 1975). *Cf.* Hesiod *Works and Days* 694 and Theognis 876, 614, 694.

drunkenness of an over-mighty feeling; what, compared with this, did the psalm-singing artist of Apollo signify, with the timorously hinted-at sounds of his *cithara?* The element of music had hitherto been propagated in caste-like guilds and thereby kept at a distance from all profane involvement; it had also been forced by the might of the Apolline genius to remain on the level of simple architectonics; here, however, it cast off all constraints. Rhythm, which had previously moved only in the simplest zig-zag pattern, now loosened its limbs for a Bacchanalian dance; *musical sound* rang out, no longer in ghost-like attenuation, but in the thousand-fold intensification of the mass and in the accompaniment of deep-voiced wind instruments. And the most mysterious thing of all occurred: here harmony was born, which, in its movement, makes the will of nature immediately intelligible. Things in the ambit of Dionysos became audible which had lain artificially hidden in the Apolline world: all the shimmering light of the Olympian gods paled before the wisdom of Silenus. A kind of art which spoke the truth in its ecstatic intoxication chased away the Muses of the arts of semblance; in the self-oblivion of the Dionysiac states the individual with all his limits and measures sank out of sight; a twilight of the gods was imminent.

What did the Will, which, after all, is ultimately a *single* entity, intend when it granted admission to the Dionysiac elements, contrary to its own Apolline creation?

The goal was a new and higher *mechane*[14] of existence, the birth of the *tragic thought.*

3

The ecstasy of the Dionysiac state, which destroys the usual barriers and limits of existence, contains, for as long as it lasts, a *lethargic* element in which all personal experiences from the past are submerged. This gulf of oblivion thus separates the worlds of everyday life and Dionysiac experience from one another. But as soon as daily reality re-enters consciousness, it is experienced as such with a sense of *revulsion*; the fruit of these states is an *ascetic*, will-negating mood. In thought the Dionysiac, as a higher order of the world, is contrasted with a common and bad order of things; the Greek desired to flee absolutely from this world of guilt and fate. He hardly sought comfort in looking forward to a world beyond death; his yearning

[14] Means.

went higher, beyond the gods, he negated existence and its gay, treacherous mirage of gods. In the consciousness that follows his awakening from intoxication he sees the terrible and absurd aspects of human existence wherever he looks; it disgusts him. Now he understands the wisdom of the wood-god.

Here the most dangerous limit had been reached which the Hellenic Will, with its fundamental principle of Apolline optimism, could permit. Here it immediately began to put its natural healing powers into effect in order to turn around that mood of negation; its means are the tragic work of art and the tragic idea. It could certainly not be its intention to weaken or indeed suppress the Dionysiac state; it was not possible to force it directly into submission, and if it was possible, then it was far too dangerous; for if a barrier was erected to the discharge of the element, it would find an outlet elsewhere and penetrate all the arteries of life.

What mattered above all was to transform those repulsive thoughts about the terrible and absurd aspects of existence into representations with which it was possible to live; these representations are the *sublime*, whereby the terrible is tamed by artistic means, and the *comical*, whereby disgust at absurdity is discharged by artistic means. These two interwoven elements are unified in a work of art which imitates and plays with intoxication.

The sublime and the comical are a step beyond the world of beautiful semblance, for a contradiction is felt in both concepts. On the other hand, they are in no sense identical with truth; they cast a veil over truth, which, although it is more transparent than beauty, nevertheless remains a veil. Thus what we have in these two things is a *middle world* between beauty and truth; here it is possible to deny Dionysos and Apollo. This world reveals itself in a playing with intoxication, not in complete entrapment by it. In the actor we recognize Dionysiac man, the instinctive poet, singer, dancer, but Dionysiac man as he is *played*. He seeks to emulate his model in the emotional upheaval of the sublime or of laughter; he goes beyond beauty and yet he does not seek truth. He remains hovering half-way between these things. He does not strive after beautiful semblance, but he does strive after semblance, not after truth, but after *probability*. (Symbol, sign of truth.) Of course, the actor was originally not a single individual; the intention was to represent the Dionysiac mass, the people; hence the dithyrambic chorus. By playing with intoxication the aim was, as it were, to discharge the intoxication of the actor and of the surrounding chorus of spectators. From the standpoint of the Apolline world, the Hellenic character was to be *healed* and *expiated*: Apollo, the true god of healing and expiation, saved the Greeks from clear-sighted, prophetic ecstasy and revulsion at existence – through the work of art which embodied tragicomical thought.

The new art-world, that of the sublime and the comical, the art world of 'probability', rested on a different view of the gods and the world than the older art world of beautiful semblance. Recognition of the terrors and absurdities of existence, of the disturbed order and the unreasonable but planned nature of events, indeed of the most enormous *suffering* throughout the whole of nature, had removed the veil from the artificially hidden figures of *moira* and the Erinyes, of Medusa and the Gorgon: the Olympian gods were in the greatest danger. In the tragi-comical work of art they were saved in that they too were plunged into the sea of the sublime and the comical; they cease to be only 'beautiful'; they absorbed, as it were, the older order of gods and their sublimity. They now split into two groups, with only a few hovering in between, deities who were sometimes sublime and at other times comical. Above all, Dionysos himself was given this divided character.

Two types, Aeschylus and Sophocles, best demonstrate how it was now possible to live in the tragic period of Greek culture. The former sees the sublime chiefly in magnificent justice. He sees men and gods in the closest subjective commonality: the divine, the just, the moral, and the *happy* are seen by him as being intertwined in a unified whole. The individual, whether man or Titan, is weighed in the same scales. The gods are reconstructed in accordance with this norm of justice. Thus, for example, the popular belief in a daemon who blinds men and seduces them into guilt – a remnant of that ancient pantheon which was dethroned by the Olympians – was corrected by making this daemon a tool in the hands of Zeus who punishes justly. The equally ancient thought, one that was also alien to the Olympians, that a whole family could be cursed, is divested of all its acerbity, since, in Aeschylus' view, there is no *necessity* for the individual to commit a crime, so that everyone can escape unharmed.

Whereas Aeschylus sees the sublime in the sublimity of Olympian justice, Sophocles sees it – strangely enough – in the sublime obscurity of Olympian justice. He restores the standpoint of the people on every count. The undeservedness of a terrible fate seemed sublime to him, the truly insoluble puzzles of human existence were his tragic muse. Suffering undergoes transfiguration in his work; it is understood as something sanctifying. The distance between the human and the divine is immeasurable; thus propriety demands the most profound submission and resignation. The true virtue is *sophrosyne*,[15] actually a negative virtue. Heroic mankind is noblest mankind without that virtue; its fate demonstrates that infinite gulf. *Guilt* hardly exists, only a lack of insight into the worth of man and his limits.[16]

This standpoint is at any rate deeper and more inward than that of Aeschylus; it comes significantly closer to the Dionysiac truth and expresses it without using many symbols – and nevertheless we can recognize here the ethical principle of Apollo woven into the Dionysiac view of the world. In the case of Aeschylus revulsion is dissolved in a sublime shiver of awe at the wisdom of the world's order, an order which is only *difficult* to recognize because of human weakness. In the case of Sophocles the shiver of awe is even greater because that wisdom is quite unfathomable. It is the pure mood of piety which does not struggle, whereas the Aeschylean view always has the task of justifying divine justice and is therefore brought to a standstill by ever new problems. In Sophocles' view the 'limit of man', which Apollo commands us to search for, is knowable, but it is narrower and more confined than Apollo meant it to be in the pre-Dionysiac period. Man's lack of knowledge about himself is the Sophoclean problem; man's lack of knowledge about the gods is that of Aeschylus.

Piety, most wondrous mask of the drive for life! Devotion to a perfected *dream-world*, endowed with the highest moral *wisdom*. A flight from truth in order to be able to worship it from afar, shrouded in clouds! Reconciliation with reality *because* it is mysterious! A disinclination to solve puzzles because we are not gods! The pleasure found in falling in the dust, the peace of happiness in misfortune! The supreme self-abandonment of man in his supreme expression! Glorification and transfiguration of the devices of terror and atrocities of existence as the means to cure us *of* existence! Living joyfully in scorn of life! The triumph of the will in its negation!

On this level of knowledge there are only two paths, the path of the *saint* and the path of the *tragic artist*; what they both have in common is the ability to carry on living even in the clearest knowledge of the nullity of

---

15 Traditionally translated as 'temperance'.
16 The German is ambiguous at this point: *seine Grenzen* may mean 'his' (man's) or 'its' limits (the limits of the worth of man).

existence, without sensing a rupture in their view of the world. Disgust at the continuation of life is felt to be a means of creation, either saintly creation or artistic. The terrifying or the absurd is uplifting because it is only *seemingly* terrible or absurd. The Dionysiac power of enchantment proves itself even here, at the very summit of this view of the world: all that is real is dissolved in semblance, and behind it the unified *nature of the Will* manifests itself, completely cloaked in the glory of wisdom and truth and in blinding radiance. *Illusion, delusion is at its peak.*

It will now no longer strike anyone as incomprehensible that the same Will which, in its Apolline form, ordered the Hellenic world, also incorporated its other manifestation, the Dionysiac Will. The struggle between both manifestations of the Will had an extraordinary goal, the creation of a *higher possibility of existence* and the attainment thereby of a yet *higher glorification* (through art). The form of glorification was no longer the art of semblance but rather the tragic art, in which, however, the art of semblance has been entirely absorbed. Apollo and Dionysos have become united. Just as the Dionysiac element penetrated Apolline life, just as semblance established itself as a limit here too, so, equally, Dionysiac-tragic art is no longer 'truth'. In tragedy the singing and dancing is no longer the instinctive intoxication of nature; no longer is the Dionysiacally excited mass of the chorus the popular mass which has been seized unconsciously by the drive of spring. Truth is now *symbolized*, it makes use of semblance, it therefore can and must also use the arts of semblance. But here already there emerges a great difference from earlier art, in that all the artistic means of semblance are *jointly* called on to assist, so that the statue now walks about, the painted scenery moves about on the periacts,[17] the same rear wall presenting first a temple, then a palace to the spectator's gaze. Thus we observe at the same time a certain *indifference to semblance* which now has to give up its eternal claims, its sovereign demands. Semblance is certainly not enjoyed as *semblance* any longer, but rather as a *symbol*, as a sign of truth. Hence the – inherently objectionable – fusing of the artistic means. The clearest indication of this lack of regard for semblance is the *mask*.

Thus a Dionysiac demand is made of the spectator, namely that everything should be imagined as having been transformed by magic, that he should always see more than the symbol, that the entire, visible world of the stage and the orchestra is the *realm of wonder*. But where is the power

17 Machines for shifting the painted backdrops that formed the scenery in a Greek theatre.

which transports him into the mood where he believes in wonders, so that he sees everything as having been enchanted? Who defeats the power of semblance and reduces it to the status of a symbol?

This power is *music*.

4

The philosophy which follows the lead given by Schopenhauer teaches us that what we call 'feeling' is to be understood as a complex of unconscious representations and states of will. The exertions of the will express themselves, however, as pleasure or lack of pleasure, and in this they exhibit only quantitative differences. There are no kinds of pleasure, but there are degrees of pleasure and a vast number of accompanying representations. Pleasure is to be understood as the satisfaction of the *one* will, the lack of pleasure as its non-satisfaction.

In what way does feeling convey itself? In part, but only in small part, it can be transposed into thoughts, which is to say, into conscious representations; this of course only applies to the part made up of the accompanying representations. But in this area of feeling there always remains an indissoluble residue. It is only the dissoluble part that language, which is to say, concepts, has anything to do with; this defines the limit of '*poetry*' as far as its ability to express feeling is concerned.

The two other forms of emotional expression are thoroughly instinctive, without consciousness, and yet they operate in a purposive way; these are the language of *gesture* and *musical tone*. The language of gesture consists of generally intelligible symbols and is produced by reflex movements. These symbols are visible; the eye which sees them immediately conveys the state which gave rise to the gesture and which it symbolizes; mostly the spectator feels a sympathetic innervation of the same parts of the face or limbs which he sees in motion. Here 'symbol' means a quite imperfect, partial copy, an allusive sign which requires agreement for its comprehension; except that in this case the general understanding is *instinctive*, not one which has passed through a clear state of consciousness.

What, then, does *gesture* symbolize of that double-natured being that is feeling?

Clearly, the *accompanying representation*, for this alone can be alluded to, in an imperfect and partial manner, by the visible gesture; an image can only be symbolized by an image.

Painting and sculpture represent human beings through gesture; i.e. they imitate the symbol and have achieved their effects when we have understood the symbol. The pleasure of looking at them consists in understanding the symbol, despite the fact that it is semblance.

The actor, by contrast, represents the symbol in reality, not just in semblance; but his effect on us does not rest on our understanding the symbol; rather we immerse ourselves in the feeling which is being symbolized and do not merely take pleasure in semblance, in beautiful semblance.

Thus stage decoration does not excite the pleasure of semblance at all; rather we take it to be a symbol and understand the reality it alludes to. We find wax dolls and real flowers quite acceptable alongside others which are merely painted, which proves that what we bring to mind here is reality and not artistic semblance. Here the task is no longer beauty but probability.

But what is beauty? 'The rose is beautiful' means only that the rose has a good appearance (*Schein*), it has a pleasingly luminous quality. There is no intention to say anything about its essence. It pleases, it arouses pleasure, as appearance, i.e. the Will is satisfied by the way it appears, pleasure in existence is promoted thereby. The rose is, in its appearance, a faithful copy of its Will, which is identical with this form; in its appearance it corresponds to the purpose intended for its species. The more it does so, the more beautiful it is; if its character corresponds to the purpose intended, the rose is 'good'.

'A beautiful painting' simply means: our idea of a painting is fulfilled here; but when we call a painting 'good' we define our idea of a painting as one which corresponds to the *essence* of a painting. Mostly, however, what is meant by 'a beautiful painting' is a painting which represents something beautiful; this is how laymen judge paintings. They enjoy the beauty of the subject; *this* is how we are meant to enjoy the plastic arts in drama, except that it cannot be the task here to represent only beautiful things; it is enough for things to appear *true*. The object represented is meant to be received in as lively and sensuous a manner as possible; it is meant to have the effect of truth; the entirely *opposite* demand is made by every work of beautiful semblance.

But if gesture symbolizes the representations which accompany feeling, by what symbol are the stirrings of the *Will* itself *conveyed* to us? Which is the instinctive mediation here?

Mediation by *musical sound*. To be more precise, what is symbolized by musical sound is the various modes of pleasure and displeasure – without any accompanying representation.

Everything we can say to characterize the various feelings of displeasure are images of the representations which have become clear through the symbolism of gesture, as when we speak, for example, about pain as something which 'beats, aches, twitches, stabs, cuts, bites, or tickles'. These seem to express certain 'frequencies' of the Will – in short, to use the language of musical sound, they express *rhythm*. In the *dynamics* of musical sound we recognize the degree of the intensifications of the Will, the varying quantity of pleasure and displeasure. But its true essence conceals itself, without allowing itself to be expressed symbolically, in *harmony*. The Will and its symbol – harmony – are both, ultimately, *pure logic*! Whereas rhythm and dynamics are still to a certain extent the external aspect of the Will as it reveals itself in symbols, whereas they still almost have something of the type 'phenomenon' about them, harmony is the symbol of the pure essence of the Will. Accordingly, the individual phenomenon can still be characterized *as* a phenomenon in rhythm and dynamics; *approached from this angle, music can be developed into an art of semblance*. The indissoluble residue, harmony, speaks of the Will outside and within all phenomenal forms; thus it is a *symbol*, not just of feeling but of the *world*. In *its* sphere the concept is quite powerless.

We now understand the significance of the language of gesture and musical sound for the *Dionysiac work of art*. In the primitive, popular dithyramb of Spring man wants to express himself not as an individual but as the *human species*. The fact that he has ceased to be an individual human being is expressed by the symbolism of the eyes, the language of gesture, for in his gestures he speaks as a *satyr*, as a creature of nature amongst other creatures of nature, and, what is more, he does so in the intensified language of gesture, in the *gestures of dance*. By means of musical sound, however, he expresses the innermost thoughts of nature; it is not just the genius of the species (which is expressed by *gesture*), rather it is the genius of existence itself, the Will, which makes itself understood directly in this way. When he uses gesture man remains within the limits of the species, which is to say, within the limits of the phenomenal world; when he produces musical sound, however, he dissolves the phenomenal world, as it were, into its original unity; the world of maya disappears before the magic of music.

But when does natural man attain to the symbolism of musical sound? When does the language of gesture no longer suffice? When does sound become music? Above all, in the supreme states of pleasure and displeasure experienced by the will, as a will which rejoices or a will which is frightened to death, in short *in the intoxication of feeling*: in the *shout*. How much more powerful and immediate is a shout, compared with something seen! But the gentler stirrings of the will, too, have their symbols in sound; in general, there is a sound to parallel every gesture; but its intensification to pure musical sound can only be achieved through the intoxication of feeling.

The most intimate and frequent fusion of a kind of gestural language with sound is called *language*. In the tone and cadence of a word, by the strength and rhythm of its sound, the essence of a thing is symbolized, by the gesture of the mouth the accompanying representation is shown, the image, the appearance of its essence. Symbols can and must be many things; but they grow instinctively and with great and wise conformity to a law. A symbol that is remembered is a *concept*; since the sound fades away entirely when preserved in memory, only the symbol of the accompanying representation is present in the concept. One 'understands' things which one can designate and differentiate.

When emotion is intensified the essence of the word reveals itself more clearly and more sensuously in the symbol of sound; which is why it resounds more. The *Sprechgesang* is, as it were, a return to nature; the symbol which gets blunted in use regains its original strength once more.

In a sequence of words, i.e. by a chain of symbols, something new and greater is to be represented; rhythm, dynamics and harmony again become necessary on this level of expression. This higher sphere now governs the more limited sphere of the individual word; it becomes necessary to select words, to put them in a new order; poetry begins. The spoken melody of a sentence is not just the sequence of the sounds of the words; for a word has only a quite relative sound, because its character, the content presented by the symbol, varies according to its position. In other words: the individual symbol of the word is constantly being re-defined by the higher unity of the sentence and the character this symbolizes. A chain of concepts is a thought; in other words, this is the higher unity of the accompanying representations. The essence of the thing is inaccessible to thought; the fact that it has an effect on us as a motive, as a stimulant of the will, can be explained by the fact that the thought has already become a remembered symbol for a manifestation of the will, for a movement and a phenomenon of the will in one. But when it is spoken, i.e. with the symbolism of sound, its effect is incomparably more powerful and direct. When it is sung, when melody is the intelligible symbol of its will, it reaches the summit of its effect; if this is not the case, it is the sequence of sounds which affects us, and the sequence of words, the thought, remains something distant and indifferent.

Now, depending on whether the effect of a word is mainly intended to be the symbol of an accompanying representation or the symbol of the original movement of the will, depending, in other words, on whether images or feelings are to be symbolized, two separate paths open up for poetry: the epic and the lyric. The former leads to the plastic arts, the latter to music. Pleasure in the phenomenal world governs epic poetry; the will reveals itself in lyric poetry. The former sets itself free of music, the latter remains bound up with it.

In the Dionysiac dithyramb the Dionysiac enthusiast is stimulated to the utmost intensity of all his symbolic powers; something never felt before demands to be expressed: the annihilation of *individuatio*, one-ness in the genius of the species, indeed of nature. Now the essence of nature is to be expressed; a new world of symbols is needed; the accompanying representations acquire a symbol in the images of an intensified human being; they are represented with supreme physical energy by the whole symbolism of the body, in the gesture of dance. But the world of the Will, too, demands to be expressed symbolically in an unheard-of manner, the powers of harmony, dynamics, and rhythm suddenly grow tempestuously. Shared between both worlds, poetry, too, attains to a new sphere where there is, at one and the same time, sensuousness of imagery, as in epic poetry, and the emotional intoxication of sound, as in lyric. To grasp this complete unleashing of all symbolic energies, the same intensification of the essence which created them is needed; the servant of Dionysos can be understood only by those who are like him. For that reason this whole new world of art, in all its utterly strange, seductive wonder, advances through the Apolline culture of the Hellenes amidst terrible *struggles*.

(Written in 1870; unpublished in Nietzsche's lifetime.)

On Truth and Lying in a Non–Moral Sense

I

In some remote corner of the universe, flickering in the light of the countless solar systems into which it had been poured, there was once a planet
on which clever animals invented cognition. It was the most arrogant and
most mendacious minute in the 'history of the world'; but a minute was all
it was. After nature had drawn just a few more breaths the planet froze and
the clever animals had to die. Someone could invent a fable like this and yet
they would still not have given a satisfactory illustration of just how piti-
ful, how insubstantial and transitory, how purposeless and arbitrary the
human intellect looks within nature; there were eternities during which
it did not exist; and when it has disappeared again, nothing will have happened. For this intellect has no further mission that might extend beyond
the bounds of human life. Rather, the intellect is human, and only its own
possessor and progenitor regards it with such pathos, as if it housed the axis
around which the entire world revolved. But if we could communicate with
a midge we would hear that it too floats through the air with the very same
pathos, feeling that it too contains within itself the flying centre of this
world. There is nothing in nature so despicable and mean that would not
immediately swell up like a balloon from just one little puff of that force
of cognition; and just as every bearer of burdens wants to be admired, so
the proudest man of all, the philosopher, wants to see, on all sides, the
eyes of the universe trained, as through telescopes, on his thoughts and
deeds.

It is odd that the intellect can produce this effect, since it is nothing
other than an aid supplied to the most unfortunate, most delicate and most
transient of beings so as to detain them for a minute within existence;
otherwise, without this supplement, they would have every reason to flee

existence as quickly as did Lessing's infant son.[1] The arrogance inherent in cognition and feeling casts a blinding fog over the eyes and senses of human beings, and because it contains within itself the most flattering evaluation of cognition it deceives them about the value of existence. Its most general effect is deception – but each of its separate effects also has something of the same character.

As a means for the preservation of the individual, the intellect shows its greatest strengths in dissimulation, since this is the means to preserve those weaker, less robust individuals who, by nature, are denied horns or the sharp fangs of a beast of prey with which to wage the struggle for existence. This art of dissimulation reaches its peak in humankind, where deception, flattery, lying and cheating, speaking behind the backs of others, keeping up appearances,[2] living in borrowed finery, wearing masks, the drapery of convention, play-acting for the benefit of others and oneself – in short, the constant fluttering of human beings around the one flame of vanity is so much the rule and the law that there is virtually nothing which defies understanding so much as the fact that an honest and pure drive towards truth should ever have emerged in them. They are deeply immersed in illusions and dream-images; their eyes merely glide across the surface of things and see 'forms'; nowhere does their perception lead into truth; instead it is content to receive stimuli and, as it were, to play with its fingers on the back of things. What is more, human beings allow themselves to be lied to in dreams every night of their lives, without their moral sense ever seeking to prevent this happening, whereas it is said that some people have even eliminated snoring by will-power. What do human beings really know about themselves? Are they even capable of perceiving themselves in their entirety just once, stretched out as in an illuminated glass case? Does nature not remain silent about almost everything, even about our bodies, banishing and enclosing us within a proud, illusory consciousness, far away from the twists and turns of the bowels, the rapid flow of the blood stream and the complicated tremblings of the nerve-fibres? Nature has thrown away the key, and woe betide fateful curiosity should it ever succeed in peering through a crack in the chamber of consciousness, out and down

---

[1] Lessing's first and only son died immediately after birth, followed soon after by his mother. This drew from Lessing the comment: 'Was it good sense that they had to pull him into the world with iron tongs, or that he noticed the filth so quickly? Was it not good sense that he took the first opportunity to leave it again?' (Letter to Eschenburg, 10 January 1778).

[2] The verb Nietzsche uses is *repräsentieren*. This means keeping up a show in public, representing one's family, country, or social group before the eyes of the world.

into the depths, and thus gain an intimation of the fact that humanity, in the indifference of its ignorance, rests on the pitiless, the greedy, the insatiable, the murderous – clinging in dreams, as it were, to the back of a tiger. Given this constellation, where on earth can the drive to truth possibly have come from?

Insofar as the individual wishes to preserve himself in relation to other individuals, in the state of nature he mostly used his intellect for concealment and dissimulation; however, because necessity and boredom also lead men to want to live in societies and herds, they need a peace treaty, and so they endeavour to eliminate from their world at least the crudest forms of the *bellum omnium contra omnes*.[3] In the wake of this peace treaty, however, comes something which looks like the first step towards the acquisition of that mysterious drive for truth. For that which is to count as 'truth' from this point onwards now becomes fixed, i.e. a way of designating things is invented which has the same validity and force everywhere, and the legislation of language also produces the first laws of truth, for the contrast between truth and lying comes into existence here for the first time: the liar uses the valid tokens of designation – words – to make the unreal appear to be real; he says, for example, 'I am rich', whereas the correct designation for this condition would be, precisely, 'poor'. He misuses the established conventions by arbitrarily switching or even inverting the names for things. If he does this in a manner that is selfish and otherwise harmful, society will no longer trust him and therefore exclude him from its ranks. Human beings do not so much flee from being tricked as from being harmed by being tricked. Even on this level they do not hate deception but rather the damaging, inimical consequences of certain species of deception. Truth, too, is only desired by human beings in a similarly limited sense. They desire the pleasant, life-preserving consequences of truth; they are indifferent to pure knowledge if it has no consequences, but they are actually hostile towards truths which may be harmful and destructive. And, besides, what is the status of those conventions of language? Are they perhaps products of knowledge, of the sense of truth? Is there a perfect match between things and their designations? Is language the full and adequate expression of all realities?

Only through forgetfulness could human beings ever entertain the illusion that they possess truth to the degree described above. If they will not

---

[3] 'war of all against all': phrase associated with Thomas Hobbes' description of the state of nature before the institution of political authority (*cf.* Hobbes, *De cive* I.12 and *Leviathan*, chapter XIII).

content themselves with truth in the form of tautology, i.e. with empty husks, they will for ever exchange illusions for truth. What is a word? The copy of a nervous stimulation in sounds. To infer from the fact of the nervous stimulation that there exists a cause outside us is already the result of applying the principle of sufficient reason wrongly. If truth alone had been decisive in the genesis of language, if the viewpoint of certainty had been decisive in creating designations, how could we possibly be permitted to say, 'The stone is hard', as if 'hard' were something known to us in some other way, and not merely as an entirely subjective stimulus? We divide things up by gender, describing a tree as masculine and a plant as feminine[4] – how arbitrary these translations are! How far they have flown beyond the canon of certainty! We speak of a snake; the designation captures only its twisting movements and thus could equally well apply to a worm. How arbitrarily these borders are drawn, how one-sided the preference for this or that property of a thing! When different languages are set alongside one another it becomes clear that, where words are concerned, what matters is never truth, never the full and adequate expression;[5] otherwise there would not be so many languages. The 'thing-in-itself' (which would be, precisely, pure truth, truth without consequences) is impossible for even the creator of language to grasp, and indeed this is not at all desirable. He designates only the relations of things to human beings, and in order to express them he avails himself of the boldest metaphors. The stimulation of a nerve is first translated into an image: first metaphor! The image is then imitated by a sound: second metaphor! And each time there is a complete leap from one sphere into the heart of another, new sphere. One can conceive of a profoundly deaf human being who has never experienced sound or music; just as such a person will gaze in astonishment at the Chladnian sound-figures in sand,[6] find their cause in the vibration of a string, and swear that he must now know what men call sound – this is precisely what happens to all of us with language. We believe that when we speak of trees, colours, snow, and flowers, we have knowledge of the things themselves, and yet we possess only metaphors of things which in no way correspond to the original entities. Just as the musical sound

---

[4] 'Tree' is masculine in German (*der Baum*) and 'plant' (*die Pflanze*) is feminine.

[5] Nietzsche uses the term *adäquat* which indicates that the meaning of something is fully conveyed by a word or expression; English 'adequate' alone does not convey this sense completely.

[6] The vibration of a string can create figures in the sand (in an appropriately constructed sand-box) which give a visual representation of that which the human ear perceives as a tone. The term comes from the name of the physicist Ernst Chladni, whose experiments demonstrated the effect.

appears as a figure in the sand, so the mysterious 'X' of the thing-in-itself appears first as a nervous stimulus, then as an image, and finally as an articulated sound. At all events, things do not proceed logically when language comes into being, and the entire material in and with which the man of truth, the researcher, the philosopher, works and builds, stems, if not from cloud-cuckoo land, then certainly not from the essence of things.

Let us consider in particular how concepts are formed; each word immediately becomes a concept, not by virtue of the fact that it is intended to serve as a memory (say) of the unique, utterly individualized, primary experience to which it owes its existence, but because at the same time it must fit countless other, more or less similar cases, i.e. cases which, strictly speaking, are never equivalent, and thus nothing other than non-equivalent cases. Every concept comes into being by making equivalent that which is non-equivalent. Just as it is certain that no leaf is ever exactly the same as any other leaf, it is equally certain that the concept 'leaf' is formed by dropping these individual differences arbitrarily, by forgetting those features which differentiate one thing from another, so that the concept then gives rise to the notion that something other than leaves exists in nature, something which would be 'leaf', a primal form, say, from which all leaves were woven, drawn, delineated, dyed, curled, painted – but by a clumsy pair of hands, so that no single example turned out to be a faithful, correct, and reliable copy of the primal form. We call a man honest; we ask, 'Why did he act so honestly today?' Our answer is usually: 'Because of his honesty.' Honesty! – yet again, this means that the leaf is the cause of the leaves. We have no knowledge of an essential quality which might be called honesty, but we do know of numerous individualized and hence non-equivalent actions which we equate with each other by omitting what is unlike, and which we now designate as honest actions; finally we formulate from them a *qualitas occulta*[7] with the name 'honesty'.

Like form, a concept is produced by overlooking what is individual and real, whereas nature knows neither forms nor concepts and hence no species, but only an 'X' which is inaccessible to us and indefinable by us. For the opposition we make between individual and species is also anthropomorphic and does not stem from the essence of things, although we equally do not dare to say that it does *not* correspond to the essence of things, since that would be a dogmatic assertion and, as such, just as incapable of being proved as its opposite.

---

[7] Hidden property.

What, then, is truth? A mobile army of metaphors, metonymies, anthropomorphisms, in short a sum of human relations which have been subjected to poetic and rhetorical intensification, translation, and decoration, and which, after they have been in use for a long time, strike a people as firmly established, canonical, and binding; truths are illusions of which we have forgotten that they are illusions, metaphors which have become worn by frequent use and have lost all sensuous vigour, coins which, having lost their stamp, are now regarded as metal and no longer as coins. Yet we still do not know where the drive to truth comes from, for so far we have only heard about the obligation to be truthful which society imposes in order to exist, i.e. the obligation to use the customary metaphors, or, to put it in moral terms, the obligation to lie in accordance with firmly established convention, to lie *en masse* and in a style that is binding for all. Now, it is true that human beings forget that this is how things are; thus they lie unconsciously in the way we have described, and in accordance with centuries-old habits – and precisely *because of this unconsciousness*, precisely because of this forgetting, they arrive at the feeling of truth. The feeling that one is obliged to describe one thing as red, another as cold, and a third as dumb, prompts a moral impulse which pertains to truth; from its opposite, the liar whom no one trusts and all exclude, human beings demonstrate to themselves just how honourable, confidence-inspiring and useful truth is. As creatures of *reason*, human beings now make their actions subject to the rule of abstractions; they no longer tolerate being swept away by sudden impressions and sensuous perceptions; they now generalize all these impressions first, turning them into cooler, less colourful concepts in order to harness the vehicle of their lives and actions to them. Everything which distinguishes human beings from animals depends on this ability to sublimate sensuous metaphors into a schema, in other words, to dissolve an image into a concept. This is because something becomes possible in the realm of these schemata which could never be achieved in the realm of those sensuous first impressions, namely the construction of a pyramidal order based on castes and degrees, the creation of a new world of laws, privileges, subordinations, definitions of borders, which now confronts the other, sensuously perceived world as something firmer, more general, more familiar, more human, and hence as something regulatory and imperative. Whereas every metaphor standing for a sensuous perception is individual and unique and is therefore always able to escape classification, the great edifice of concepts exhibits the rigid regularity of a

Roman *columbarium*,[8] while logic breathes out that air of severity and coolness which is peculiar to mathematics. Anyone who has been touched by that cool breath will scarcely believe that concepts too, which are as bony and eight-cornered as a dice and just as capable of being shifted around, are only the left-over *residue of a metaphor*, and that the illusion produced by the artistic translation of a nervous stimulus into images is, if not the mother, then at least the grandmother of each and every concept. Within this conceptual game of dice, however, 'truth' means using each die in accordance with its designation, counting its spots precisely, forming correct classifications, and never offending against the order of castes nor against the sequence of classes of rank. Just as the Romans and the Etruscans divided up the sky with rigid mathematical lines and confined a god in a space which they had thus delimited as in a *templum*, all peoples have just such a mathematically divided firmament of concepts above them, and they understand the demand of truth to mean that the god of every concept is to be sought only in *his* sphere. Here one can certainly admire humanity as a mighty architectural genius who succeeds in erecting the infinitely complicated cathedral of concepts on moving foundations, or even, one might say, on flowing water; admittedly, in order to rest on such foundations, it has to be like a thing constructed from cobwebs, so delicate that it can be carried off on the waves and yet so firm as not to be blown apart by the wind. By these standards the human being is an architectural genius who is far superior to the bee; the latter builds with wax which she gathers from nature, whereas the human being builds with the far more delicate material of concepts which he must first manufacture from himself. In this he is to be much admired – but just not for his impulse to truth, to the pure cognition of things. If someone hides something behind a bush, looks for it in the same place and then finds it there, his seeking and finding is nothing much to boast about; but this is exactly how things are as far as the seeking and finding of 'truth' within the territory of reason is concerned. If I create the definition of a mammal and then, having inspected a camel, declare, 'Behold, a mammal', then a truth has certainly been brought to light, but it is of limited value, by which I mean that it is anthropomorphic through and through and contains not a single point which could be said to be 'true in itself', really and in a generally valid sense, regardless of mankind. Anyone who researches for truths of that

[8] Originally a dovecot, then a catacomb with niches at regular intervals for urns containing the ashes of the dead.

kind is basically only seeking the metamorphosis of the world in human beings; he strives for an understanding of the world as something which is similar in kind to humanity, and what he gains by his efforts is at best a feeling of assimilation. Rather as the astrologer studies the stars in the service of human beings and in relation to humanity's happiness and suffering, this type of researcher regards the whole world as linked to humankind, as the infinitely refracted echo of an original sound, that of humanity, and as the multiple copy of a single, original image, that of humanity. His procedure is to measure all things against man, and in doing so he takes as his point of departure the erroneous belief that he has these things directly before him, as pure objects. Thus, forgetting that the original metaphors of perception were indeed metaphors, he takes them for the things themselves.

Only by forgetting this primitive world of metaphor, only by virtue of the fact that a mass of images, which originally flowed in a hot, liquid stream from the primal power of the human imagination, has become hard and rigid, only because of the invincible faith that *this* sun, *this* window, this table is a truth in itself – in short only because man forgets himself as a subject, and indeed as *an artistically creative* subject, does he live with some degree of peace, security, and consistency; if he could escape for just a moment from the prison walls of this faith, it would mean the end of his 'consciousness of self'.[9] He even has to make an effort to admit to himself that insects or birds perceive a quite different world from that of human beings, and that the question as to which of these two perceptions of the world is the more correct is quite meaningless, since this would require them to be measured by the criterion of the *correct perception*, i.e. by a *non-existent* criterion. But generally it seems to me that the correct perception – which would mean the full and adequate expression of an object in the subject – is something contradictory and impossible; for between two absolutely different spheres, such as subject and object are, there is no causality, no correctness, no expression, but at most an *aesthetic* way of relating, by which I mean an allusive transference, a stammering translation into a quite different language. For which purpose a middle sphere and mediating force is certainly required which can freely invent and freely create poetry. The word appearance (*Erscheinung*) contains many seductions, and for this reason I avoid using it as far as possible; for it is not true that the essence of things appears in the empirical world. A painter who has no hands and who wished to express in song the image hovering before him

---

[9] The word Nietzsche uses here – *Selbstbewußtsein* – could also mean 'self-confidence'.

will still reveal more through this substitution of one sphere for another than the empirical world betrays of the essence of things. Even the relation of a nervous stimulus to the image produced thereby is inherently not a necessary relationship; but when that same image has been produced millions of times and has been passed down through many generations of humanity, indeed eventually appears in the whole of humanity as a consequence of the same occasion, it finally acquires the same significance for all human beings, as if it were the only necessary image and as if that relation of the original nervous stimulus to the image produced were a relation of strict causality – in exactly the same way as a dream, if repeated eternally, would be felt and judged entirely as reality. But the fact that a metaphor becomes hard and rigid is absolutely no guarantee of the necessity and exclusive justification of that metaphor.

Anyone who is at home in such considerations will certainly have felt a deep mistrust of this kind of idealism when he has once become clearly convinced of the eternal consistency, ubiquitousness and infallibility of the laws of nature; he will then conclude that everything, as far as we can penetrate, whether to the heights of the telescopic world or the depths of the microscopic world, is so sure, so elaborated, so endless, so much in conformity to laws, and so free of lacunae, that science will be able to mine these shafts successfully for ever, and that everything found there will be in agreement and without self-contradiction. How little all of this resembles a product of the imagination, for if it were such a thing, the illusion and the unreality would be bound to be detectable somewhere. The first thing to be said against this view is this: if each of us still had a different kind of sensuous perception, if we ourselves could only perceive things as, variously, a bird, a worm, or a plant does, or if one of us were to see a stimulus as red, a second person were to see the same stimulus as blue, while a third were even to hear it as a sound, nobody would ever speak of nature as something conforming to laws; rather they would take it to be nothing other than a highly subjective formation. Consequently, what is a law of nature for us at all? It is not known to us in itself but only in its effects, i.e. in its relations to other laws of nature which are in turn known to us only as relations. Thus, all these relations refer only to one another, and they are utterly incomprehensible to us in their essential nature; the only things we really know about them are things which we bring to bear on them: time and space, in other words, relations of succession and number. But everything which is wonderful and which elicits our astonishment at precisely these laws of nature, everything which demands explanation of us and could seduce us into being suspicious of idealism, is attributable precisely and exclusively to the rigour and universal validity of the representations of time and space. But these we produce within ourselves and from ourselves with the same necessity as a spider spins; if we are forced to comprehend all things under these forms alone, then it is no longer wonderful that what we comprehend in all these things is actually nothing other than these very forms; for all of them must exhibit the laws of number, and number is precisely that which is most astonishing about things. All the conformity to laws which we find so imposing in the orbits of the stars and chemical processes is basically identical with those qualities which we ourselves bring to bear on things, so that what we find imposing is our own activity. Of course the consequence of this is that the artistic production of metaphor, with which every sensation begins within us, already presupposes those forms, and is thus executed in them; only from the stability of these original forms can one explain how it is possible for an edifice of concepts to be constituted in its turn from the metaphors themselves. For this conceptual edifice is an imitation of the relations of time, space, and number on the foundations of metaphor.

2

Originally, as we have seen, it is *language* which works on building the edifice of concepts; later it is *science*. Just as the bee simultaneously builds the cells of its comb and fills them with honey, so science works unceasingly at that great *columbarium* of concepts, the burial site of perceptions, builds ever-new, ever-higher tiers, supports, cleans, renews the old cells, and strives above all to fill that framework which towers up to vast heights, and to fit into it in an orderly way the whole empirical world, i.e. the anthropomorphic world. If even the man of action binds his life to reason and its concepts, so as not to be swept away and lose himself, the researcher builds his hut close by the tower of science so that he can lend a hand with the building and find protection for himself beneath its already existing bulwarks. And he has need of protection, for there exist fearful powers which constantly press in on him and which confront scientific truth with 'truths' of quite another kind, on shields emblazoned with the most multifarious emblems.

That drive to form metaphors, that fundamental human drive which cannot be left out of consideration for even a second without also leaving out human beings themselves, is in truth not defeated, indeed hardly even tamed, by the process whereby a regular and rigid new world is built from its own sublimated products – concepts – in order to imprison it in a fortress. The drive seeks out a channel and a new area for its activity, and finds it in myth and in art generally. It constantly confuses the cells and the classifications of concepts by setting up new translations, metaphors, metonymies; it constantly manifests the desire to shape the given world of the waking human being in ways which are just as multiform, irregular, inconsequential, incoherent, charming and ever-new, as things are in the world of dream. Actually the waking human being is only clear about the fact that he is awake thanks to the rigid and regular web of concepts, and for that reason he sometimes comes to believe that he is dreaming if once that web of concepts is torn apart by art. Pascal is right to maintain that if the same dream were to come to us every night we would occupy ourselves with it just as much as we do with the things we see every day: 'If an artisan could be sure to dream each night for a full twelve hours that he was a king,' says Pascal, 'I believe he would be just as happy as a king who dreamt for twelve hours each night that he was an artisan.'[10] Thanks to the constantly effective miracle assumed by myth, the waking day of a people who are stimulated by myth, as the ancient Greeks were, does indeed resemble dream more than it does the day of a thinker whose mind has been sobered by science. If, one day, any tree may speak as a nymph, or if a god can carry off virgins in the guise of a bull, if the goddess Athene herself is suddenly seen riding on a beautiful chariot in the company of Pisistratus through the market-places of Athens[11] – and that was what the honest Athenian believed – then anything is possible at any time, as it is in dream, and the whole of nature cavorts around men as if it were just a masquerade of the gods who are merely having fun by deceiving men in every shape and form.

But human beings themselves have an unconquerable urge to let themselves be deceived, and they are as if enchanted with happiness when the bard recites epic fairy-tales as if they were true, or when the actor in a play acts the king more regally than reality shows him to be. The intellect, that master of pretence, is free and absolved of its usual slavery for as long as it can deceive without *doing harm*, and it celebrates its Saturnalian festivals when it does so; at no time is it richer, more luxuriant, more proud, skilful, and bold. Full of creative contentment, it jumbles up metaphors and shifts

10 *Pensées* VI. 386.   11 Herodotus I. 60.

the boundary stones of abstraction, describing a river, for example, as a moving road that carries men to destinations to which they normally walk. The intellect has now cast off the mark of servitude; whereas it normally labours, with dull-spirited industry, to show to some poor individual who lusts after life the road and the tools he needs, and rides out in search of spoils and booty for its master, here the intellect has become the master itself and is permitted to wipe the expression of neediness from its face. Whatever the intellect now does, all of it, compared with what it did before, bears the mark of pretence, just as what it did before bore the mark of distortion. It copies human life, but it takes it to be something good and appears to be fairly content with it. That vast assembly of beams and boards to which needy man clings, thereby saving himself on his journey through life, is used by the liberated intellect as a mere climbing frame and plaything on which to perform its most reckless tricks; and when it smashes this framework, jumbles it up and ironically re-assembles it, pairing the most unlike things and dividing those things which are closest to one another, it reveals the fact that it does not require those makeshift aids of neediness, and that it is now guided, not by concepts but by intuitions. No regular way leads from these intuitions into the land of the ghostly schemata and abstractions; words are not made for them; man is struck dumb when he sees them, or he will speak only in forbidden metaphors and unheard-of combinations of concepts so that, by at least demolishing and deriding the old conceptual barriers, he may do creative justice to the impression made on him by the mighty, present intuition.

There are epochs in which the man of reason and the man of intuition stand side by side, the one fearful of intuition, the other filled with scorn for abstraction, the latter as unreasonable as the former is unartistic. They both desire to rule over life; the one by his knowledge of how to cope with the chief calamities of life by providing for the future, by prudence and regularity, the other by being an 'exuberant hero'[12] who does not see those calamities and who only acknowledges life as real when it is disguised as beauty and appearance. Where the man of intuition, as was once the case in ancient Greece, wields his weapons more mightily and victoriously than his contrary, a culture can take shape, given favourable conditions, and the rule of art over life can become established; all the expressions of a life lived thus are accompanied by pretence, by the denial of neediness, by the radiance of metaphorical visions, and indeed generally by the immediacy

---

[12] Phrase used of Siegfried in Wagner's *Götterdämmerung* (act III).

of deception. Neither the house, nor the gait, nor the clothing, nor the pitcher of clay gives any hint that these things were invented by neediness; it seems as if all of them were intended to express sublime happiness and Olympian cloudlessness and, as it were, a playing with earnest things. Whereas the man who is guided by concepts and abstractions only succeeds thereby in warding off misfortune, is unable to compel the abstractions themselves to yield him happiness, and strives merely to be as free as possible of pain, the man of intuition, standing in the midst of a culture, reaps directly from his intuitions not just protection from harm but also a constant stream of brightness, a lightening of the spirit, redemption, and release. Of course, *when* he suffers, he suffers more severely; indeed he suffers more frequently because he does not know how to learn from experience and keeps on falling into the very same trap time after time. When he is suffering he is just as unreasonable as he is when happy, he shouts out loudly and knows no solace. How differently the same misfortune is endured by the stoic who has learned from experience and who governs himself by means of concepts! This man, who otherwise seeks only honesty, truth, freedom from illusions, and protection from the onslaughts of things which might distract him, now performs, in the midst of misfortune, a masterpiece of pretence, just as the other did in the midst of happiness: he does not wear a twitching, mobile, human face, but rather a mask, as it were, with its features in dignified equilibrium; he does not shout, nor does he even change his tone of voice. If a veritable storm-cloud empties itself on his head, he wraps himself in his cloak and slowly walks away from under it.

(Written in 1873; unpublished in Nietzsche's lifetime.)

Glossary

Nietzsche's use of language in *The Birth of Tragedy* differs from that of most philosophers in certain respects, most notably in the extent to which his arguments rely on the 'poetic' devices of metaphor, etymological linkage and word-play. These peculiarities create difficulties for translator and reader alike, since the English equivalent seldom conveys the multi-layered character of the original German and thus obscures the patterns Nietzsche creates from the German terms.

By settling, eventually, on 'The *Birth* of Tragedy' as the title of his first book, Nietzsche drew attention to the imagery of sexuality and reproduction which pervades it, in elaboration of Schopenhauer's assertion that sex is the 'Brennpunkt des Willens' (focus of the Will). This lexical network encompasses both the orgiastic rites of Dionysos and 'sublimated', intellectual, and artistic expressions of the same *Trieb* ('drive'); thus such terms as *Befriedigung, brünstig, entladen, Erguß, Zeugung* appear in contexts which are not obviously sexual. The central term in this complex is *Lust*, which is much broader than modern English 'lust' but which, in *The Birth of Tragedy*, still connotes this kind of desire even when referring to the highest forms of delight.

The second main complex of imagery centres on *Schein* and the associated verb *scheinen* which can mean both 'to give off light' and 'to appear'. Thus Nietzsche links Apollo, the 'shining one', with the world of 'appearances' (*Erscheinungen*), 'semblance' (*Schein*) and beauty (*Schönheit*, which like *Schein*, derives from Old German *skôni*, meaning 'bright', 'gleaming' and hence 'magnificent'). This network in turn is related to a set of words centred on *Bild* ('image'), namely *Abbild, Lichtbild, Traumbild, Urbild, Götterbild, Bildner, bilden* and *Bildung*.

Abbild copy

Ahnung intimation, intuition, premonition

Anschauung contemplation, perception; a Goethean term which denotes direct, intuitive understanding of a sense-impression

Askese asceticism; self-denial of *Lust* and avoidance of *Rausch*

aufgehoben extinguished, preserved and raised to a higher level

Befriedigung satisfaction (in the sense of giving peace – *Friede* – to the Will)

Begrenzung limitation

Bild image

bilden to form

Bildner sculptor, maker of images

Bildung formation, education

entladen discharge, in the sense of relieve of a burden

ergießen cause to flow, ejaculate

Erguß outpouring, ejaculation

Erlösung release and redemption. One of a set of (Christian) religious terms to which Nietzsche assigns a new meaning, in this case by bringing the word closer to its root *lösen*, to set free or loose (from the pressure of pent-up, contradictory drives)

Erscheinung appearance; here mostly in the sense of phenomenon

Genius genius; here an impersonal, universal force cognate with the creative Will

gerechtfertigt justified

Gleichnis symbol, symbolic likeness No English term permits a consistent translation of Neitzsche's variation between '*Gleichnis*' and *Symbol*. The variation does not however reflect consistent distinctions in meaning

gleichnishaft symbolic

Götterbild image of the gods

heiter, Heiterkeit serene, serenity or, as terms of disapproval, cheerful, cheerfulness

idealisch ideal; here in the sense of belonging to the realm of ideas

Können ability, *Kunst* (art) derives from the same root

Lichtbild image of light

löst loosens, releases

Lust desire and delight, lust; basis of the Will's creativity ('Everything exists thanks to *Lust*')

Maß measure, proportion

Mäßigung moderation; like *Begrenzung*, an effect of Apolline control *maßvoll*   measured

Optik   prism or lens

Rausch   intoxication; not simply an effect of alcohol or drugs, in Nietzsche's view, but an expansive, heightened sense of being associated particularly with creativity

Rechtfertigung   justification; one of the religious-moral terms re-interpreted by Nietzsche

reizen   to stimulate, excite or provoke

schauen   to gaze, see; the verb has visionary or symbolic connotations

Schauer   seer

Schein   semblance; here in the sense that all appearances are an inadequate symbolic likeness (*Gleichnis*) of the Will which defies containment in the forms of time and space

Schönheit   beauty; see remarks above on *Schein*

sentimentalisch   sentimental, reflective; contrasted with *naiv* in Schiller's aesthetics

Spiegelung   reflection, mirage

Spiel   play

Sprechgesang   the German term for this operatic technique has now been adopted in English to distinguish it from 'recitative'.

Täuschung   deception

Trieb   drive, impulse, instinct

Übermaß   excess

übersehen   overlook or oversee

uigeheuer   monstrous, enormous; in the sense of *nicht geheuer*, uncanny or disturbing

Untergrund   deep or hidden ground; literally what lies below the surface, but here punning on *Grund* (ground or reason) to suggest the foundations of being

Ur-   prefix meaning original or primal, both in a temporal sense and in the sense of an ever-present source

Urbild   original

Ur-Eine (das)   the primal unity; a paradoxical concept as Nietzsche understood it, in that it was characterized by *Urwiderspruch* (primal contradiction)

Vorstellung   representation

Wissenschaft   science; includes all branches of scholarship

Zeugung   procreation

Zuhörer   listener, member of an audience

Index

(The index contains no general entries for 'Apollo'/'Apolline', 'Dionysos'/'Dionysiac', 'music', or 'tragedy' because these terms occur on virtually every page.)

Index

Cambridge texts in the history of philosophy

Titles published in the series thus far

Antoine Arnauld and Pierre Nicole *Logic or the Art of Thinking* (edited by Jill Vance Buroker)

Boyle *A Free Enquiry into the Vulgarly Received Notion of Nature* (edited by Edward B. Davis and Michael Hunter)

Bruno *Cause, Principle and Unity* and *Essays on Magic* (edited by Richard Blackwell and Robert de Lucca with an introduction by Alfonso Ingegno)

Clarke *A Demonstration of the Being and Attributes of God and Other Writings* (edited by Ezio Vailati)

Conway *The Principles of the Most Ancient and Modern Philosophy* (edited by Allison P. Coudert and Taylor Corse)

Cudworth *A Treatise Concerning Eternal and Immutable Morality with A Treatise of Freewill* (edited by Sarah Hutton)

Descartes *Meditations on First Philosophy*, with selections from the *Objections and Replies* (edited with an introduction by John Cottingham)

Descartes *The World and Other Writings* (edited by Stephen Gaukroger)

Hobbes and Bramhall on Liberty and Necessity (edited by Vere Chappell)

Kant *Critique of Practical Reason* (edited by Mary Gregor with an introduction by Andrews Reath)

Kant *Groundwork of the Metaphysics of Morals* (edited by Mary Gregor with an introduction by Christine M. Korsgaard)

Kant *The Metaphysics of Morals* (edited by Mary Gregor with an introduction by Roger Sullivan)

Kant *Prolegomena to any Future Metaphysics* (edited by Gary Hatfield)

Kant *Religion within the Boundaries of Mere Reason and Other Writings* (edited by Allen Wood and George di Giovanni with an introduction by Robert Merrihew Adams)

La Mettrie *Machine Man and Other Writings* (edited by Ann Thomson)

Leibniz *New Essays on Human Understanding* (edited by Peter Remnant and Jonathan Bennett)

Malebranche *Dialogues on Metaphysics and on Religion* (edited by Nicholas Jolley and David Scott)

Malebranche *The Search after Truth* (edited by Thomas M. Lennon and Paul J. Olscamp)

Melanchthon *Orations on Philosophy and Education* (edited by Sachiko Kusukawa, translated by Christine Salazar)

Mendelssohn *Philosophical Writings* (edited by Daniel O. Dahlstrom)

Nietzsche *The Birth of Tragedy and Other Writings* (edited by Raymond Geuss and Ronald Speirs)

Nietzsche *Daybreak* (edited by Maudemarie Clark and Brian Leiter, translated by R. J. Hollingdale)

Nietzsche *Human, All Too Human* (translated by R. J. Hollingdale with an introduction by Richard Schacht)

Nietzsche *Untimely Meditations* (edited by Daniel Breazeale, translated by R. J. Hollingdale)

Schleiermacher *Hermeneutics and Criticism* (edited by Andrew Bowie)
Schleiermacher *On Religion: Speeches to its Cultured Despisers* (edited by Richard Crouter)
Schopenhauer *Prize Essay on the Freedom of the Will* (edited by Günter Zöller)